John Dewey's Theory of Community

American University Studies

Series V
Philosophy

Vol. 40

PETER LANG
New York · Bern · Frankfurt am Main · Paris

Feodor F. Cruz

John Dewey's Theory of Community

PETER LANG

New York · Bern · Frankfurt am Main · Paris

Library of Congress Cataloging-in-Publication Data

Cruz, Feodor F.
  John Dewey's theory of community.

  (American university studies. Series V. Philosophy ;
vol. 40)
  Bibliography: p.
  Includes index.
  1. Community. 2. Dewey, John, 1859–1952—Views on
community. I. Title. II. Series: American university
studies. Series V, Philosophy ; v. 40.
  HT65.C78 1988   301′.01   87-17251
  ISBN 0-8204-0488-8
  ISSN 0739-6392

CIP-Kurztitelaufnahme der Deutschen Bibliothek

Cruz, Feodor F.:
John Dewey's theory of community / Feodor F.
Cruz. – New York; Bern; Frankfurt am Main;
Paris: Lang, 1987.
  (American University Studies: Ser. 5,
  Philosophy; Vol. 40)
  ISBN 0-8204-0488-8

NE: American University Studies /

© Peter Lang Publishing, Inc., New York 1987

Printed by Weihert-Druck GmbH, Darmstadt, West Germany

TO MY FATHER AND MOTHER

TABLE OF CONTENTS

PREFACE

The highest tribute ever paid to John Dewey as a philosopher was, perhaps, what was recently accorded to him by Richard Rorty in a book entitled **Philosophy and the Mirror of Nature** (Princeton, N. J.: Princeton University Press, 1979). In it, Rorty named Dewey, Heidegger, and Wittgenstein as the three great 'edifying' philosophers. By the qualification 'edifying,' he meant to extol and identify them as reactive philosophers who offered satires, parodies, aphorisms, and to distinguish them from systematic and constructive ones who offered arguments along normal professional lines.

The preference for the former ('edifying' philosophies) is based on the view that the latter (traditional systematic and contemporary analytic thought) have reached an impasse that cannot be broken through because they are built on the notion of mind as a mirror of nature. In abandoning this framework, the aim of philosophy (without mirrors) will no longer be to provide a tribunal of pure reason which judges other areas of knowledge and culture, pronouncing on their results from an ahistorical point of view. In place, Rorty suggests, it will continue the conversation which constitutes our culture, forming no tradition, distrusting the idea that man's essence is to be a knower of essences, and doubting the value of the whole project of universal commensuration. (Cf. op. cit., p. 367f.)

Whether or not the outlook favored by Rorty will in any way benefit philosophy is a question that cannot be decided here and now. He himself is not quite sure what form or forms this conversation will take. But what can and must be immediately attended to, for the sake of Deweyan scholarship, is the validity of his characterization of Dewey as a non-systematic and a non-constructive philosopher. Is it really the case that Dewey was "intentionally peripheral," and that he avoided putting his subject on the secure path of science, as Rorty alleges? These are points that will be considered in the present study. The effort will be to show that Dewey did have a systematic framework, a set of categories that was indeed different from those of traditional metaphysics but one that, nevertheless, was intended to function in the same way, and that his "conversations" were designed to be meaningful only if interpreted according to that framework and those categories of experience and reality. In fact, as is proposed here, **community** is a concept and a theory that is at the center of his biological pragmatism and, hence, serves as the key to his entire philosophical system.

The reading approach taken in this study was intentionally textual. It stayed as close to the sources as was workable. While unclear areas were freely interpreted to produce an intelligible and coherent explanation, their contexts and the support of relevant commentaries on them guided the process.

Also, some sections may appear to have been written without sufficient regard for the requirements of good writing style. But, in those occasions, the result was unavoidable. It was considered a small price to pay, if it could also be seen that the intention was to maintain fidelity to Dewey's own thoughts, which oftentimes were inextricably tied up with his own expressions. In any event, it is hoped that this work would be of assistance to those who wish to get beyond the popular impression that Dewey was a bad writer and was an "intentionally peripheral" thinker, as they explore and determine for themselves the value of what can be found in his engaging "conversations."

The theme and the spirit of this work have been inspired by Dr. Vincent C. Punzo of St. Louis University, a deeply respected mentor. It is through this project that I wish to thank him for his sustained encouragement and friendship over the years. I also wish to thank members of my family and friends who patiently waited from a distance until the completion of this work.

Dubuque, Iowa
May 1987

INTRODUCTION

The popular view that the heart of John Dewey's entire philosophy lies in his theory of experience and the ways in which experience is related to nature is incontrovertible. But, the statement is too broad a summation of its multi-faceted content and is hardly helpful in understanding his difficult thoughts dispersed in his copious writings of more than sixty five active years. For, within the general theory of experience, there is a more specific account which, it can be argued, is the center of his biological pragmatism and, hence, the ultimate key to his entire philosophic system. Here can be found the route of his departure from Hegel's absolute idealism leading to a new conception of the universe. And, more significantly, here is where the two critically related events - the abandonment of the subject-object dualism latent in traditional western thought and its replacement by a radically different framework with its own set of categories - can be seen to occur. This theory is what may be conveniently referred to as his theory of the human community.

This theory is the subject-matter of this study. The central problems that will be considered can be posed thus: How do human associations develop into human communities? How does the human environment bring about the emergence of 'mind'? How can intelligence and freedom, which is the product of social conditions, be also the creative agency of a community's culture? It may be suggested that the difficulty inherent in Dewey's naturalistic humanism consists in the fact that it takes the dialectical relations of human freedom and natural-social conditions as one radical principle with two sides. Traditionally, the two sides have been regarded as distinct and separate, although, at times, the direction in which human freedom controls the contingencies of nature and culture has been emphasized while, at other times, the dominance over men of natural and social necessities has been given prominence. For Dewey, these are but two aspects of one and the same reality rather than two competing forces that often collide to the success of one and the failure of the other. Whether this double-barrelled principle is tenable or is a form of fatalistic humanism (as Hendrik Hart believes it to be) is a question that needs to be settled.

The overwhelming impulse to devote yet another study of John Dewey's work is occasioned by the lack of due attention given to the subject-matter at hand. This is surprising, considering the importance of the issue not only in understanding Dewey's system but also in weighing the merits of his contribution to the eternal project of solving the 'problems of men.' Only a few commentaries have dealt with it and have done so only in an indirect way. Among these are those authored by Richard H. Bernstein, Emmanuel G. Mesthene, Hendrik Hart, Abdukarim H. Somjee, and a few others. (Cf. Bibliography for work titles.)

Bernstein's **John Dewey** is an enlightening edition making available an extensive but rather schematic account of Dewey's most salient doctrines, including that of community. It also discusses connected issues of significance to the concern of this study. But the book, as a whole, lacks both direction and focus in its treatment of selected popular topics from Dewey. Mesthene's analysis of Dewey's reply to the problem of intelligibility is a faithful rendition of the instrumental theory of scientific inquiry. His explicit identification of language as the agent in the knowing process is definitely Deweyan. The result of his study on this point deserves, however, further development and needs, for better understanding, incorporation immediately into the context of language and ultimately into that of the human community.

Hart's commentary on the functional relation between the testing of truth and the community of men in Dewey's theory of verification is a good supplement to Mesthene's effort. Its negative tone is also useful because that contributes balance to the heap of sympathetic interpretations already available on the subject. It is, however, too destructively critical, to the degree of overshadowing some important positive points in Dewey - points which the author, perhaps, unwittingly, missed - particularly Dewey's constructive insights on science and culture. Somjee's study is fundamentally a critique of the methodology of Dewey's political analysis. The present endeavor extends beyond such an aim in that it includes the study of non-political aspects of human transactions (which Somjee, by the requirement of his theme, justifiably ignored).

The sequence to be followed in this work is unavoidably non-chronological. The nature of available materials demands a topical handling. Dewey left only scattered thoughts on the subject with no definite continuity, clear structure, or immediately visible consistency. It would, therefore, be a more fruitful procedure to reconstruct and interpret his theory of community from suitable texts regardless of the dates when these were completed than to follow a temporally sequential method of forcefully threading ideas together. The stipulation is, of course, that such texts have to be coherent with the mature naturalistic phase of his philosophical development. This phase can roughly be located between a decade before the publication of **Experience and Nature** in 1925 and some fourteen years thereafter with the release of **Freedom and Culture** in 1949.

Since the primary objective of this work is reconstructive, the effort in the first four chapters will be directed to organizing ideas rather than dramatizing conflicting thoughts. The last chapter will, however, point out major problems encountered along the way. The stages of development will pierce through Dewey's deliberations from the metaphysical to the psychological, social, political, and moral planes in succession. The first chapter will introduce the setting - how Dewey sees the universe, i. e., what lines demarcate the real from the unreal. From the

mirror of naturalism, the world would show itself to be characterized by distinctive features. These may be regarded as categories that are descriptive of whatever is. But is naturalism,
with its own methodology, a legitimate form of metaphysics? Can
it adequately account for the differences in beings, for purposive growth toward life and mind?

The second chapter will carry the discussion to the level
of human existence. In Dewey's thinking, language and meaning
are achievements of higher but still natural transactions. Communication widens the field of signification. It comprises science
(which becomes, in Dewey's purview, the instrumentality for resolving conflicts and directing contingencies in both nature and
society) and art (which serves, in his social theory, as a medium
of culture and acts as the stimulus of aesthetic experience). The
third chapter will focus on the individual in the community, en-
gulfed as it were by a sea of cultural interchanges. Does freedom
have any reality or meaning in this context? What is the function
of education in relation to the attainment of freedom? Can it
transmit customs and traditions and still, simultaneously, liberate minds?

The fourth chapter delineates the foundation of human communities. What are the factors which determine the character of a
community? Is there one dominant aspect of social existence that
directs the forms of its institutions and dictates the quality
of its morals? What is the requirement for political authority?
Is the existence of political authority in society compatible
with the exercise of personal liberties of individuals constituting that society? Is democracy, as a form of political organization, ethically justifiable? In this discussion, Dewey endorses democracy not only as a system of organized intelligence
but, more significantly, as a communal way of life. In fact, it
constitutes for him an ideal condition to be aspired for by all
humans. Whether or not this conclusion follows from the arguments and conclusions of earlier chapters will be considered in
the final chapter. Here, too, will be faced the question (quite
crucial in evaluating the merit of Dewey's political philosophy)
concerning the possibility of that Great Community he envisions.

#

THE METAPHYSICAL BASIS OF DEWEY"S THEORY OF COMMUNITY: THE THREE LEVELS OF TRANSACTIONS

A. Naturalism as a Metaphysics

1. Towards a Definition of Naturalistic Metaphysics

John Dewey, like Immanuel Kant, rejects transcendental metaphysics, the view which presumes to teach ultimate origins and ends that lie beyond the realm of actual and possible experience. For him, preoccupation with "problems which do not rise out of experience and for which solutions are sought outside of experience"[1] is from the start, a losing proposition. Of this sort is the search for ultimate traits (in the sense of essential and necessary attributes) and causes (in the sense of efficiencies that can explain the existence and evolution of the universe).

But there could be, for him, a legitimate type of metaphysical inquiry, one that inspects the character of nature without going beyond it. This may be called 'immanent metaphysics.' Its function is to delineate the most general and pervasive traits of existence. Experience itself is the avenue that leads to the discovery of these traits. And if the testimony of what he calls 'primary nonreflectional experience' or the 'unbiased evidence of experience in gross' is to be accepted, what would be found are not eternally permanent (self-existing things or substances but simply 'qualitied' events and temporal processes. It is from these events or processes that the general traits of existence can be derived. When so derived, it will appear that they really are not traits in watertight compartments. On the contrary, they are "so intimately intermixed that all important issues are concerned with their degrees and the ratio they sustain to one another."[2]

The objective, then, of metaphysics is to arrive at a structural cataloguing of things but without giving any synthetic interpretation of them that is based on one selected feature as the principle of unity for the whole. Fidelity to experience and nature cannot allow one to commit such a fallacy of arbitrary selection. Furthermore, the results of the inquiry cannot be taken as dogmatic conclusions. These cannot be more than descriptive and hypothetical. The method of deducing necessary principles from the categories of existence that may be found is a logical leap quite inconsistent with a thoroughgoing empiricism of the sort espoused by Dewey.

But the function of thought does not terminate in merely revealing by analysis and description the traits and characters of natural existence. The very nature of such traits and characters forbids such an unfruitful conclusion. As he says quite directly:

> Qualitative individuality and constant rela-
> tions, contingency and need, movement and
> arrest are common traits of all existence.
> This fact is source both of values and their
> precariousness; both of immediate possession
> which is causal and of reflection which is a
> precondition of secure atttainment and appro-
> priation.[3]

The point is to make generalizations applicable to specific aims. The more certain one is that the world is of such and such a cha- racter, the more he is committed to try to direct his conduct in life on the basis of that character. As A. E. Murphy observes, to note that contingency is a pervasive trait of events and to bring this into connection with concrete situations of life is to provide a metaphysical basis for criticism of values and mea- nings.[4]

For Dewey the idea is far-reaching. It brings to the fore the relation between existence and value, between the general traits of the universe and the issues of life and death.[5] If nature is indeed an evolving affair marked by precariousness and instability, man should learn how to accommodate to such a condition not only by making life stable for survival but by enhancing its useful and aesthetic qualities. Furthermore, the fact that the baselines marked down by metaphysics do not ex- tend beyond nature indicates that man is a being in and of na- ture, a creature firmly planted in the natural processes. Conse- quently, his values can be found only in nature.

This unqualified naturalism flatly rejects any form of supernaturalism or extra-naturalism which, by definition locates ultimate human values in a transcendental order. It closes the door to any spiritual interpretation of life based on the rea- lity of the hereafter. It, however, opens a new religious dimen- sion. In Dewey's estimation, this is the only form of religion that is both realistic and truly accessible.

Finally, the naturalistic outlook finds in the method of natural science a suitable tool for the secure attainment and appreciation of values. As it has wrought wonders in the explo- ration of physical events, likewise will it do so in human affairs. Thus, it can easily be noticed, the alliance between philosophy and science has been one of Dewey's more outstanding and consistent affirmations. This is also why he hails the pub- lication of Charles Darwin's celebrated work, Origin of Species, as a significant leap in the direction of naturalism. It did not only mark "an epoch in the development of natural sciences" but also rendered philosophy its "biological contribution."[6] Such a contribution consists in giving prominence to change over fixity in the science of evolution by showing that what used to be regarded as fixed forms indeed have origins. He prophesies that this was bound to transform the logic of knowledge and, hence, the treatment of morals, politics and religion. Commenting on the point, J. E. Smith sums up what he thinks Dewey saw in Darwinism:

> The contribution of Darwinism is the estab-
> lishing of the primacy of change and the banis-
> hing of ultimate origins and finalities; the
> focus upon specific problems and changes; the
> discovery of the outcomes of such change for the
> purpose of inserting ourselves and our knowledge
> into the stream of things so as to influence the
> the results in accord with human plans and pur-
> poses; the shift of interest in philosophy away
> from wholesale and ultimate questions.[7]

For Dewey, change could mean development (if it occurs in a suitable environment), and such is a process with a direction. He makes this point in clarifying the meaning of potentiality:

> Anything might be said to exhibit potentiality
> with respect to two facts; first, that the change
> exhibits (in connection with interaction with new
> elements in its surroundings) qualities it did
> not show till it was exposed to them, and, secondly,
> that the changes in which these qualities are shown
> run a certain course.[8]

In the final analysis, as will be shown below, the aim toward which the course of change can be directed to is vital and intelligent organization, i. e., life and mind.[9]

Given the last statements, it will now appear that Dewey's naturalism includes not only a procedural proposal but a truly cosmic setting. It is important to take note of this point since naturalists are often charged of committing their primary allegiance to their preferred method of inquiry, to the point of obscuring (if not dissolving) their substantive views of things in general.[10] Dewey does not fail in this regard. In fact, as will be shown later, his logical, just as much as his ethical and political, inquiries are conducted within the framework of a well-rounded theory of existence. The following paragraphs will explore some of the more salient substantive elements of his theory.

2. Dewey's Categoreal Scheme

Just as any metaphysics is framed according to an order of ideas by which nature and experience is read, so also Dewey's metaphysics is contrived in terms of some basic categories. These categories, inextricably biological in origin and implications, permeate his reconstruction of philosophy and direct his treatment of special topics. In fact, it is only in the light of this biologically rooted categories that Dewey's writings can become intelligible and coherent.

That categories function in the background of any field of study needs no demonstration. They are necessary elements in the very activity of building theories or general conceptions of particular phenomena. Thus, "the psychologist is seeking to dissect 'forms of the understanding,' the logician is intent upon enumerating 'types of order,' the metaphysician is engaged in discovering and describing 'kinds of structure.'"[11] What such categories may specifically be is, however, a matter of controversy. Sidney Hook suggests that they are identifiable as those irreducible differentials of explanation. They are ideas of explanation because they are given and accepted as answers to questions. They are irreducible because they are ultimate in a series of explanation. And they are differentials because when a term is explained, words by which they are expressed belong to a specific group.[12]

Hook raises another issue quite useful in understanding Dewey's categories. Why are categories explanatory concepts? In virtue of what do they serve? He explains that there are two accounts that can be found in traditional discussions: the structural and the conceptual. In both, they are regarded as forms of understanding. But in the first (represented by Aristotle's metaphysics), they are forms of understanding because "they possess distinctive character and instrumental efficiencies only insofar as they represent, reflect or signify certain pervasive natural traits, patterns and kinds."[13] In the second (represented by Kant's revision), mental activity is not simply registering passively a succession of atomic events. Expressed through specific judgments, it must not only be introduced to hold together for analysis the natural structures and laws which are said to condition the very possiblity of that mental activity, but also "spontaneously operates to construct and produce, if not create, its own objects out of an unorganized sensuous manifold."[14]

The difficulty in the first view, as Hook sees it, consists in that it cannot show that categories do reflect actually existing structures without establishing them as synthesizing apparatus for fusing experience and organizing situations. For one thing, there are concepts that are adopted as having no correspondence in existence but are, nevertheless, accepted because they are fruitful in unifying and predicting phenomena (e. g., ideal laws of physics or legal fictions). This suggests that these structural configurations reflect habits of mind rather than actual traits of existence. The alleged traits, if they are not actually so, could be but different ways of thinking about things specifically when the purpose is to convert them into scientific objects.

The defect in the second interpretation consists in its positing the mind outside of the empirical order as if for the sole purpose of explaining its ability to perform activities with the use of the categories. Also, it cannot account for why precisely the selected categories, rather than others, are ones that are fruitful and applicable, without invoking the agency of an influence external but compelling to the movement of thought.

Hook presents Dewey (together with Peirce) as providing a third alternative in which the difficulties involved with the two traditional interpretations are avoided. According to it, categories are explanatory concepts precisely because they are forms of a mind, which is a mode or consequence of behavior in a natural context of things and events. The categories validly apply to all objects and qualities, since they characterize mind in its operations. In this way, the subjective is actually subsumed under the objective and not posed diametrically to it as belonging to a different order of reality. In this way, too, the synthetic quality or unity of thought is explained. The selection of categories is formed not by any power external to thought, but by the phenomenon of 'interest.'[15]

In looking for the categories, the inquirer may ignore language, since language differs from one culture to another and from one type (say common parlance) to another (say technical lexicon). Rather, he should examine the forms of social organization and the bodies of scientific knowledge. Dewey would accept the view that categories are bound with social interchanges and distinctions made in scientific and philosophical analyses. Yet, he would not concede that they cannot be found in language. The reason for this posture will become apparent in the discussion below (Chapter III). It suffices to state here that this theory of language and meaning considers language not merely as a vehicle of thought but as thought-itself-expressed.

As far as the number of categories is concerned, Dewey, unlike Aristotle, gives no definite and closed listing. This openness can be attributed to his fidelity to the disclosure of nature that diversity is a prime characteristic of that nature. The same attitude also follows logically from the perpective that takes temporal process and 'qualitied' events as central. There are two primary sources in Dewey's works if a list of fundamental categories will be made.[16] One is the essay entitled "The Subject-matter of Metaphysical Inquiry" (1915), in which Dewey describes the province of First Philosophy as the "irreducible traits in any and every subject of scientific inquiry." Here, only three instances are named: diversity, interaction, and change (or process). The other source is Experience and Nature, where a more comprehensive (not in the sense of complete) list is provided. Taking Lewis E. Hahn's study[17] as guide, the last mentioned work of Dewey includes the categories of potentiality, continuity (or evolution), texture, context, strand, quality, fusion, reference, order, and (to add to Hahn's list) selection, and instrument. These concepts are not, however, disparate and self-enclosed. By a process of 'deduction,'[18] one category can be derived from another. Process, for instance, can (by implication) yield continuity or interaction.

Here are some of the categories and their respective meanings in Dewey's usage. Understanding them would certainly ligh-
ten the task of reading his intentions behind concrete passages
in his works.

1. Potentiality. This refers to the existential capacity
that is actualizable in interactions.

> ...the qualities of things associated are dis-
> played only in association, since in interactions
> alone are potentialities released and actualized.
> Furthermore, the manifestation of potentialities
> varies with the manner and range of association.
> This statement is only a formal way of calling at-
> tention to the fact that we charactrize an element,
> say hydrogen, not only, as the name implies, in
> terms of its waterforming potentiality but ulti-
> mately in terms of consequences effected in a whole
> range of modes of conjoint behavior.[19]

Potentiality is sometimes used in the field of inquiry. It is
the name given to the observed existing facts that are taken to
locate and delimit the problem in a problematic situation. It
is opposed to 'possibilities' which, in logic, are identified
with operability. Possibilities, as distinct from existential
potentialities, are abstract. Things acquire meanings and thereby enter into inquiry by virtue of their potentialities. If not
for the fact that they are found in events (rather than in substances) they would be equivalent to Aristotle's 'causa materia-
lis.' In Experience and Nature, events are described not as
lumpy substances but as ongoing and, hence, unfinished, incomplete, and indeterminate process.[20] In Logic, crude materials
are called potentialities because they possess qualities so as
to permit and promote the performance of specific operations
which result in formed-matter as means to end.[21]

From a broader perspective, the original state of existences described as matter potential to life and mind.[22] This
implies evolution. Rejecting the idea of an originally bio-
centric world, life is proposed to be the result of change
having a direction.

> Starting where we must start, with the present,
> the fact of organization shows that the world is
> of a certain kind. In spots, it has organization.
> Reference to the evolution of this organization
> out of an earlier world in which such organization
> was not found, means something about that earlier
> condition - it means that it was characterized by
> a change having direction - that is, in the direc-
> tion of vital and intelligent organization.[23]

There is, thus, an ineradicable teleology in Dewey's world of processes.

Affairs in nature turns out, in his gaze, to be most human. The premise that everything is in the making involves man in the process. Things are not just there as brute facts. They assume beneficial or harmful characters insofar as they contribute or block the maintenance of life. The notions of potentiality and evolution are directed against ultimate origins and absolute finalities. They mark a turnabout from wholesale questions and lead to specific issues and changes. The effect on attitude is trust, trust in the ability of intelligence to insert human purposes into the stream of things so as to ascertain good results. The empirical method and concern for the future spring from the conception of the universe which is still in the process of becoming and, up to a certain point, still plastic. This is the universe where thought makes a difference, for, here, it has really constructive and creative functions.[24]

The description of the world as inescapably precarious, the trust in the power of intelligence, the emphasis on action, the concern for consequences, the futuristic outlook, are expressions not only of his naturalism but also of his pragmatic concerns. But naturalism and pragmatism are not two distinct perspectives in Dewey. As a metaphysical inquirer, Dewey is a committed naturalist. As a social reformer, he is an avowed pragmatist. But the naturalistic movement of his thoughts leads to the knowledge that consequences of the transactive process of cosmic existence generate its structure, and that the meaning of existence is the control of these consequences. If consequences condition us, we must condition them, Dewey strongly believes and advocates.

The pragmatic movement of his thoughts is an affirmation of his confidence in the meaning of life. He gives assurance that any person can get firm hold of the consequences of transactions. Anyone can start again to believe in the value of life when he is confronted with the worth of the fruits of his works and doings. "The statement that as we sow, so shall we reap, is trite. But there is no field of life in which it applies so aptly and fully as in that of belief and the methods employed to affect belief."[25] Hope is alive when future consequences are foreseen and controlled, and knowledge makes it so. He affirms that "action, when directed by knowledge, is method and means, not an end. The aim and end is the securer, freer and more widely shared embodiment of values in experience by means of that active control of objects which knowledge alone makes possible."[26]

2. Continuity. This category is Dewey's answer to the problems brought about by the dualisms and bifurcations instituted by traditional philosophy. It eradicates the mysteries surrounding the 'body-mind problem,' most particularly. It is his description of the vertical or longitudinal aspect of experience

(as distinct from interaction, which is its horizontal or late-
ral aspect).[27] Dewey explains:

> To live signifies that a connected continuity of
> acts is effected in which preceding ones prepare
> the conditions, under which later ones occur. there
> is a chain of causes and effects, of course, in
> what happens with inanimate things. but for living
> creatures, the chain has a particular cumulative
> continuity, or else death ensues.[28]

In terms of experience, continuity means integrity: "Every experience takes up something from those which have gone before and
modifies in some way the qualities of those which come after."[29]
In terms of events, these are said to be passing into other
things, in such a way that a later occurrence is actually an
integral part of the character or nature of present existence.[30]
But there is no reduction of complex transactions to atomic
elements. Rather, it is the case of events exhibiting its rela-
tional structure, "it is an affair of tracing patterns of change
following threads of reference or connection from one situation
or transaction to another which affords a convenient instrument
of control."[31]

From the logical standpoint, the continuity of the lower
(i. e., simple) and higher (i. e., complex) activities and forms
is presented as the primary postulate of a naturalistic logic.[32]
Also, the integrity of experience and nature is affirmed. It is
explained as the absence of breach between operations of inquiry
and biological and physical activities, but, again, without reducing the former to the latter. The totality of these continuities
is expressed thus:

> ...neither the plain man nor the scientific inqui-
> rer is aware, as he engages in his reflective acti-
> vity, of any transition from one sphere of exis-
> tence to another. He knows no two fixed worlds -
> reality on one side and mere subjective ideas on
> the other; he is aware of no gulf to cross. He
> assumes uninterrupted, free, and fluid passage
> from ordinary experience to abstract thinking,
> from thought to fact, from things to theories
> and back again. Observation passes into develop-
> ment hypothesis; deductive methods pass into use
> in description of the particular; inference passes
> into action, all with no sense of difficulty save
> those found in the particular task in question. The
> fundamental assumption is continuity.[33]

Metaphysically, the category of continuity rules out the
possibility of the appearance in the scene of nature both of a
completely new being and of an outside force as cause of changes

that occur. Environment and living beings make adjustments to preserve the continuity. On the part of man, this is set off by deliberate purpose. Psychologically, the same category connects mind and nature through the empirical facts of biological impulse and habit.[34] Sociologically, the same principle unites the natural and social sciences, just as it makes continuous the speculative and practical pursuits, the physical and moral, etc.[35]

The concepts 'temporality,' 'unity,' and 'diversity' are deducible from Dewey's use of the category 'continuity.' 'Temporality' is only another term for the transitory character of an order that is never finished and consequently has no fixed laws.[36] The 'nature of things,' if the term 'nature' has to be used with real meaning, would designate their historical career. Individuality is also achieved in the same way, i. e., in relation to time. It is represented by an historical career, which is a series of interactions the uniqueness of which consists in the way encountered situations are responded to.

'Unity' is postulated as the prestine condition of existence. Matter that is potential to life is the original constitution of nature. Diversity of modes of existence is a development which results from various interactions in an evolutionary progression. Differentiation by way of external addition is dismissed, since it is a form of dualism and, hence, contraposes continuity. "The difference between the animate plant and the inanimate iron molecule is not that the former has something in addition..."[37] Rather, multiplicity and difference are events of increasing complexity accomplished through diversification of common properties. This outlook, according to Hart, makes Dewey a 'genetic structural monist.'[38]

Dewey's emphasis on continuity and unity is not, however, identical with Hegel's holistic idealism. Dewey does not patronize the idea of multiplicity by way of 'coincidentia oppositorum,' the continuous movement of things back and forth into their self-generated opposites. Diversification is not the outcome of opposition between poles but rather of contrasts within a unified whole. "If the word 'polarities' were used by me," he writes Bentley, "it would be a synonym for 'distinctions', not as that from which they arise."[39] Thus, Dewey's monism would, for instance, contrast, within one field of motion, random physical motion and organic movement instead of positing motion and rest as original contradictories generating one another. By the same token, it would explain conscious and unconscious behavior not as contradictories but as contrasts within one field of or-organic behavior (conscious behavior being a product of evolutionary diversification). "The beginning is with action in which the entire organism is involved as a specialized differentiation of an inclusive whole of behavior."[40] Incidentally, the basic contrasts in Dewey's scheme are organic-inorganic and physical-mental.

Perceiving the monistic undertones in Dewey's discussion presents no special difficulty. His constant refutation of various forms of dualism sufficiently indicates it. What does present considerable difficulty, however, is determining his real affiliation with respect to the opposition between individualism and universalism. In axiological discussions, this opposition appears as the tension between the between the individual as the reconstructive agency in society versus the communal efforts of individuals or between the passive citizens and the dominant socio-political forces. It can be safely stated though, for the time being, that (at least on the metaphysical plane) his position is one of compromise between the two extremes. He has always maintained both, stressing one or the other on different occasions.

In his early writings, the universalistic (in the sense of holistic) trend is quite pronounced. In 1898, he writes: "Life tends to maintain itself because it is life. The particular acts which are put forth are the particular outcome of the life that is there; they are its expression, its manifestation."[41] In later thoughts, the strong universalistic tone loses fervor, although without completely disappearing. While he rejects in his mature view a block universe monism, he also dismisses an inclusive individualism as "itself a product of a cultural individualistic movement."[42]

His definitive position (as proposed in his later works) shows the two tendencies becoming fused. In his description of the scene of life, he observes that individual organisms are partial (i. e., never complete and separate) developments within the universal process of growth tending to life.

> The creature is not equal to the task of indefinite self-renewal. But continuity of the life process is not dependent upon the prolongation of the existence of any one individual. Reproduction of other forms of life goes on in continuous sequence. And though, as the geological record shows, not merely individuals but also species die out, the life process continues in increasingly complex forms.[43]

Life, then, is constantly renewed by transmission. But the individual is not without an important role in the process. It stimulates renewal and triggers new developments. Thus, the universal and the individual interact so as to maintain life both universally and individually.

> There is the individual that belongs in a continuous system of connected events which reinforce its activities and which form a world in which it is at home, consistently at one with its own preferences, satisfying its requirements. Such an individual is in its world as a member,

extending as far as the moving equilibrium of
which it is a part lends support.[44]

Levi's summation of the present issue corroborates the proposed
interpretation:

> His (Dewey's) picture of the world envisages both
> atomicity and continuity, and it avoids the danger
> of both the Hegelian and the Leibnizian alterna-
> tives. It skirts the dangers of both a world of
> individuals so hermetically sealed and autonomous
> that they are practically relationless, and of a
> world of unity so holistic and so organically inter-
> related that real individuality is swallowed up in
> the midst of totality.[45]

The condition of interdependence of the universal and the individual is, incidentally, one of the reasons for the terminological preference for 'transaction' instead of 'interaction.'
With Arthur F. Bentley, Dewey discusses the problems connected
with the relationship between total context and individual centers. In this discussion, he makes an effort to depart from a
homogeneous universe without distinctions, while at the same
time moving away from a heterogeneous aggregate of disjointed
existences.[46] This point will further be developed below.

3. Transaction. The discussion of the category of continuity brings to the fore the idea of original unity of existence
in terms of matter-in-potency-for-life. Movements toward diversification evolve as the result of various types of interactions
among things and environment. Interaction can, therefore, be
seen as a universal trait of all existences. There are what
Dewey calls 'intra-organic or organic and environ-energies'
types. When and where these occur, new energies are released.
"We observe," he says, "that the qualities of things associated
are displayed only in association, since in interactions alone
are potentialities released and actualized."[47]

Dewey's universe contains no void, no isolated parts, no
passive elements. It is not a Parminidean being but a Heracli-
tean becoming. It is "a moving whole of interacting parts." The
very act of be-ing is interaction. Undifferentiated, inert, and
unrelated existences are, hence, abstractions. To think of them
as concretely real is to commit a logical error similar to what
whitehead calls the 'fallacy of misplaced concreteness.'[48] Even
the terms involved in an interaction are not existentially distinct. Only by analysis and selective abstraction can the actual
occurrence be differentiated into two factors, the organism and
the environment. There are, however, degrees of participation.
Ratner, distinguishing Whitehead and Newton from Dewey, says on
behalf of Dewey:

16

"Once with interactions, always with interactions,"
but the relations between systems of interactions
or interactive continua (societies, situations or
local histories) may be "external" depending upon
the extent and quality of the interactivity between
the systems of interaction or interactive continua
involved. When by virtue of "inhibitions and atte-
nuations" the interactivity has decreased so that
there are no appreciable consequences of the interactivity in the members in that interactive system,
then the members are in so far external to each
other.[49]

In the Knowing and the Known, Dewey (with Bentley) revises his
terminology to underscore the distinctiveness of his category.
Here, he differentiates three types of action: self-action,
interaction, and transaction. 'Self-action,' a basic concept in
ancient and medieval physics, designates the activity which arises from the capacity intrinsic to an entity; the entity acts
on and by its own power. Greek atomism and Newtonian mechanics
brought to light a new idea of action which can be referred to
as 'interaction.' In this case, the entities in act are virtually
unchangeable; the action proceeds not from themselves but among
them, much like the way the Leibnizian monads are pre-established.

The first type of action is dismissed by Dewey, being inconsistent with the category of continuity. The second is an instance of the 'static fallacy,' incompatible with the termporal
character of things in nature.[50] Dewey's choice as the term more
expressive of the naturalistic view of reality is 'transaction.'
Different from the two other types, this kind of action arises
not from any principle intrinsic to things nor from independently
existing entities. Rather, the elements involved in the action
are elements precisely because of their function in it. This
means that they are subject to change so much so that the action
affects both in one way or another.

Dewey's terminological preference has some far-reaching
consequences. Two are worth mentioning from the standpoint of
this study. For one thing, the adopted term implies a different
conception of subject-object relationship and stimulus-response
interaction. For another, it transfers the locus of qualities
from substances (either mind or external objects) to situations
or contexts. The first consequence is well-illustrated in the
case of perception. Dewey explains:

...the stimulus or perceive object is a part of
the process of determining the response; nay, in
its growing completeness, it is the determining
of the response. As soon as an integral and clear-
cut object stands out, then the response is decided, and the only intelligent way of choosing the
response is by forming its stimulus. the change

effected in the environment by the final total organic act is just a consummation of the partial
changes effected all through the process of perception by the partial reactions that finally
determine a clear-cut object of perception.[51]

The text indicates that the stimulus of perception does not
attain the status of object by itself. The perceiver somehow
'forms' its object, thereby determining it. There is notably a
Kantian flavor in this conception. In the second consequence,
it is denied that qualities are 'in' the organism. They are
rather 'of' interactions, in which both extra-organic things
and organism partake.[52]

The preference for 'transaction' is not, however, a formal
revision of views held prior to its introduction. The doctrines
mentioned are part and parcel of Dewey's views all along. As
early as 1876, he must have been already looking into the philosophical implication of the interaction model formulated in physics by Maxwell. Hegel, Darwin, and the biologistic school of
psychology prevalent in the first quarter of the century supplied content to the model. Nature and experience, as Dewey en-
counters them, lend heavy support to the view. As he declares,
"In nature there are no actions which are stripped to the bare
state of homogeneous oneness. All actions are themselves consequences of systems of interactions of various complexities of
organization."[53] In agreement with Dewey, Lamprecht says that,
in experience, life is seen as

a more or less correlated group of interactions
between lungs and air; digestion is an interaction
between stomach (and other internal organs) and
food; seeing is an interaction between eye (and
optic nerve and other parts of the visual apparatus) and various objects in the vicinity of the
animal body. So with other human activities...[54]

That the direction of Dewey's teleology is life and intelligence, and that life and intelligence are products of interactions, lead to the conception of the 'social' as an all-embracing philosophical idea. Notice that it is not described as a
metaphysical category in the strict sense of the term. The reason is, it may be suspected, that it is a derivative of 'transaction'; it is, therefore, presented not as a general trait of
all existences but as a special mode of interaction. It is employed to mark clearly the distinctive quality of human transaction. As Bernstein points out, "Dewey argues that the social
is a philosophic category because it is needed to account for
distinctively human experience in which physical and psycho-
physical phenomena are transformed."[55] It indicates the richest,
fullest, and most subtle mode of natural transaction, for it is
in the social level that the lower forms of reality take on new

significance. And this significance, "according to the findings
of science, appear(s) only late in time."[56]

   4. **Selective Behavior.** Dewey's ontology also points to the
presence of bias in nature. Natural events (which are organisms
in interaction with other natural events) manifest bias by exhibiting elementary and unsophisticated patterns of response -
satisfaction and dissatisfaction, pursuance and avoidance, etc.
Organisms "find" that the ordering of the environment depends,
up to a certain extent, on their own activities in response to
their needs.

   In "Context and Thought," Dewey calls it 'selective interest.'[57] But this is a particular type of natural selection
found only in man and, therefore, only an aspect of the more
general trait presented under the name 'context.' But in "Philosophies of Freedom," it is treated as a general trait, and,
hence, considered a metaphysical category.

      Preferential action in the sense of selective be-
      havior is a universal trait of all things, atoms
      and molecules as well as plants, animals, and man.
      Existences, universally as far as we can tell, are
      cold and indifferent in the presence of some things
      and react energetically in either positive or nega-
      tive way to other things. These "preferences" or
      differential responses of behavior, are due to
      their own constitution; they "express" the nature
      of things in question. They mark a distinctive
      contribution to what takes place. In other words,
      while changes in one thing may be described on the
      basis of changes that take place in other things,
      the existence of things which make certain changes
      having a certain quality and direction occur cannot
      be so explained.[58]

   The importance of this category consists in the fact that
it is taken as the principle of individuality in or uniqueness
of things. By extension, it is also the root of freedom. Choice,
says Dewey, is more than this preferential action, but it is,
at least, this. The significance of this point will be seen in
Chapter IV below.

B. The Three Levels of Transaction

The main issue in the following discussion is the differentiation of things in nature. By 'differentiation,' the reference
is not to numerical distinction but to qualitative diversification. According to Dewey, classical Greek philosophies, followed by their medieval counterparts, committed themselves to a
metaphysics of pre-established forms (substantial or accidental)
and, hence, did not have to make an issue of specific differences. What they had to contend with was the problem of multiplicity. They had to concentrate their efforts to devising theories that would solve the perennial question of the "one and the
many."

   In Dewey's genetic monism, no ready-made forms are assumed.
With this stipulation, the burden of his philosophy becomes one
of demonstrating the emergence of qualitative diversification.
It is to this end that he, in practice, fixes much of his attention. In the process, the concomitant problem of multiplicity
is simultaneously considered. Following the traditional understanding of qualitative distinction as relating to physical and
psychical differences, he resolves the issue in the context of
the perennial 'body-mind' problem. He suggests that the way out
of this snarl is to re-think those concepts in virtue of which
the problem arose. When this is accomplished, he is certain,
those concepts will be found to have primarily nothing to do
with body-mind.[59] Their true import is, in fact, connected with
justifying the metaphysical presupposition from which they have
been conceived and have been sustained.

   In Dewey's analysis, the classical metaphysics initiated
by Plato and Aristotle assumes a radical distinction between
body and mind. The term 'Body' or the 'physical' is, on the one
hand, that sort of thing caught up within the spatio-temporal
dimensions of the sensible world. In man, it is the head, the
trunk, the limbs; the collection of cells consisting of skin
and cells inside it; the assemblage of flesh, bones, and organs
which can anatomically be pointed to; the mass of matter with
weight and extension.[60] 'Mind' or the 'psychical' is, on the
other hand, that sort of thing or faculty which senses, perceives, conceives, thinks, remembers, imagines, believes, intends, decides, aims, acts, wants; which is subject to emotions,
impulses, habits.

   The sharp distinction between the two sorts of things or
functions is made the basis of the conclusion that these, in
fact, are separate substances or 'principles' of being, and each
belong to distinct orders of reality. 'Body' is confined to the
realm of the purely physical nature. Understandably, only the
positive sciences, such as physics, biology, physiology, anatomy,
can investigate its properties and the laws governing it through
the use of the scientific method of experimentation and inductive
analysis. 'Mind' has been washed off of its contamination with
matter and, hence, assigned to the world of 'pure spirits.' Only
the philosophical and theological disciplines have legitimate

claim to dealing with it through the method of introspection
and deductive reasoning. In Dewey's judgment, this is the standpoint that led to the growth and harmful effects of doctrines
splitting off from each other religion, morals, science, philosophy, arts and conduct, knowledge and practice.[61]

After the separation of body from mind, of the purely physical from the purely psychical or spiritual, the difficulty
that traditional philosophers had wrought themselves into was
how to put back what has been sundered. the question thereafter
had become (as Campbell expresses it): What is the relation, in
man, between his mind and his body?[62] Formulated from the perspective of psycho-physical parallelism, it asked: How does a
psychic factor influence a physical factor? From the standpoint
of the Cartesian form of dualism, the problem was to explain how
a spiritual substance could affect change in a physical mechanism.

Dewey believes that these formulations have no empirical
reference. They are as nonsensical as the assumption of dualism
upon which they are based. The solutions that have been offered,
ranging "from the materialism of Hobbes, the apparatus of soul,
pineal gland, animal spirits of Descartes, to interactionism,
pre-established harmony, occasionalism, parallelism, panpsychic
idealism, epiphenomenalism, and the 'elan vital' - a portentous
array,"[63] are conceived within the same framework and, hence,
retain the same deficiencies.

In summary, the traditional outlook, taken as whole, fails
for a number of reasons. First, its metaphysics of substance
hypostatizes mind and renders it impregnable to empiricial analysis and verification. Second, it separates body from mind,
thereby overlooking the inherent continuity in them. Third, it
downgrades the physical, reducing it to a state of passivity
and subservience to the mind. Mind, being the efficient cause
of distinctively human acts, such as thinking and willing, is
elevated to an inviolable order, given priority and supremacy
in the graded scale of 'Being.' Fourth, in separating mind from
body, mind is likewise cut off from its natural environment, both
physical and social. In so doing, humane interests and values are
placed outside the boundaries of nature. Dewey refutes the old
theory by declaring that it denies quality in general from natural events, ignores in particular their temporal context, and
promulgates the dogma of the superior reality of 'causes.'[64]

Dewey finds that the dualistic interpretation, inspite of
its unwarranted assumptions, has deeply permeated western culture and civilization in all its facets. This process of assi-
milation has become virtually a tacit assent, if not a conscious
commitment. In this way, the disastrous effects of the old theory continue to flourish. The manifestations and consequences are
not hard to find. Specialization in science and technology and
(even) in the liberal arts has and continue to create two extreme
classes of people: the mechanical, whose function and mode of
life is 'nutritional' and 'appetitive' - not quite unlike the

slaves of ancient Greek society, and the high-brow elite with
unsoiled hands pursuing knowledge for its own sake - maintaining
the tradition of the philosophers of ancient Athens.[65]

On another score, morals is pushed within, to the innermost
self. This is to be expected in a viewpoint where essential personality is located in a mind or a consciousness that is disconnected from the world of matter. For the same reason, freedom,
is interpreted to mean, not the power to do or refrain from doing, but the virtue of interior assent or intention identified
as purity of soul. Consequently, social change is claimed to be
attainable only through sanctity, instead of labor and scientific efforts.

The same kind of dualism has penetrated human discourse,
Dewey continues to observe. In his estimation, it has made the
situation such that in order to gain a unified outlook of the
connection of events or of reality as a whole, one has first to
wrestle with linguistic difficulties. Dewey cites some instances.
The term 'self' is used as if it were a self-contained entity
separate from body and action. Thoughts are said to be 'in the
mind.' Consciousness is sometimes described as 'lost,' as if
these are complete substances. If such usages are meant to be
taken literally, the only impression that can be obtained is
that whatever exists fall into two mutually exclusive realms
called matter and mind, nature and experience, physical and psy-
psychical, etc.[66]

Dewey believes that the linguistic problem poses a special
difficulty when speaking about the unity of man removed from di-
chotomous implications. The term 'human life,' for example,
would hardly lead to the recognition that it is the unity of
mind and body that is being referred to.

> Consequently, we discuss the matter, when we talk
> of the relations of mind "and" body and endeavor
> to establish their unity in human conduct, we
> still speak of body "and" mind and thus uncon-
> sciously perpetuate the very division we are stri-
> ving to deny.[67]

This point might sound trivial. But, its has a significance,
one that will surface once the issue concerning the connection
between language and thought is confronted.

Thus, if more positive steps would be taken, the old metaphysics has to be abandoned in favor of a naturalistic ontology.
In doing so, Dewey believes, the problem will appear altogether
in a different light and with less mystery. If metaphysics were
not assigned the project of reaching out for ultimate origins
and ends, then its claims would not be permitted to transcend
the confines of experience. If the general traits nature presents and science discovers are were not rigid enclosures but

qualitative individualities, constant relations, contingency, process, evolution, then the search would be, not for substances and essences, but for qualities. The philosophical quest would, as a consequence, be not for 'what' but for 'how.'

In Dewey's observation, history has been witness to the fact the it is the search of substances that led to the separation of the psychical from the physical and all the errors entailed in such a separation. In his words, "...the habit of regarding the mental and physical as separate things has its roots in regarding them as substances or processes instead of as functions and qualities of action."[68] In this shift in the direction of inquiry from the substantial to the functional plane constitutes Dewey's first move toward a naturalistic view of the world.

By the term 'quality,' he is not referring to immediate qualities, the 'sense' of events (wet and dry, hot and cold, light and heavy, up and down), but to primary qualities, signifying qualites treated not as additives but as relations.[69] By the term 'function,' he does not mean simply 'disposition' or 'immanent action' but interaction. The interaction meant is not, however, one between two disparate terms but instead one between continuous events, as pointed out above. For the sake of linguistic clarity, 'body' and 'mind' can be better employed adverbially or adjectivally, instead of nominally. In this way, many confusions, caused by terms of the sort being interpreted in the substantial sense, can be avoided. In fact, Dewey says, it is in virtue of the different qualities and effects revealed in one and the same world of objects and events that we say something, at one point or time, acts like a lump of matter, at another, like an animal blinded by a glare of light.

Because appropriate changes in linguistic usages are virtually impossible to realize, Dewey contents himself with giving new signification to old terms. The functional framework now substituting for the substantial, his next move is to propose a method of analysis adequate to the data given in experience. For this, he calls on the empirical approach - that treatment of data so well tested as effective and fruitful in scientific disciplines. This move is not as unexpected as it may seem. His reasoning does not beg the question. He does not think that because a method is found useful in some area, a set of data under consideration should, therefore, be accommodated to it. Rather, he sees that the data are such that they cannot be appropriately dealt with by means other than the application of scientific procedures. Thus, because nature and experience present no gaps, the method adequate to the task of inquiry should be faithful to that given character. That method is the scientific method.

"Other methods," he says "begin with results of reflection that has already torn in two the subject-matter experienced and the operations and states of experiencing."[70] The scientific method alone takes the integrated unity of experience as the valid starting point of philosophical thought. It takes the subject-matter in its unanalyzed totality and through reflective analysis renders it puposeful. The analysis, it is true, leads to distinctions. But the kind and intent of the distinctions are not to divide what is initially unified, but to discover tools for conducting natural processes to consummatory ends.

> To distinguish in reflection the physical and to
> hold it in temporary detachment is to be set
> upon the road that conducts to tools and tech-
> technologies, to construction of mechanisms, to
> the arts that ensue in the wake of the sciences...
> Along with this added ability in regulation goes
> enriched meaning and values in things, clarifi-
> cation, increased depth and continuity - a re-
> sult even more precious than is the added power
> of control.[71]

As it stands now, the body-mind problem or the physical-psychical dichotomy no longer consists in how to explain the relation between the two completely heterogeneous substances or substantial principles but in how such and such an event having such and such a quality actually occurs; how a functionally physical quality is beneficial or harmful to life; how living environment is conducive or detrimental to the emergence of mind.[72] Formulated in such ways, the problem now appears less mysterious. For, as Dewey would summarily put it, "in the ultimate analysis the mystery that mind should use a body, or that a body should have a mind, is like the mystery that a man cultivating plants should use the soil; or that the soil which grows plants at all should grow those adapted to its own physico-chemical properties and relations."[73]

The alternative approach Dewey proposes does not, however, deny the reality of 'grades.' But this does not mean admission of distinct orders of reality. What it denies is precisely the postulation of different natures, principles or causes operating in each level and making the difference in the qualities of their activities. In the first place, concluding to the reality of such agencies constitutes a leap from what Dewey perceives as given to an unknown and unknowable realm transcending experience, which, for being such, is utterly unverifiable. In the second place, doing so would imply admitting a breach in the continuity of historic processes of things in nature. It is for the same reasons that Dewey rejects both the mechanistic theory (which makes the physical alone account for the existence and functions of the psychical) and the teleological or spiritualistic metaphysics (which considers happenings that precede the appearance of the psychical or the mental as mere preparations for the sake of the latter). Again, both can be seen to commit what has already been described as a false start - the assumption that the physical and the psychical are two separate things.

In place of these untenable accounts, the alternative theory

explains grades as empirical traits in nature having their own
respective categories. The categories do not, however, point to
the operations of ontologically distinct forces or causes. They
are but categories of description - conceptions required to state
the fact in questions.[74] If the concept of causation is to be introduced at all, Dewey concedes, it must be interpreted in the
manner that not the physical as such but some natural events having physical qualities be taken as the 'causes' of life and
mind. For, indeed, what such events do is mark the release of
potentialities as a given thing is engaged in diverse modes of
interactions. The wider and more complex the associations are
involved, the more fully are potentialities released and properties modified. It is in this way, too, that the phrase 'degrees
of reality' has to be understood.[75]

Dewey cautions that the case so described is not as ludic-
rous as suggesting that one phenomenon lies on top of the other.
Speaking of the social level as continuous with the physical,
he explains:

> What would social phenomena be without the phy-
> sical factor of land, including all the natural
> resources (and obstacles) and forms of energy for
> which the world "land" stands? What would social
> phenomena be without the tools and machines by
> which physical energies are utilized... The view
> is superficial of those who fail to see that in
> the social the physical is taken up into a wider
> and more complex and delicate system of inter-
> actions so that it takes on new properties by
> release of potentialities previously confined
> because of absence of full interaction.[76]

The account emphasizes that the situation is one in which the
vital or organic is included within the social. In more constructive studies, Dewey identifies and describes three distinct
grades or levels of transaction. These are as follows:

1. **The Physical.** This level (otherwise known as the inanimate field) is the scene of narrower and more external interactions, although not without qualitative diversification. It
is the scene where physico-chemical activities can be observed.
As such, it is "subject to conditions of disturbed inner equilibrium, which lead to activity in relation to surrounding
things and which terminate after a cycle of changes - terminus
termed saturation.[77] The terminus does not, however, lead to
the preservation of its integrity or 'nature' (if the term may
be used in Dewey's sense of 'qualitative manifestation'), for
the saturation occurs indifferently, in such a way that the
tendency is not towards the maintenance of a temporal pattern
of activity. Iron, for example, although exhibiting characteristic bias or selective reactions, does not tend to keeping

itself simple iron. The moment it interacts with specific elements, it is modified according to the factors involved in the
process. To illustrate: if it interacts, say, with water, it
becomes iron-oxide.

The breadth of Dewey's vision, extending to the highest
possibility of natural transactions (which he assigns to intelligence) places qualities in the inanimate field as insignificant in themselves, i. e., when divorced from their functional
value in enhancing life and mind. "The most that can be said
about qualities in the inanimate field is that they mark the
limit of the contact of historical affairs, being abrupt ends
or termini, boundaries of beginning and closing where a particular interaction ceases."[78]

But because physical things have or can acquire the added
property of being a stimulus in evoking responses in an organism,
they merit being made objects of scientific analysis.[79] Thus,
when dealing with psycho-physical occurrences, Dewey observes
the importance of taking note of the physical processes involved,
viz. those processes which the organism shares with inanimate
things.

> When they (organic processes and changes) are
> seen to be shared with processes going on in
> inanimate nature, all that is discovered without
> about the latter becomes an intellectual tool
> for the systematic knowledge of vital processes
> and the apparatus and technics for directing
> physical nature are capable of utilization in
> hygienic, medical and surgical treatment of bodiy
> changes.[80]

2. **The Psycho-Physical.** The second level of transaction
brings out the quality of life. It is here that plant and animal forms emerge. Their activities are ordered according to
needs, efforts, and satisfaction. Need is "a condition of un-
easy or unstable equilibrium;" effort is manifested in the
"movements which modify environing bodies in ways which react
upon the body, so that its characteristic pattern of active
equilibrium is restored;" satisfaction is the "recovery of equilibrium pattern, consequent upon the changes of environment due
to interactions with the active demands of the organism."[81]

Dewey explains that these concrete states of events, are
as a matter course, observable also in the physico-chemical functions of inanimate bodies. But, there is a difference - in the
way in which physico-chemical energies act and react in internally interconnected ways. In inanimate bodies, interconnectedness is random and external, and activities themselves occur
indifferently (i. e., they do not tend to maintain a temporal
pattern of activities, they do not lead to the perpetuation of
their identifying characteristics).

Dewey continues to observe that in inanimate bodies, activities, such as those that are directed toward restoration of equilibrium pattern, run through a complex integrated course or history. Interactions of various parts take place in such a way "as to tend to continue a characteristically organized activity. They tend to utilize conserved consequences of past activities so as to adapt to subsequent changes to the needs of the integral system to which they belong."[82] In Dewey's terminology, as it may now be understood, The compound term 'psycho-physical' does not denote addition of a psychic force superimposed upon matter. Rather, it means that "physical activities have acquired additional properties, those of ability to procure a peculiar kind of interactive support of needs from surrounding media."[83]

The gradual ascent of beings to a higher (in the sense of more complex) level of transaction is also explicable in no other way than in a naturalistic sense and, hence, opposed to a transcendentalist version. Consequently, technically contextual notions, such as those fundamental categories of traditional psychology ('organization,' 'sensitivity,' 'feeling,' etc.), have and can be given no more than functional (never essentialistic) definitions. 'Organization' means the presence of the whole in the parts and of the parts in the whole. The organized pattern of activity leading to the perpetuation of that condition is the basis of 'sensitivity.' Sensitivity essentially occurs when responses become not merely selective but discriminatory in behalf of some results rather than others. In those animals equipped with locomotive and distance receptors, sensitivity is realized as feeling. This happens when susceptibility to the useful and harmful elements in the animal's surrounding become premonitory. For example, an immediate quality, such as color or sound, instigates a determinate mode of action, such as one of pursuance or avoidance. This response to qualities becomes productive of results, viz., satisfaction of a need.

3. The Psychical. The third plateau of transaction is that of association, communication, participation. Here is where mind - the possession of and response to meanings - trully appears. In Dewey's description, mind arises when feelings had are not just had but are known to be had. It surfaces when the qualities of feelings become significant of objective differentiations. It comes about when those qualities are no longer just felt but make sense. This results from language - that organized system of interactions among other living creatures.

Language is the verbal formulation of meanings. For Dewey, it is quite obvious that language is a necessary condition of knowledge and, consequently, of mind. "Without language, the qualities of organic action that are feelings are pains, pleasures, odors, colors, noises, tones only potentially and proleptically. With language they are discriminated and identified."[84] This point is critical, and bears some weighty implications in any inquiry concerning man. It, therefore, deserves the separate and larger treatment that is aimed at in the following chapter.

It suffices to say here that Dewey's theory postulates that affections can be discriminated and identified as being colors, sounds, etc. only through discourse. Affections (as a whole) are those he refers to by the term 'sentience.' This (sentence) is taken up into a system of signs indicating a definite active relationship of organism and environment. He explains: "To term a quality 'hunger,' to name it, is to refer to an object, to food, to that which will satisfy it, towards which the active situation moves."[85]

This means that, for Dewey, the clear manifestation of the occurrence of mind is the presence of what he calls the double function of meaning: sense and signification. Both are quite distinct from mere feeling. On the one hand, sense has a recognized reference, feeling does not. The reference of sense is actually an immediate and immanent meaning - the qualitative characteristic of something, not just a submerged unidentified quality or tone. On the other hand, signification involves the use of quality as a sign of something else (e. g., red to mean danger). The phenomenon of signification, says Dewey, coincides with the attainment of mental quality.

He surmises that it is this transformation of the purely organic by inclusion within the more complex type of transaction just described that led to the belief in the intrusive intervention of unnatural or supernatural factors. This belief, then, is summoned in accounting for the differences between the psychophysical and the psychical fields, between the animal and the human. 'Mind,' he is convinced, comes as a distinctive trait of certain events. But its advent does not, in any manner, indicate the introduction of a foreign reality by some transcendental cause. Mind remains to be rooted in organic or psycho-physical activities, for these remain to be the conditions for the presence and operation of meanings.

The need for organic and psycho-physical basis cannot be over-emphasized. It supplies mind with its footing and connection in nature. It provides meanings with their existential stuff. But, for Dewey, meanings, ideas, etc. when they occur, are not simply characters of new interactions of events; "they are characters which in their corporation with sentiency transform organic action, furnishing it with new properties."[86] The case is analogous to sound becoming articulate speech. While speech remains to be sound, it is sound with a new property - that of meaningfulness. The property thus acquired by organic action become both instrumental (as a means of communication) and consummatory (as an event to be enjoyed).

In the context of Dewey's version of naturalism thus described, the term 'mind' applies to that "whole system of meanings as they are embodied in the workings of organic life."[87] In an article entitled "Affective Thought," he calls on the findings of physiology and psychology to corroborate his view. He reads these findings as showing the continuous development from lower to higher functions, i. e., from affectivity to reasoning.

The idea of 'affectivity,' he contends, expresses the fact that an organism has certain basic needs which are supplied only by activities modifying the surroundings. When the equilibration between the organism and its environment is disturbed, its needs become urgent or, in Dewey's word, restless, a condition which continues to be so until integration is achieved. 'Reasoning' refers to that which enters as a phase of the generic function of bringing about integration. The source from which thinking draws its 'stuff' to satisfy need is found in habits, that is, the changes wrought in ways of acting and undergoing by prior experiences.[88]

Before turning to a more detailed treatment of the complex nature of the third level of transaction,[89] two major issues (on unity and continuity[90]) raised by Dewey's critics concerning this level need to be recalled, if the more serious implications of this new framework have to be confronted. The first concerns the adequacy of Dewey's solution to the problem of the unity of man (understood as the integration of physical and psy-psychical functions) and/or the continuity of the three grades of transaction. The second pertains to the judgment that such an account of unity and continuity is tantamount to pure materialism or reductionism.

The question of adequacy is not too bothersome for Dewey. He assures his readers that the unification of being, in which-ever level of transaction, is not undermined. As already seen in his metaphysical scheme, unity and continuity are included in the list of nature's given traits. Consistently, the distinctions he makes to refer to physical, psycho-physical, and psy-chical or mental events are not intended to draw lines marking separate realms. They are, instead, meant to indicate "levels of increasing complexity and intimacy of interaction among natural events."[91] Though they are all aspects of and within nature, each plateau has its own qualities and patterns of behaving which are continuous with, yet distinguishable from, the others. In a more lucid language, Dewey describes the delicate balance between continuity and uniqueness thus:

> ...While there is no isolated occurrence in nature, yet interaction are not wholesale and homogenous. Interacting events have tighter and looser ties, which qualify them with certain beginnings and endings, and which mark them off from other fields of interaction.[92]

The problems which are more applicable to the dynamic situation are not those requiring identification of permanent boundaries and static beings. Rather, these are more pragmatic concerns, such as, how loose ends can be tightened, how a relatively close field can come into conjunction of more intimate nature with another, how new energies may be released so as to bring about new qualities, how physical condition can lead to

the emergence of mental qualities.[93] And to find solutions to
these, the adoption of the regulative and directive power of
science is recommended. This instrument is suitable not only to
smooth over rough junctures but "to give facility and security
in utilizing the simpler manageable field to predict and modify
the course of the more complete and highly organized."[94]

Summarily, the differences in qualities must be understood
as ones of degree and emphasis, and always within the basic background of unity and continuity. Thus, as Dewey suggests, in the
analysis of behavior, some functions may still be treated as
primarily physical (e. g., digestion, reproduction, and locomo-
tion), since they are conspicuously so, and others as mental
(e. g., thinking, desiring, hoping, loving, fearing), since they
are distinctively so. Yet, he cautions,

> if we are wise, we shall not regard the diffe-
> rence as other than one of degree and emphasis.
> If we go beyond and draw a sharp line between
> them, consigning one set to body exclusively and
> the other to mind exclusively we are at once
> confronted with undeniable facts. The being who
> eats and digests is also the one who at the same
> time is sorrowing and rejoicing; it is a common-
> place that he eats and digests in one way to one
> effect when glad, and to another when sad.[95]

The so-called body-mind relation may likewise be understood no
longer as a mystery. For,

> In the hyphenated phrase body-mind, "body" desig-
> nates the continued and conserved, the registered
> and cumulative operation of factors continuous
> with the rest of nature, inanimate as well as ani-
> mate; while "mind" designates the characters and
> consequences which are differential, indicative
> of features which emerge when "body" is engaged
> in a wider, more complex and interdependent
> situation.[96]

Simply, from the standpoint of human action - of life in operation - 'body' presents itself as the mechanism, the instrumentality of behavior, while 'mind' as its function, its fruit,
and consummation.[97]

If some sense is to be given to the question 'where' the
mind is, an intelligible reply (limiting the application to the
organic individual) would be saying:

> the "seat" or locus of mind - its static phase -

is the qualities of organic action, as far as
these qualities have been conditioned by language
and its consequences. It is usual for those who
are posed by the question of "where" and who are
reluctant to answer that mind is "where" there is
a spaceless separate realm of existence, to fall
back in general on the nervous system, and specifically upon the brain or its cortex as the "seat"
of mind. But the organism is not just a structure;
it is a characteristic way of interactivity which
is not simultaneous, all at once but serial.[98]

Dewey believes that the functioning of mind involves not only
the brain but also other organs of the body. Furthermore, the
physiological processes can take place only insofar as they
interact with or adjust to events outside the boundary of the
body. In this view of unity, he is convinced, lies the answer
to the problems that haunt philosophy since the Pre-socratics.
Here, too, with analogous application, he sees the solution to
the failures of specialization.

Those who talk most of the organism, physio-
logists and psychologists, are often just those
who display least sense of the intimate, delicate
and subtle interdependence of all organic structures and processes with one another. The world
seems mad in pre-occupaton with what is specific,
particular, disconnected in medicine, politics,
science, industry, education. In terms of a conscious control of inclusive wholes, search for
those links which occupy key positions and which
affect critical connections is indispensable. But
recovery of sanity depends upon seeing and using
these specifiable things "as" links functionally
significant in process. To see the organism in
nature, the nervous system in the organism, the
brain in the nervous system, the cortex in the
brain is the answer to the problems that haunt
philosophy.[99]

A more difficult issue Dewey has to confront is that pertaining to reductionism or materialism he has been accused of
maintaining. To this charge he reacts quite sanguinely. The reason is not distaste for the stigma the name bears, a name which
now is being associated with him. It is, rather, the fear that
such an accusation could place him in bad company and simultaneously lead to misunderstanding his genuine thoughts. But, in
noting his strong protest to name-calling and explicit disavowal
of materialism, it remains to be seen if, in fact, he does succeed in extricating himself from the charge. Such a determination is obviously hinged on what 'materialism' means, that sort
of materialism he specifically rejects. The term, historically,

is both equivocal and ambiguous, judging from the different meanings it has received from the early Greeks to the most recent
British Empiricists. The term 'matter' by itself is already quite
problematic, to say the least.

But, if 'matter' does mean something, it cannot but be conceived as a measurable, perceivable entity or event. And if such
were the case, the charge would immediately appear unjustified.
For, in Dewey's usage, 'matter' or the 'physical' refers to that
character of events occurring at a certain level of interaction.
Assuredly,

> ...what we call matter is that character of na-
> tural events which is so tied up with changes
> that are sufficiently rapid to be perceptible as
> to give the latter a characteristic source of
> events or processes; no absolute monarch; no
> principle of explanation; no substance in which
> a man well fortified with this world's goods,
> and hence able to maintain himself through vicis-
> situdes of surroundings, is a man of substance.
> The name designates a character in operation, not
> an entity.[100]

Hence, Dewey's 'matter' has nothing in common with the 'matter'
of classical materialists like Democritus and Hobbes.

Considering Dewey's system itself which has been labeled as
a form of materialism, it may the case be that critics are making
a similar misapprehension? To arrive at a fair judgment, classical materialism needs to be compared with his brand of naturalism. A convenient procedure is to start with an enumeration of
some propositions ordinarily accepted as tenets of materialism.
An exhaustive list is, obviously, both uncalled for and unnecessary. It is sufficient to cite only those representative statements made by materialists and which Dewey's critics themselves
take to be claims of true materialists. The process will help
determine in what specific sense Dewey is or is not a materialist.

1. If one who does not regard "this world and all that is
in it, as dust and ashes, compared with the value of a single
soul...," who does not consider "the action of this world and
the action of the soul simply incommensurate,"[101] is a materialist, then Dewey is truly a materialist. For, indeed, he rejects
the idea that the soul and its action, as supernatural realities,
are in opposition to the natural world and its action. He likewise eschews the thought that the natural is basically corrupt.
He is quick, however, to make a qualification. His form of naturalism does not fly to the opposite extreme.

It holds to the possibility of discovering by

natural means those conditions in human nature
and in the environment which work concretely
toward production of concrete forms of social
health and social disease - just as the possibility of knowledge and of control in action by
adequate knowledge are in process of actual
demonstration in the case of medicine.[102]

It is true that naturalism "regards everything that exists
or occurs to be conditioned in its existence or occurrence by
causal factors within one all-encompassing system of nature,
however 'spiritual' or purposeful or rational some of these
things and events may in their functions and values prove to
be," But it does not deny that a distinction should be made between the causal factors and the values conditioned by those factors. The qualitative nature of the cause does not necessarily
condition the qualitative nature of its effect, Dewey maintains.
Life and mind, he admits, can occur only in certain conditions
as the result of suitable causes; but the causes may not altogether be living and mental. But origination from a lowly cause
needs not be taken as a reason for demoting the result, just as
the excellence of the effect need not be attributed to the cause.
Simply stated, what conditions an event is not necessarily the
measure of value of that event.

In Dewey's naturalism, then, there is no reduction of a result to its conditions. Concretely, there is no reduction of the
mental to its physical matrix. On the contrary, it recognizes
"in their full force all the observed facts which constitute the
differences that exist between man and other animals as well as
those fact which constitute strands of continuity between the
different modes of living."[103] In an uncharacteristically sharp
tone, Dewey leaves no room for doubt with respect to his denial
of reductionism: "Any notion that human action is identical with
that of non-living things or with that of the "lower" animals
is silly."[104]

Even when considering the wider scope of evolution, he consistently maintains the same posture. He declares that it is possible, and sometimes, desirable, to state the processes of an organized being in physico-chemical terms. But this does not mean
that the peculiar features of living and thinking beings are to
be eliminated or explained away by resolution into the features
found in non-living things.

Organic life which defies total explanation in
the categorial concepts of mechanics typifies a
freedom which is not possessed by the inorganic
world. Consciousness insofar as it cannot be completely defined in biological terms is characterized by a quality of freedom lacking in the
organic world.[105]

He is saying that a purely mechanistic or vitalistic metaphysics
is an inadequate account of real affairs. For, the nature of
the changes of physico-chemical things, as they enter into more
and complex interactions, exhibit capacities - vital, intellectual, moral, social - never to be found in an exclusively mechanical world.[106]

    Particularly in the level of human intercourse, Dewey
observes, one should not fail to recognize the qualifying factor
that modifies what may, at first glance, appear as a strictly
physical event. Taking a case from an ordinary social experience
to illustrate the point, he states:

> When one of us steps on the toes of his neighbor
> in a crowded place, we offer regrets - since
> otherwise we are likely to subject ourselves
> to sour looks, irritation and resentment. A
> strictly physical event has taken place, but
> even from an ordinary common-sense point of view,
> the physical is not the whole of the matter. The
> presence of a personal relation introduces a qua-
> lifying factor.[107]

And, as a marked indication of dissociation from reductionist
materialism, he rebukes those who deny "higher" phenomena under
the pretext of being faithfully scientific in the approach.

> Take the case of those who revolt against the
> old dualism and who because of their revolt
> imagine they must throw away and deny the exis-
> tence of all phenomena that go by the names of
> "higher", intellectual and moral. Such persons
> exist. they suppose they are not scientific un-
> less they reduce everything to the exclusively
> somatic and physiological.[108]

    What he warns against is the employment of those differen-
tial qualities exhibited by mental or psychical events as basis
for arguing that such events are cut off or separate from the
physical. For Dewey, reality is the growth-process itself, where
events are phases of a continuity, of a history. To suppose a
breach in the historical process, as supernaturalists do, is to
alienate an event from its natural environment, to stifle it, to
render it impertinent to the direction of the process. He declares:

> Unless vital organizations were organizations of
> antecedent natural events, the living creature
> would have no natural connections; it would not
> be pertinent to its environment nor its environ-

ment relevant to it; the latter would not be usable, material of nutrition and defence. In similar fashion, unless "mind" was, in its existential occurrence, an organization of physiological or vital affairs and unless its functions developed out of the patterns of organic behavior, it would have no pertinency to nature, and nature would not be the appropriate scene of its inventions and plans, nor the subject-matter of its miracle, that a separate mind is inserted abruptly in nature, its operation would be wholly dialectical, and in a sense of dialectic which is non-existential not only for the time being, but forever; that is dialectic would be without any possible reference to existence.[109]

Thus, Dewey is opposed to reductionism in either extreme - the kind called 'pure materialism' or the sort referred to as 'unadulterated idealism.' He is against materialism in which material and mechanical means are severed from the consequences which give them meaning and value. He is also opposed to spiritualistic idealism in which intellectual and spiritual functions are disengaged from the ultimate conditions and means of all achievement, namely, the physical.[110]

2. A materialist (or, more technically, a mechanist) is one who denies the existence of a life-force or a substantial soul in a living body distinct or separate from the body itself. He does so on the basis of two fundamental reasons. First, a life-force or a soul is a superfluous addition insofar as life and mind can be adequately explained by the physico-chemical energies and reactions of matter. Second, a living body (organism) is merely the sum-total of its material parts with their respective physico-chemical properties. Krikorian, writing on the naturalistic view of mind, sums up the wider meaning of mechanism as that which "may be identified with causal explanation, where the relations employed are non-teleological, causal relations, that is to say, invariant correlations, and where the entities employed are physico-chemical entities."[111]

Is Dewey a mechanist in the sense so described? Clearly not. For, while he denies the reality of soul in the traditional concept of it as a substance, passages quoted above show that he never identifies the phenomena of life and mind with the purely physico-chemical energies and reactions of matter. What he insistently maintains is that the matrix or condition of life and mind is the physical. This, however, is not reductionism. It does not follow that, because life is described to exist within the medium of mechanism, it is thereby defined in terms of mechanism. While living beings are through and through physico-chemical in composition, there is no purely mechanical definition of life. Life, in Dewey's account, is purposive behavior.

Krikorian's terminology is helpful. The difference between

a mechanist and a naturalist lies in the fact that the former explains life and mind in terms of additive organizations, while the latter explains the same in terms of non-additive ones. The first explains life as the sum of the (physico-chemical) units constituting an organism; the second takes into account the differential quality or purpose exhibited on account of the organization.[112] As already stated above, in Dewey's language, the organism is not just a structure but a characteristic way of interactivity. "It is a way impossible without structures for its mechanism, but it differs from structure as walking differs from legs or breathing from lungs."[113]

3. Perhaps, the aspect of Dewey's naturalism which is more oftenly criticized is his fundamental belief in the universal application of the empirical or scientific method. Such a belief, the criticism argues, implies a reductionist view. The argument to this effect states: method is not independent of subject-matter. As Sheldon points out, we do not use telescope to dissect the seeds of a plant.[114] The scientific method is ordered to the study of material subject-matter; it is suitable only to the observable or physical. Since Dewey, as a naturalist philosopher, appropriates this method, employs it exclusively, and endorses its application to the study of mind and behavior, he (as any naturalist adopting solely the same method) thereby, reduces mind and behavior to the purely physical. The naturalist is, in fact, a materialist, reducing all states and events to a degree of being wholly at the beck of the states and processes called material or physical.

The argument, in all appearances, is a serious one. For, it is a fact that this is one aspect of Dewey's naturalism in which he shares the intent and cultural motivation of materialism. It is also a fact that he confines the real to the natural order. He proposes that the various features of reality (the mind not excepting) should be examined as a natural phenomena. For, everything has its origin, growth, and decay within the physical, biological and social setting.

Do these affirmations make Dewey a materialist? Again, a negative reply is quite tenable. He favors the scientific method generally because he recognizes its efficacy; it is the only me-method that submits its material to thorough experimentation and verification. (As will appear in the following chapter, there are other reasons for this preference.) Thus, without being dogmatic, it allows no room for obscurantism. The traditional conception of mind, Dewey observes, is infected by so many mysteries precisely because it had been the result of a non-empirical approach. Such an approach proceeds by introspection and, by it, arrives at non-verifiable conclusions. The naturalistic method takes behavior as its object of analysis. Being a phenomenon open to public examination, findings can be treated, tested, and verified in a truly objective manner. That the application of this procedure is not 'ipso facto' the adoption of materialism is born by the fact that conclusions arrived at do not classify all modes of behavior identically.

Dewey complains of the narrownes of his critics' conception
of 'matter.' They identify what is material with what is spatially and temporally limited. If to confine reality to nature
is what materialism means, then he would have no quarrel about
being named under it. But, he insists that his brand of naturalism does not limit all events to the physical or material boundaries. What he finds fault in is the unfounded belief of the
same critics to the classification of reality into two mutually
exclusive and unbridgeable realms.

Take Sheldon's critique as an instance. Its premise that
scientific method is ordered solely to the study of the material,
and, hence, observable subject-matter is hardly true. It confuses
the notion of 'method' with that of 'instrument.' A scientific
method, Dewey would explains, is a manner of approach, a system
of analysis, which makes use of observation. This is why it has
to have what is observable for its subject-matter. but an observable datum is not necessarily material. Mental events are observable, at least to the thinking subject. They are also accessible
to others, being externally communicable via speech and behavioral language. Yet, these are not material.[115] The fact that they
can be treated scientifically needs no demonstration. It is sufficient to point to the existence of the sciences of psychoana-
lysis and psychiatry.

Furthermore, the scientific method does not end in mere
observation and collection of data. It includes interpretation
as its consummatory stage. Significantly, it is precisely in
this phase that an inquirer could end up being a mechanist, a
naturalist, or an idealist. On this point, Krikorian observes:

> Experimentalism does not mean that we can under-
> stand nature by merely gathering facts, but ra-
> ther by interpreting them after they are gathered.
> Mechanism is one form of interpretation; purpose
> is another. It may be that the two are not incom-
> patible - that certain objects are both mechanical
> and puruposive. Living beings are through and
> through physico-chemical, yet there is no mecha-
> nical definition of life. Life is a purposive
> behavior, and our task will be so to define life
> that it may dwell in the world of mechanism and
> be of it, yet without being turned into mechanism
> or without mechanism being turned into it.[116]

In the final analysis, the worth of an interpretation depends on
whether or not it can be verified in experience. Dewey is confident that his view, not that of the materialist or the transcendentalist, can pass this test.

###

CHAPTER II

COMMUNITY AND COMMUNICATION

The word 'communication' does not bear an univocal signification in Dewey's philosophical lexicon. He shifts from one sense to a another, often without warning. While it would be useful to make a complete listing of his meanings for the term, such a tedious task is quite unnecessary forthe purpose of the present study. It is sufficient to identify two of his fundamental usages: 1) in the usual sense, as a medium of transmitting thoughts, feelings, etc.; and 2) in a broad sense, as descriptive of the shared life of people in society. The first refers more directly to the ins- trumental aspect of communication, viz., language as a form of communication that makes knowledge possible. The second points clearly, but in an oblique way, to the consummatory aspect, which consists in the the aesthetic enjoyment of shared experience. The The fact that Dewey's theory allows communication to be both ins- trumental and final presents particular difficulty in ascertai- ning his meanings in specific locations. The best guide in all cases is, of course, the context of the discussion.

The deliberation on the third plataeu of interaction directs attention to communication, specifically language, as the condi- tion for the emergence of mind (cf. above, p.26). It indicates the continuity of physical interaction with organic and psycho- physical activities without, however, diminishing the distinctive character of the the psycho-physical. But the account in that setting is more descriptive than demonstrative. It depicts the resulting condition of the process of evolution, but it does not show how such an evolution takes place. It signals the time when mind appears, but it does not explicate how it becomes. These shortcomings are partly due to Dewey's wandering style of expo- sition (which, nevertheless, has been closely followed in that section so as to preserve his original thoughts) and partly due to the elusive nature of the phenomenon under consideration.

In this chapter, then, what has been thus far an incomplete treatment of the subject will be resumed and expanded. Here, Dewey's theory of language will be reconstructed along the lines of four of his major claims. These are as follows: First, his contention that the origin of language, and, hence, of mind, is biological - a claim that strategically provides empirical foun- dation to his behavioristic theory of human nature and conduct. Second, his account of meanings as consequence of communication, i. e., of shared experience among men. Third, his conclusion that language is a necessary condition of thought and knowledge and, hence, shapes them according to its established categories, as is shown by the fact that language reflects the the culture in which it is in use. Fourth, his affirmation that language (and communication at large) is both instrumental (in the sense that it is an agency of social education and the medium by which a society of beings is transformed into a community of humans) and

38

consummatory (in that it consists in "sharing in the objects and arts precious to a community... a sharing whereby meanings are enhanced, deepened, and solidified"[1]).

A. Language and Meaning

One of Dewey's disagreements with both transcendentalists and empiricists concerns their treatment of social institutions as if it were the result of "ready made specific physical or mental endowment of a self-sufficing individual wherein language acts as a mechanical go-between, to convey observations and ideas that have prior and independent existence."[2] Language is taken by them as mere words or sounds that happen to be associated with perceptions, sentiments, and thoughts which are already complete prior to language.

Dewey believes that such a conception does not tally with the biological pattern of mental development. According to him, it reverses the actual order of relation between psychic response and linguistic forms. "Organic and psycho-physical activities with their qualities are conditions which have to come into existence before mind, the presence and operations of meanings, ideas, is possible."[3] The former may not yet constitute meanings, but they provide the latter with existential stuff. For example, he explains that some organic act of absorption or elimination of seeking or turning away from, destroying or caring for, signaling or responding, all serve as footing in nature to thought and meaning. Conversely, without language, all there is in private consciousness is a substratum of psycho-physical actions.

Elsewhere,[4] Dewey traces the origin of language (signs and significance), not from intent and ready-made minds, but as the result of overflow or as by-products of gestures and sounds which are not yet expressive. In that original condition, these gestures and sounds are still forms of organic behavior and, hence, not yet communicative. The description is vaguely reminiscent of the Aristotelian concept of potency-act development. But the similarity is too superficial to be made a basis for an argument showing intellectual kinship. The category of continuity implying historical process allows no room even for the most mitigated type of dualism such as what hylomorphism appears to be. He is quick to explain:

> When mind is said to be implicit, involved,
> latent, or potential in matter, and subsequent
> change is asserted to be an affair of making
> it explicit, evolved, manifest, actual, what
> happens is that a natural history is first cut
> arbitrarily and unconsciously into two, and then
> the severance, is consciously and arbitrarily

cancelled. It is simpler not to start by engaging in such maneuvers.[5]

Dewey simply cannot accept the idea of language, thought,
or mind as separate from nature. For (as has already been cited
above), if such were indeed the case, mental operations would
be wholly dialectical, i. e., without any possible reference to
existence. It is only when mind occurs as an organization of physiological affairs and developed out of the patterns of organic
behavior that it would have relevance to nature and that nature
would be the fitting scene of its inventions and the subject-
matter of its knowledge. What must be noted in this open declaration is an implicit proposal on how to face the issue concerning truth - to take it as a pseudo-problem and, hence, meriting
no serious philosophical attention. The fact is, a mind which has
developed from nature must bear the impress of nature's structure. It will naturally find at least some of its categories to
be concordant with nature's. It is only from this standpoint that
philosophy can extricate itself from the dilemma which British
Empiricism left it in. It will, then, appear that their quarrels
are no more than a petty exercise in dialectic.

The theory tracing the origin of language from biological
roots equips Dewey with an empirical ground for a behavioristic
account of meaning. Meaning, he says, is not a psychic existence
but a property of behavior. This is why it is inherently objective; it is a habit of response which people have and which is
open to stimulation by many things.[65] Following this direction
leads to the consideration of all mental activities, including
intelligence, as natural capacities. So understood, intelligence
would be that "peculiar aptitude for the conservation of meanings which is a natural consequence of the forms of human interaction."[7]

If the question were to be asked: What causes or what occasions lead to the assumption of psychic quality by a psycho-physical event? Dewey's answer would be, the context of mutual
assistance and direction, i. e., communication. This organized
interaction brings about the transformation of sounds into signs
and of words into meanings that make up language. Viewed from a
behavioristic standpoint, the event can be described as 'cooperative,' "in that response to another's act involves contempora-
neous response to a thing as entering into the other's behavior,
and this upon both sides."[8] Language, in turn, makes organic
psycho-physical actions identifiable objects and events, with
perceptible character.[9] This is saying that the linguistic media
(speech, gestures, etc.) are what make possible ideas and emotions. In its original form, language serves to coordinate the
behavior of one organism with that of another. This is why it is
a form of communication! Under more sophisticated conditions,
it can add qualitative functions, such as scientific and artistic
ones.

The setting, where the pervading quality is communication,

is distinctively human precisely because of that quality. With
it, a particular event becomes characterized, enriched with the
additive of ideas or meanings. Clearly, Dewey is referring here
to the level where knowledge is attained. In the human psyche,
it stands for thought or 'reflection.' The former term is basic;
the latter is more significant. It implies necessary dependence
on association. It is domesticated speech which arises in the
course of social living. Actually, even in its privacy, it is
submerged in a network of relations. Thus, it is analyzable only
as an internal dialogue; it is a mental soliloquy, and "soliloquy
is the product and reflex of converse with others...[10] If we have
not talked with others and they with us, no reflection is ever
possible.

In a typical Deweyan twist, mind-in-action becomes describ-
able only as a mode of behavior, i. e., not substantially. Reflection, for instance, is considered reflective not because it
is a self-enclosed Cartesian 'res cogitans,' but because it is
a mirror of the various strands of social life. Studies of various linguistic phenomena through which mind is expressed, he
believes, lend support to his claim. Levi points out what Dewey
sees, "mind and self originates within the matrix of society
and the clue to social nature is to be found in the uses of language."[11] Tesconi, in defense of the idea, cites an interesting
paper by a black actor and author, Ossie Davis, published in
the Saturday Review[12] which relates how language supports and
sustains (not only expresses) prejudicial thought in regard to
race. A close examination of dictionaries and thesaurus brought
Davis to that conclusion. In Roget's Thesaurus, for example, he
counted, on the one hand, 120 synonyms for 'blackness' and most
of them with connotations that are vulgar, like smut, soot,
blotch, unclean, foul, sinister, etc. For the word 'white,' on
the other hand, the 134 synonyms have favorable connotations:
purity, cleanness, honorable, innocent, and the like.

For the very reason that language presupposes shared experience and joint activities, it cannot be realistically treated
as an external of private mental processes. Rather, the use made
of gestures, sound, and marks within the social context has to
be explored. The error of nominalism, Dewey suggests, consists
in its failure to follow this prescription. In denying interaction, the only alternative left for it is to insist that the
words we use are expressions of pre-formed, exclusively individual, mental states.[13] Furthermore, in ignoring organization,
it makes nonsense of 'meaning.' For, meanings do occur only when
forms of linguistic media (sounds, gestures, or written marks)
establish a genuine community of action.

Dewey's version of the Copernican revolution appears in
this context. In his analysis, the Greeks, on the one hand, took
the structure of discourse for the structure of things. This is
what led them to the subject-object categories. "They conceived
of ideal meanings as the ultimate framework of events, in which
a system of substances and properties corresponded to subjects
and predicates of the uttered proposition."[14] Moreover, they as-

sume that the correspondence of things and meanings is prior to
social intercourse and language. He, on the other hand, takes
the structure of discourse for the forms things assume under the
pressure of social cooperation and exchange, a reversal that
avoids the paradoxes of a representative theory of knowledge
sustained in traditional epistemologies.

For the sake of clarification, the phrase 'forms which
things assume under the pressure of communication' can be equated with Dewey's meaning of 'meaning.' The rule is the same: no
person or thing can possess any designated meaning prior to or
outside conjoint existence.

> The meaning of signs moreover always includes
> something common as between persons and object.
> When we attribute meaning to the speaker as his
> intent, we take for granted another person who
> is to share in the execution of the intent, and
> also something independent of the persons con-
> cerned, through which the intent is to be rea-
> lized. Persons and thing must alike serve as
> means in a common shared consequences. This
> community of partaking is meaning.[15]

In his reply to Prof. Everett Hall's critique of the meaning of meaning in Experience and Nature, Dewey adds some qua-
lifications to his statement on the identification of community
of partaking with meaning. While reiterating the principle that
events "acquire" meaning through the fact of human intercourse,
he also makes clear to Hall and what Hall believes to be the
confused readers of Experience and Nature that to say meanings
are begotten of communication is "neither to say, nor imply,
that conditions of origin are identical with those of all subsequent status."[16] This assertion refutes Hall's imputation
that he is restricting meanings to linguistic behavior. On the
contrary, he is postulating that language has the consequence
of reaction, of reacting upon other events (physical or human)
giving them meaning and significance. "After communication has
been instituted," Dewey says, "its pattern is extended to all
sorts of acts and things, so that they become signs of other
things."[17] He calls this the 'language of nature.'

But even with this extension, the dependence of meaning on
communication and the social participation based on it is not
eliminated. For, without the latter, such a 'language of nature'
is not possible. Prior to communication, Dewey admits, there are
indeed some indispensable natural prerequisites to meaning, such
as immediate qualities and 'feelings.' But he does not regard
these as 'per se' meanings. They function more as existential
basis to or as 'stuff' of meanings. In themselves, they have
no recognized reference; they are but submerged and unidentified
quality or tone. Meaning appears as 'sense' only when they become a qualitative characteristic of something, or as 'signifi-

cation' when they are used as signs of something else.[19]

A further development of the doctrine concerning the dependence of meaning on communication is the relation between knowledge (and, for that matter, mind) and language. At first glance, the question seems to be adequately covered in the foregoing. For, if meaning depends on communication and language, then, knowledge (which is nothing more than the system of meanings) is 'ipso facto' similarly based on language. But this conclusion runs counter to the evolutionary perspective Dewey so tenaciously adheres to. According to that perspective, language is a development from the animal-function of signaling and similar acts and, hence, must be a later occurrence.[20] If it comes later, how can it provide psychic qualities to said animal acts? In other words, how can knowledge occur when the condition for its occurrence is yet to exist? If psychic or mental phenomenon is begotten of language, how can it come about when language is yet to become?

Of course, it can be argued that language is not necessarily identical with communication, as Dewey seems to be explaining on a point in an earlier part of this chapter. So distinguished, communication can explain the achievement of language, and language can account for the attainment of cognitive quality. This interpretation is not too farfetched. Dewey, in fact, accepts some forms of communication which are non-linguistic. But the difficulty is not yet resolved by so admitting. For, at the same time, Dewey does not identify language merely with verbal transmission of ready-made thoughts, as has been cited above. 'Language,' 'discourse,' 'communication' are almost indistinguishable in his vocabulary, whatever he may say to the contrary on specific occasions. These all denote the humanly shared experience saturated with meanings. Thus, he unhesitatingly declares: "In the human being, this function (of signaling acts) becomes language, communication, discourse, in virtue of which the consequences of the experience of one form of life are integrated in the behavior of others."[21] Even when literary propriety compels him to sharpen his usage, verbal forms or 'recorded speech' is given no privileged status.

What is clear, however, is that verbal communication and communication as shared experience are intrinsically related. The fact is, Dewey would perhaps argue that the former cannot be truly communicative without the latter. This is why Dewey does not tire of insisting on the contextual value of meanings. There can be no transmission of meanings without a sharing in a common situation, a situation vaguely described in his discussion of the third plateau of transaction as 'complex.' This is the essential peculiarity of language. Participation, instead of egocentric activity, puts man "at the standpoint of a situation in which two parties share."[22]

To support his claim, Dewey draws heavily from Ogden and Richards' "The Meaning of Meaning."[23] In his reply to Hall, he directs attention to an account in it about an incident described by J. H. Weeks in his book entitled **Among Congo Cannibals**. The

narrative, says Dewey, amply demonstrates the difficulty of
understanding among people with different cultural backgrounds.
It tells that there is more to communication than mere use of
verbal signs. Words may be arbitrary, but the meanings they stand
for are begotten of culture.

The notion of shared experience is indispensable for the
occurrence of meanings leads to a new conception of objectivity
that can be assigned to them. Linguistic media are said to be
objective because they have marks and are capable of connotation
and denotation. Thus, they are more than just events; they are
infused with consequences and implications. From them, other logical operations, such as inference and reasoning follows; "these
operations are reading the message of things, which things utter
because they are involved in human associations."[24] Objectivity
is accounted for by the fact that meanings are a socio-cultural
phenomenon. This is saying that linguistic media take on meanings
or become 'objectified' as the ideas and emotions related to
these media are experienced by more than one person, by at least
two different centers of behavior. It is in this way that a meaning involves a set of expectations stimulated by some existential events such as linguistic media, objects of experience,
etc.[25] Dewey's example in **Experience and Nature** is conveniently
illustrative:

> A traffic policeman holds up his hand or blows his
> whistle. His act operates as a signal to direct
> movements. But it is more than an episodic sti-
> mulus. It embodies a rule of social action. Its
> proximate meaning is its near-by consequences in
> coordination of movements of persons and vehicles;
> its ulterior and permanent meaning - essence - is
> its consequence in the way of security of social
> movements.[26]

The point he is making is quite clear. Communication is a presupposition of meaning. In relation to knowledge, communication
(specifically the linguistic sort) is similarly required. But
how can knowledge arise when it is precisely such type of interaction that is lacking in those levels where knowledge is absent
(as in the first and second level of interaction or in the level
of infancy)? The difficulty here, in validating the claim that
knowledge arises from language, appears greater than explaining
how meaningful conversations result as an overflow or by-product
of gestures and sounds.

Dewey's mind is not easy to read through the contexts of relevant passages. Of themselves, the texts are not clear. Taking
a constructive approach, however, is helpful. If the development
of applicable materials would be followed to its logical conclusion, then we have to admit the simultaneity of knowledge and
language, so that the achievement of language is likewise the
attainment of knowledge. E. G. Mesthene, in an essay entitled

"How Language Makes Us Know" goes farther than taking them to be simultaneous. He attributes to Dewey the postulate that the process of acquiring knowledge (he terms 'inquiry') is identical with the process of formulating that knowledge into language. Emphatically, he regards this view as one of the most important conclusions of Dewey's Logic.[27]

There is no metaphor in his statement. Mesthene means it literally, so he says. Language is important not only for storing and transmitting knowledge. It is essential for getting it in the first place. He admits that formulation, as a phase of inquiry, can be distinguished from other elements of knowledge for ana- lytic purposes. But he insists that inquiry and formulation are not (in Dewey), two separate processes. He invokes a number of passages from the Logic. One bears an indirect reference to the point. Speaking of the logical import of mapping, Dewey states: The relations of the map are similar (in the technical sense of the word) to those of the country (i. e., of which it is a map) because both are instituted by one and the same set of opera- tions."[28] In the formal definition of inquiry given earlier in the same book, the text comes closer to Mesthene's interpreta- tion.

> Inquiry is the controlled or directed transfor-
> mation of an indeterminate situation into one
> that is so determinate in its constituent dis-
> tinctions and relations as to convert the ele-
> ments of the original situation into a unified
> whole.[29]

Then, on the following page, the crucial statement on the func- tion of language or discourse in inquiry is made:

> In the intermediate course of transition and
> transformation of the indeterminate situation
> discourse through use of symbols is employed as
> means. In received logical terminology, propo-
> sitions, or terms and the relations between them
> are intrinsically involved.[30]

In these texts, Mesthene reads Dewey as saying that dis- course (the use of terms and propositions) appears as the agency of transformation from an indeterminate to a determinate situa- tion. It is the tool by which situations are manipulated to get knowledge. The same interpretation can be found in D. A. Piatt: "Granted that reasoning operates with ideas or concepts, it does so only by the manipulation of symbols arranged as terms, propo- sitions, and the like. There is no thought without language beha- vior."[31] This is why Dewey refuses to admit that speech is merely a practical convenience and bears no intellectual significance. He rejects the idea that it consists of mere words that happen to be associated with perceptions, sentiments, and thoughts which are complete prior to language. He cannot accept the analogy that language merely expresses thought as pipes conduct water without any transformation taking place in the process. Such conceptions ignore the office of signs in creating reflection, foresight, and recollection.[32]

The doctrine on the requirement of language for thought directly brings to the fore the instrumental nature of language. Language promotes consciousness - "that phase of a system of meanings which at a given time is undergoing redirection, transitive transformation."[33] It affects no only persons but events as well. For, "when communication occurs, all natural events are subject to consideration and revision. They are readapted to meet the requirements of conversation, whether it be public discourse or that preliminary discourse termed thinking."[34]

But language also signals the attainment of character. "Natural events become messages to be enjoyed and administered. Thus events come to possess characters; they are demarcated and noted."[35] When events acquire meanings, they assume representatives, surrogates, signs, implicates. They are thereby rendered more manageable. This is so because through meanings humans are oftentimes saved from serious effects of accidents as they deal with real things. Language, says Piatt, has the advantage that "it takes us away from actual smoke and fire to symbols as substitutes so as to bring us back with the means of identifying, recognizing, understanding and controlling smoke and fire."[36] Even if accidents happen in the realm of symbolic terms, the mishap is not too unfortunate because it is always corrigible. Overt activity can always be postponed until symbolic representations forecast an outcome which might be favorable. In this way, energy is economized and the release of nature's powers is made more effectively useful.

From a humanistic standpoint, communication is no less valuable. In fact, it is the means by which natural environment is converted into a cultural setting. Events are made no longer indifferent to human response. In taking on meanings through language, they can now be passed around, from on to another. Wants and inmpulses are, then, attached to them. These, in turn, are transformed into desires and purposes, implicated as they are in a common meaning and new ties. It is in this sense that Dewey speaks of the generation of what may be metaphorically called 'general will' and 'social consciousness': "Desire and choice on the part of individuals in behalf of activities that, by means of symbols, are communicable and shared by all concerned."[37]

The ideas of 'general will' and 'social consciousness' are synonymous to the notion of community in two related senses. In the first place, the environment is cultural and, therefore, contains "charged stimuli," i. e., conditions favorable to characteristic human activities. In the second place, the persons involved present an order of energies transmuted into one of mea-

nings which are mutually appreciated and consulted when engaged
in combined action. But the idea is an ideal, in the sense that
it is not an achieved fact but a prospective one. "We are born
organic beings associated with others, but we are not born members of a community."[38] To be actualized, the idea entails two
prescriptions: First, humans are asked to promote the cultural
environment through a process of continuous refinement. Second,
they are directed to bring the young within the traditions, outlook, and interests inherent in the community and by which that
community is identified. As he says For, "everything which is
distinctively human is learned, not native, even though it could
not be learned without native structures which mark man off from
other animals."[39]

The method proposed by Dewey, particularly for the latter
project, is education. The educational system, however, is not
closed within the school walls, at least not for him. Society
itself, he says, is the great educator.

> ...society with its meanings stored in books, tech-
> niques, occupations, customs, mores, and institu-
> tions, constitutes an objective realm of mind. It
> is this society with its established modes of ac-
> tion and thought which patterns the conduct of the
> child, and which, therefore, functions as the great
> educator.[40]

Again, communication is the basic instrument that society employs. In fact, social life is a life of communication. And all
aspects of communication (and, hence, all of social life) is
educative. Communication enlarges and modifies experience with
an effect that transpires not only on the recipient but also on
the original source of communication. This is so since experience
has first to be formulated before being transmitted. It loses its
educative power only when it becomes cast in a mold and runs as
a matter of routine.

Dewey is obviously citing the wonders of communication. He
views it as the instrument which enable humans beings to teach
their fellows ways and means of adjusting to natural and cultural
forces. It also allows them to continuously make and remake themselves as better and better modes of communication are invented
and adopted.

B. Communication as Common Inquiry

The preceding section has shown the requirement for language
(and communication, in general,) in the transformation of events
into objects with meanings. And it is this transformation that
render problems concerning such events to become soluble or, at
least, manageable. In this section, a more specialized use of

language and organized kind of communication will be considered. The importance of this theme consists in the fact that Dewey views the scientific community as the paradigm of all social organizations. He endorses the adoption of the scientific method not only in exploring the forces and structure of reality but also in securing social objectives. To examine the nature of science through its character as shared knowledge, through its activities as common inquiry, and through its principles as conditioned by the very process of inquiry, is, therefore, fruitful not only in itself but also in gaining insights into how a society can become a community.

As can be expected, Dewey extols science because of the wonders of its consequences. He is convinced that it cannot yield such bountiful harvests if its method were not adapted to the subject-matter it has thus far been applied. The use of the empirical method constitutes, in his judgment, the union of experience and nature, a condition that is not greeted by its practitioners as a monstrosity, but is rather accepted matter-of-factly. Reasonably so, since experience, controlled in specifiable ways, is the avenue that leads to the facts and laws of nature. Indeed, it is the only effective medium for getting at nature. The scientific environment is, therefore, the context where both experience and nature go harmoniously together. For, nature, once empirically disclosed, in turn, deepens and directs the further development of nature.

Dewey's espousal of the scientific method is at the same time his rejection of dogmatism. In its application, ultimate and immutable truths are eliminated in favor of systematic, extensive, and careful use of unprejudiced observation. The data are collected, arranged, and experimented upon. Then, the findings are interpreted and subjected to further testing. Conclusions are never absolute; they are maintained as hypotheses.

Dewey finds particularly significant the manner by which science draws its materials from primary or crude experience and refers back to it for validation and confirmation. The process promotes primary experience to a more meaningful order as interpretation about it is enriched. The same approach rules out arbitrary selection and pays due regard to the general traits nature presents as it gives tribute to the exclusive integrity of experience.

The faith in the scientific method is not, however, a surrender to materialism, Dewey already made clear in an earlier discussion. He sees no merit in the objection that a method applicable to physical subject-matter may not be equally suitable to non-physical phenomena. He argues that those who make this protest confuse the natural with the physical. Science, he would admit is, in fact, based on experience, as experience is continuous with nature. But, nature is not all physical. There are in it ideal values, such as aesthetic and moral traits. And these are as genuinely real as the characteristics of sun and electron.

48

The empirical method is, therefore, as applicable to the
special sciences on a technical scale as it is to experienced
subject-matter on a liberal scale. In both levels, Dewey is certain, it can refine the objects of common-sense experience and
render them more useful than these already are. If such a method
has wrought profound transformation in astronomy and biology,
there is no reason to doubt that it could effect a similar transformation in the social disciplines.[41] In fact, he suggests, this
may be the only way to save mankind from the cultural lag it is
currently suffering from.

But there is more to the scientific method than the efficiency of its self-corrective steps and its direct consistency
with nature and experience. Its power is inherent in its structure as shared experience. The members of the scientific community may be poles and years apart from one another, but they
perform their individual task with mindfulness of what others
have achieved or failed to achieve. They publish their findings,
thereby contributing to enrich the fund of common knowledge. He
illustrates the process more vividly:

> A scientific work in physics or astronomy gives
> a record of calculations and deductions that were
> derived from past observations and experiments.
> But it is more than a record; it is also an indi-
> cation, an assignment, of further observations
> and experiments to be performed. No scientific
> report would get a hearing if it did not describe
> the apparatus by means of which experiments were
> carried on and results obtained; not that appa-
> ratus is worshipped, but because this procedure
> tells other inquirers how they are to go to work
> to get results which will agree or disagree in
> their experience with those previously arrived
> at, and thus confirm, modify and rectify the
> latter.[42]

Significantly, it is this scientific spirit that Dewey
desires to be absorbed in the democratic process. In **Freedom
and Culture**, he cites the parallelism betwen the two scenes.

> It is of the nature of science not so much to
> tolerate as to welcome diversity of opinion,
> while it insists that inquiry brings the evi-
> dence of observed facts to bear to effect a
> consensus of conclusions - and even then to
> hold the conclusion subject to what is ascer-
> tained and made public in further new inqui-
> ries. I would not claim that any existing democ-
> racy has ever made complete or adequate use of
> scientific method in deciding upon its policies.
> But freedom of inquiry, toleration of diverse

views, freedom of communication, the distribution of what is found out to every individual
as the ultimate intellectual consumer are involved in the democratic as in the scientific
method.[43]

But Dewey's trust in the cooperative effort of science has further consequences. Most curiously, here is where he locates the
circumstance of truth and verification. The borrowed (from
Peirce) definitions of the truth and the real in his **Logic** bear
this out: "The opinion which is fated to be ultimately agreed
to by all who investigate is what we mean by the truth, and the
object represented by this opinion is the real."[44]

Obviously, the definition thus stated is susceptible to various interpretations and vulnerable to many attacks. Bertrand
Russell, for one, takes it as tantamount to a sociological prophesy.[45] But Dewey's expression cannot be taken literally. The
key term 'ultimately' is intended to have a mathematical sense
rather than a chronological meaning. For, if it were meant chro-
nologically, it would make truth depend upon the opinion of the
last man alive, just as it depended on the opinion of everyone
in the past who investigated it! L. Nissen expresses the difficulty involved in the passage:

> In virtue of the necessity of checking in both
> directions, the definition implies that it is
> impossible to us, at this time, to know whether
> any opinion is true or not except for the last
> survivor, and then only in respect to opinions
> that no person dead could have investigated.[46]

The mathematical meaning is, therefore, more tenable. If
Dewey is following the lead of Peirce, then he would imagine,
according to Russell, "a series of opinions, analogous to a
series of numbers such as 1/2, 3/4, 7/8... tending to a limit,
and each differing less from its predecessor than any earlier
number of the series does."[47] Even in this sense, though, not
all difficulties are eliminated. In the second definition given
in the same place (also taken from Peirce), the mathematical
reading is more evident: "Truth is that concordance of an abstract statement with the ideal limit toward which endless investigation would tend to bring scientific belief, which concordance the abstract statement may possess by virtue of the confession of its inaccuracy and one-sidedness, and this confession is an essential ingredient of truth."[48] Russell finds the
phrase "confession of inaccuracy" most puzzling. Strictly, it
would mean that a statement is true because it say it is inaccu-
rate!

Still more problematic is Peirce's belief that there is an
ideal limit which endless investigation would tend to bring about

scientific belief. Russell wonders why he thinks so. Is it an empirical generalization from the history of research? an optimistic faith in the perfectibility of man? a prophesy or a prediction of what would happen if scientists grow more clever? Whichever it is commits one to an unfounded hope. Nissen rakes up more difficulties which are of the same kind as those of Russell's and, hence, need not be brought up.

What is necessary to bring up is Dewey's direct replies in view of which Russell's and similar objections appear less effective. In the first place, Dewey distinguishes truth and validity, a distinction which Russell fails to notice. Validity, on the one hand, would refer to the quality of a resolved situation, as the consequence of distinctive operations of inquiry, a determination of the truth or falsity of a given proposition here and now. The principle in this determination is the consequence which renders the problematic situation resolved. Truth, on the other hand, would mean the ideal limit of an indefinitely continuous inquiry. In this definition, Dewey quickly points out, nothing about guessing future belief is required. In fact, the truth of any present proposition is subject to the outcome of continued inquiries.

This is saying that its truth or validity (to use Dewey's preferred term for the case) is provisional, "as near the truth as inquiry has as yet come, a matter determined not by a guess at some future belief but by the care and pains with which inquiry has been conducted up to the present time."[49] To Dewey's interpretation, then, the meaning of Peirce's reference to the "confession of inaccuracy and one-sidedness" as an ingredient of the truth of a present proposition is precisely the admission of the necessary subjection of any proposition to the results of future inquiry. This admission is nearer the truth than the dogmatic claim of infallibility concerning a conclusion entertained here and now.

The distinction between truth and validity is particularly important in comparing Dewey's theory of verification and inquiry with the doctrines of absolute transcendental realists (like Locke). The latter would, for instance, contest pragmatic epistemology on the ground that, unlike their principle, it renders propositions unescapably hypothetical till doomsday and, hence, makes the scientific effort an exercise in futility. The charge is, however, unjustly levelled because Dewey never claims that no specific scientific issue is ever resolved. On the contrary, his pragmatism explicitly contains the proviso that the test of consequence is valid only if such consequence resolved the specific problem under investigation.[50] A particular method can thereby be regarded valid if it could bring about the resolution of the problem. The conclusion, though, cannot be held as an "eternal" truth, for it is subject to the results of future investigations. F. Kaufmann clarifies the same thought:

The potentially endless self-corrective procedure

of science - the "continuum of inquiry" -
is composed of well-determined specific inquiries, each of which has to be treated by the
logician as a self-contained unit. There is a
definite 'terminus a quo' for each inquiry -
the instituted problem - and there is a definite 'terminus ad quem', the solution of the
problem represented by a warranted assertion.
This definiteness is not impaired by the fact
that any assertion may have to be eliminated
from the body of knowledge if it fails to
pass subsequent tests. To state that no scientific results is 'indubitably established is
not to declare that scientific problems cannot
be solved.[51]

Dewey's second point in his reply to Russell makes clear
that Peirce's (and his) definition of truth does not assume that
propositions, which have truth and falsity as their inherent
property, are th subject-matter of inquiry. (Russell makes this
assumption in his critique.) Instead, things and events are the
material and object of inquiry. Propositions are but means in
it. Thus, as conclusions of a given inquiry, they become means
of carrying on further inquiries.[52] 'Qua' means, they are constantly modified and improved as they are used.

Moreover, the assumption that propositions are the subject-
matter of inquiry is incompatible with the empiricistic view
which is concerned with truth and falsity as existentially applicable and (to begin with) as determinable by means of inquiry into material existence. Realism demands that inquiry be
faithful to nature's bidding. And what nature presents of itself
is not a pre-established perfectly rational world. Instead, it
shows itself as having both stable and precarious sways. It cannot, therefore, prompt science to formulate laws with abiding
truth. To build a hope to the contrary "is not so much inspiration to work as it is a justification for acquiescence."[53] What
needs to be developed is that working scientific faith. This
consists in "the belief that concern for objective continual
inquiry with assiduity and courage in its performance, is capable of becoming habitual with an ever-increasing number of human
beings."[54]

Dewey's reply to Russell's critique is more of a clarification than a justification. He makes it clear that truth, in
his judgment, is provisional, in the sense that it is never ab-
solutely established; and it is ideal, in the sense that it is
not now actually attained. But where no absolute truth is successfully achieved, 'warranted assertibility' is conveniently
available. Although inquiry begins in doubt, it terminates in
the institution of conditions which remove the need for doubt.
Such a finality occurs when the opinion arrived at enables the
inquirer to secure desired results. 'Warranted assertibility' is
equivalent to that opinion. It can also be called 'designated

knowledge' or 'belief,' only if it were not for the fact that
these terms do not imply immediate relation to inquiry as its
results.[55]

The notion of 'warranted assertibility' is evidently pragmatic. It is instituted when the consequence desired is secured.
The qualification 'desired' has no psychological connotation.
'Warranted assertibility' is not identifiable with the removal
of private discomfort, contrary to Russell's supposition.[56]

> The only desire that enters, according to my view,
> is desire to resolve as honestly and impartially as
> possible the problem involved in the situation.
> "Satisfaction" is satisfaction of the conditions
> prescribed by the problem. Personal satisfaction
> may enter in as it arises when any job is well done
> according to the requirements of the job itself;
> but it does not enter in any way into the determi-
> nation of validity, because, on the contrary, it is
> conditioned by that determination.[57]

Consequence is used as the test of proposed ends or ideals.[58]
As a test, it is never meant to be taken as supreme in and of
itself.

What is supreme in inquiry is the very activity of sharing
ideas. For, it is no exaggeration that the problem of truth, validity, and verification is one with the problem of community.
In several places, this thought has been expressed. "The import
of the term (truth) remains socially determined. To represent
things as they are is to represent them in ways that tend to
maintain a common understanding,"[59] says one passage. "Indeed,
capacity to endure publicity and communication is the test by
which it is decided whether a pretended good is genuine or spurious,"[60] says another.

Implied in the last statement is the reason for which Dewey
locates the problem of truth and verification in the social center. The importance of publicity in making decisions consists
in the fact that the criteria used in testing and verifying knowledge are themselves derived from the social scene. Again, this
is indicated on several occasions. In **Democracy and Education,**
he states, "the place of communication in personal doing supplies
us with a criterion for estimating the value of informational
material in school."[61] In an article for the **Old Penn,** he expresses the same idea: "It is not, so to say, the object alone which
decides what is the proper and authorized account of itself; but
the object as a term and factor in established social
practice."[62]

That criteria for testing and verifying knowledge are derived from the social setting means that the rules and principles of inquiry result from the process itself of common inquiry.

These may, he would admit, arise out of private investigation, but they become effective only when they are shifted, refined, and sanctioned in the experience of society. As C. W. Hendel states: "The life blood of inquiry consists of rules and leading principles which become funded in the shared experience of the community of inquirers."[63] This is why, when fully tested, they are sometimes codified into explicit laws, thereby becoming part of the fabric of community life.

The intimate connections between the concepts of truth, the real, and community is also a part of Peirce's doctrine. The influence may not be direct, but similarity in its emphasis is striking. Says Peirce:

> The real, then, is that which, sooner or later, information and reasoning would finally result in, and which is therefore independent of the vagaries of me and you. Thus, the very origin of the conception of reality shows that this conception essentially involves the notion of a community, without definite limits, and capable of a definite increase of knowledge. And so those two series of cognition - the real and the unreal - consists of those which, at any time sufficiently future, the community will always continue to reaffirm; and those which, under the same conditions, will ever after be denied.[64]

But there is a difference. This can be discerned from the last statement. Dewey's theory provides no assurance for the future as the discussion above already indicated.

Like Peirce's, Dewey's logic becomes not only a formal science but also a social discipline. It is "a mode of activity which is socially conditioned and which has cultural consequences."[65] It is socially conditioned because it is formulated in terms of symbols and signs which proceed from social interchange. It has cultural consequences insofar as it concludes with the resolution of an indeterminate situation and a prescription for action. Such a resolution or prescription oftentimes becomes embodied in the living habits and rules of the community.

The activity of valuation demonstrates concretely, not only the use of the scientific method in dealing with social and moral problems, but also the dependence of sound moral judgment upon the social conditions that promote the growth of intelligence. This passage from logic to valuation, it may be noted, is not an abrupt transition. On the contrary, in Dewey, the two are continuous. As Levi confirms, "the center of importance for one who is at once social philosopher and philosopher of science, methodologist and moralist, is the point at which a generalized logic of inquiry is transformed into a logic of evaluation."[66]

The term 'value' is connected with the word 'end' in Dewey's lexicon. 'End' refers to qualitative ending of a natural trans-action. It can be the simple terminus or closure of any natural event, such as the end of a biological growth; it can be an end-in-view which is a desired imaginative projection; or it can be a consummation of a controlled experience. These are all possible sources of values. But because they proceed from intricate or complex transactions, they are always precarious, i. e., abruptly ending, ever-changing, sometimes conflicting. As he says, "some-times every immediate good or intrinsic good goes back on us... We are on the dark as to what we should regard with passionate esteem..."[67]

Oftentimes, what we use to prize is no longer worth valuing, because some growth on our part or some change in conditions around us. Sometimes we trust on luck to bring new objects to cherish or eliminate conditions we do not favor. But we do not depend always on fortuitous circumstances. Sheer impatience or urgent demand induces us to inquire, deliberate, formulate ends-in-view in order to resolve the initial conflict and bring into existence disirable objects, events, or conditions. Ends-in-view, proclaims Dewey, are shaped according to two factors: The first are the norms and standards of our shared experience in the com-munity. The second is the practical demand of the problematic situation in which we are involved. This signifies that values are not original properties of things.

> The notion that there are some value properties
> which carry their justification upon their face
> is for Dewey the snare and delusion of the whole
> axiological tradition, for it tends to isolate
> operations of the intellect from the realm of
> values and evaluation.[68]

The first factor mentioned is the source of values as imme-diately prized goods. This is the result of a long term expe-rience, thus embedded in the grooves of communal life. This is manifest in the fact that what are considered values or intrinsic goods in one culture may not be so regarded in another. The se-cond factor puts pressure on us to 'value,' i. e., to judge, appraise, or weigh certain objects or alternative actions. This is equivalent to the reflective process of deciding what should be regarded with "passionate esteem", in Dewey's description above. As an activity, it culminates in a value judgment.

A value judgment is not merelay a description of a thing which is considered good or a thing which is prized. It is an ascription of such a quality to a thing. It is a reflection, a process of finding out what one wants. Doing so requires the formation of a new desire and a direction of action. Through the process, the things "get" values, something they did not have before, whatever efficiencies they may originally have. As Dewey says, "to judge value is to engage in instituting a deter-

minate value where none is given."[69] It is on this point that
R. Bernstein raises the question:

> If ascribing value is not describing what we
> now prize or esteem or discovering a new hidden
> property, what is the difference between the
> values that we have before reflection and those
> that we have as a result of deliberation, and
> how do we decide what ought to be valued?[70]

Dewey's answer can be speculated upon, if it is recalled
that he rejects the Platonic type of valuation, one that determines values by comparing alternatives with an ideal model. He
appraises it as defective because it does not really compare
specific aims with one another. Instead, it locates the model
outside of the concrete conditions of the problematic situation.
In the process, the problematic situation becomes less intelligible because it is abstracted from actual connection with
facts. The final moral judgment is hardly the result of deliberation, for it is formed practically in an 'a priori' manner.
The truth is, there is no pat and fixed formula for solving value problems because situations differ; each has uniquely concrete features by which it is identifiable. Dewey proposes (as
an alternative to an ideal model) a standard of value which is
formed in the process of practical judgment by a mind that is
inherently conversant with facts.

A direct reply to Bernstein can be drawn from Dewey's own
thinking on the matter. He would say that the difference between
values before and after reflection consists in the simple fact
that the latter is more enlightened than the former. This is to
be expected because deliberation brings about understanding of
the specific situation and foresight of the consequences of
choice. But what is the basis for such a judgment? How does reflection determine the direction it should take? Is Dewey endorsing here a purely situational or relativistic kind of valuation?

Not quite. Although every problematic situation is, for him,
unique in itself, it bears resemblances with other situations.
This only indicates that past experiences are important because
they can guide deliberation.

> An individual within the limits of his personal
> experience revises his desires and purposes as
> he becomes aware of the consequences they have
> produced in the past. This knowledge is what ena-
> bles him to foresee probable consequences of his
> prospective activities and to direct his conduct
> accordingly.[71]

The manifold of human experiences through time provides guide-

lines for handling future problems. From the existing guidelines, improved rules can be derived. "Improved valuation must
grow out of existing valuations, subjected to critical methods
of investigation that bring them into systematic relations with
one another."[72] But these are never rigid rules. They are hypothetical norms inasmuch as they can be modified by new experiences. They are stable, but never static. They are always subject
to further re-evaluation. Thus, the standards of value are actually transvaluations of all prior value and the inquiry into
them is a self-corrective procedure.[73]

By these proposals for valuation, Dewey sets himself midway
between the two extremes of absolute objectivism and pure subjec-
tivism. The Scholastics, his instance of the first kind, rely on
a moralism based on a pre-established order. Some Existentialists
(like Sartre) exemplify the second type, by depending on the
promptings of the deepest self for guidance. Dewey trusts on
rules which, although proceeding from within the process of inquiry, are nevertheless objective in content. For, their validity comes through the agency of a socially established pool of
knowledge.

The differences among the three perspectives are significant
even to the kind of moral evaluation individuals make on a daily
basis. The first is less sensitive to the variety of individual
situations; the second allows little chance for ascertaining moral decisions in advance. In Dewey's approach, the advantages
of both sides are recognized, as their respective disadvantages
are avoided. His awareness of the temporal and historical dimensions qualifying the human situation is a recognition of individual differences. But common marks are also acknowledged. The
very fact that the question at hand is one on value already indicates that it is a distinctively human problem. Hence, it is
one which is either common to all men or one in which only humans can actually be involved.

This is stating that value is a human quality, not however
of humans in their isolation from one another but of humans-in-
community. Thus, a person, just as anyone of his kind, inspite
of the uniqueness of his situation, is bound by some rules that
do not apply to lower forms of beings. Dewey's three levels of
transaction appears in this context to be not just a metaphysical
description; it is also designation of the limits of the moral
realm. Vincent Punzo succinctly expresses the idea.

> The acknowledgment of the uniqueness of the situa-
> tions in which man finds himself should not blind
> one to the fact that in so far as these situations
> involve moral problems, they involve issues that
> relate to man as a subject in the human community.
> The uniqueness of man's situation does not mean
> that he ceases to be a member of the human commu-
> nity. A man may decide to "act like a pig," but he
> can never "be" a pig. He remains a "man-who-acts-

like-a-pig."[74]

The point being made is quite simple: no human can escape his situation of being-human. And to be human is to be a member of the human community. His individuality and the uniqueness of his situation need to be recognized. But his character as a member of the human community is at issue in all possible situations.

In the life of the community, socially established rules are not immune from deteriorating into purposeless restrictions. They can even later appear to be blind and irrational (as in the case of social rules disallowing women to vote). This is why they need to be subjected to continuous critical review. But, Dewey is quick to point out that conditions conducive to intelligent inquiry or valuation do not arise spontaneously. These are created by a long process of cultivation. Needless to say, here is where, in Dewey's mind, education is indispensable. Here, in fact, lies the basis of his philosophy of education.

There are, then, two sides to the human situation in the community. On the one hand, man stands as a critic of society to prevent it from suffering from stagnation and running off course. On the other hand, he relies on the community in shaping up his habits and dispositions; he derives from it the leading principles that guide not only his conduct but also the very critical inquiry he is expected to perform from time to time. This is why he, for his part, while acquiring a treasury of values - things to be prized - by way of inheritance from his elders and by transmission from his contempories, has to consider at the same time its relevance in his concrete situation.

But social life, for its part, simultaneously has to foster, nurture, and preserve those truly human values chief among which is intelligence. It is in the democratic way of life that Dewey sees these two sides best promoted. It is where "the balance between stability and flexibility of common interest can be achieved, where the conditions for free social inquiry, and individual responsibility, can be fostered."[75] The note on the conditions for free social inquiry directly leads to another of such conditions: art (which oftentimes is understimated as to its social significance).

C. Art as Communication

After calling attention to the need for language and communication in the development of science and valuation, Dewey points to another level of communal life, communal life carried to the limit, where such a life reaches a consummatory level - the realm of art. Art connotes the fulness of communal life because it is a distinctive medium of sharing which brings experience to its richest phase. It is also, as will be shown later, that enhancement of meanings so important to human solidarity.

Although this may appear to be an abrupt shift in perspective, particularly in a philosopher quite well known for his emphasis in instrumentalities. But such is not the case. Dewey's entire philosophic vision includes, not only as an integral part of it but as actually its culmination, the field of aesthetics and art. This follows from the fact that naturalism centers on the analysis of experience. And because art is the crystallization of experience, art cannot be an extraneous subject-matter of that vision but its fruition. Indeed, he proclaims on many occasions, "the highest because most complete incorporation of natural forces and operations in experience is found in art."[76] It can even be said that art is for him the illustration 'par excellence' of the ultimate meaning of intelligence, morals, democracy, education, and, not the least of all, of the nature of things.[77]

True, it is easy to miss the significance of art in Dewey's philosophical development. One fact is, he did not write his developed view on the theme until that monumental essay entitled Art as Experience, and this was done so when he was already in his seventies. This can easily give the impression that his main concern is logic and metaphysics and his reflections on art are mere afterthoughts. But other facts point contrariwise. If one is to read carefully his essays on Qualitative Experience, How We think, Democracy and Education, and above all Experience and Nature, the aesthetic dimensions and implications of his leading ideas are not hard to find.[78]

These writings emphasize two major points: 1) the continuity of experience and art, and 2) the interpenetration of the efficacious with the final in art, or, in his way of expressing it, art is simultaneously instrumental and consummatory. The second point has a direct bearing on the issue of community. Art, he proves, is an important fact in unifying men in society. The first point is consistent with his kind of naturalism, one that unfailingly sustains continuity. But in spite of the metaphysical overtones, his theory of art carries a proposal quite applicable to a problem prominent in industrial societies and, hence, merits special attention here.

To recall the general setting of his philosophy, Dewey explains experience as that interaction of live creatures with the environing conditions. Because this interaction is continuous (without leaps and bounds) in the same manner that the very process of living is continuous (not fragmented into bits, as the Humean time) experience occurs continuously (where subject and object are not separate). Within this continuity, however, certain conditions of resistance and conflict make aspects and elements of the self and the world (both implicated in the interaction) qualify with emotions and ideas that particular phase of the interaction. Thereafter, conscious intent emerges. When this happens, a genuine experience comes about. It is recognizable through the fact that the material experienced runs its course to fulfillment. It is thereby integrated within and demarcated in the general stream of experiences from other experiences.

The particular experience so described is an activity so rounded up that its closure is a consummation rather than a mere cessation. It is a whole and carries with it its own individualizing quality and self-sufficiency. Experience, in this sense, is defined by situations and episodes that are spontaneously refered to in common parlance as 'real experiences.' It may be something of great importance (as an event where danger is narrowly averted) or it may be a simple occurrence (as a hearty dinner in a quaint restaurant). These are those experiences with aesthetic quality.

In contrast, there are the mechanical and routine activities. These lie within two limits: "At one pole is the loose succession that does not begin at any particular place and that ends - in that sense of ceasing - at no particular place. At the other pole is arrest, constriction, proceeding from parts having only mechanical connection with one another."[79] There is actually no essential difference between this type of experiences and the aesthetic one. They have the same material, being both modes of interaction between live creatures and environment. The difference is a matter of perspective - the way the end-in-view is foreseen and applied to every instant of the activity. It lies, too, on whether or not the end is related to all that went before as the culmination of a continuous movement.

The continuity of experience and art can be viewed from another standpoint, that of means and ends. Dewey criticizes the theory that makes a sharp distinction between the two and that thinks of one as completely independent of the other. The truth is the contrary. Means and ends do not refer to different grades of reality. They are of the same order, but conceived from different vantage points. Dewey's notion of 'end' is end-in-view. It is not something remote or final which is hit upon after performing a series of disconnected acts. Illustrating the point through the activity of building a house, he says:

> The end-in-view is a plan which is "contemporaneously" operative in selecting and arranging materials. The latter, brick, stone, wood, and mortar, are means only as the end-in-view is actually incarnate in them, in forming them. literally, the are the end its present stage of realization. The end-in-view is present at each stage of the process; it is present as the "meaning" of the materials used and acts done; without its informing presence, the latter are in no sense "means"; they are merely extrinsic causal conditions.[80]

In the analogy, the completion of the house is the end or fulfillment of the acts involved in building it. Hence, it is a consummation relative to the specific situation. While being so, it also functions as a means to some further experiences. Means,

then, are not things that are external and acccidental antece-
dents of the occurrence of something else. And ends are not
independent of things that have come before. This is what Dewey
means by the phrase: "a genuine instrumentality is always an
organ of an end."[81]

But what is the relation of the theory of the continuity
of experience and the conception of means and ends to Dewey's
social and cultural views? The connection is not hard to find,
once the theory of continuity is understood as a reaction to
traditional dualisms which infects even the art world. A case
that could make the point intelligible is the play theory art
which Dewey attacks in passing in Experience and Nature but more
directly in Art as Experience. This theory underlies the idea
that aesthetic experience is a form of release or escape from
the pressures of reality. The assumption is that "freedom can
be found only when personal activity is liberated from control
by objective factors."[82] And because play is an instance of that
liberated activity, it is opposed to necessary work. Play exists
as a result of energy demanding outlet, whereas necessary activities come as the response of the demands of the environment
that must be met in the practical order.

Dewey believes that the opposition between work and play
is an artificial one. The existence of works of art is evidence
enough.

> In art, the playful attitude becomes interest in
> the transformation of material to serve the pur-
> pose of a developing experience. Desire and need
> can be fulfilled only through objective material,
> and therefore playfulness is also interest in an
> object... The spontaneity of art is not one of
> opposition to anything, but marks complete absorp-
> tion in an orderly development.[83]

The contrast between free and forced activity is externally
brought about in the human situation by social conditions, such
as the forces of industrialism and sectarianism, Dewey believes.
Such a contrast can and should, therefore, be eliminated as far
as possible, rather than be erected into a permanent 'differen-
tia' by which art is defined. Let art be art, he exclaims. "The
diffusion in one experience of the pressure upon the self of
necessary conditions and the spontaneity and novelty of individuality."[84]

It can be sensed that his observation on the relationship
between play and work extends and applies similarly to the notions of spontaneity and necessity, of freedom and law. In this
respect, he criticizes Kant for limiting freedom to moral actions
that are controlled by the rational conception of duty. He is
more sympathetic to J. Schiller's idea that "play and art occupy
an intermediate transitional place between the realm of necessary

phenomena and transcendent freedom, educating man to recognition and to assumption of the responsibilities of the latter."[85] Dewey acknowledges, without of course submitting to the idea, that this view represents a valiant attempt on the part of an artist to escape the rigid dualism introduced by Kant. The attempt is obviously unsuccessful, however, since the artist remains confined within the same framework.

Dewey's sympathy for Schiller is actually more than a feeling of kinship in intention. In more ways than one, Schiller strengthened, if not inspired, his insights into the nature of art. It was in him, before in Dewey, that a distinct justification of the artistic beauty could be found. This consisted in deducing the idea of art from a conception of reason and man and in assigning to it a purpose within practical life. Like Dewey, Schiller blazed the trail way from a dual conception of reality to a union that rises triumphantly above all cleavages. Dewey's dissatisfaction with the social conditions of his time that brought about the opposition between enjoyment and labor is also an echo of Schiller's critique of his age.

> With us there is a sharp separation of the sciences, a strict sundering of ranks and occupations, a rupture between state and church, laws and customs; enjoyment is separated rated from labor, means from end, effort from reward.[86]

While they agree on the nature of the problem, the differ on the solution to it. They both recognize that the hiatus in life must be bridged by art. But how it must do so is the question. Schiller accepts, perhaps unwillingly, the dualism of matter and spirit, force and liberty. Dewey denies that it is a valid description of the human condition.

Thus, on the one hand, the former believes that it is only by introducing a balancing factor to coordinate the poles of spirit and matter in a happy equilibrium that problems can be remedied. This third factor (or 'drive') is what Schiller calls the play impulse; this is what constitutes beauty and art. Dewey, on the other hand, is more revolutionary. He is convinced that dualism, in all its many guises is the effect or influence of unhealthy conditions, not a genuine trait of reality. In its place, continuity and integration must be asserted. The result will be art. Art, therefore, lies embedded not only in nature but in experience as well. There is, then, no necessity to introduce an external device (such as Schiller's play-drive) to account for artistic creativity and, more importantly, to solve the problem of individuals "lost" in their own society.

The doctrine of means and ends has a similar social and cultural application. In fact, this is the only way of assessing the real situation. Our profound social and practical problems reflect an artificial line divorcing means from ends. One speaks,

62

for instance, of labor as means to earning a living. We justify
the boring, often stultifying, aspects of work as being a necessary means for that end. This is when tediousness comes; when
ends become indulgent dissipations, passive amusements, and dis-
tractions.

> The notion that means are menial, instrumenta-
> lities servile, is more than a degradation of
> means to the rank of coercive and external
> necessities. It renders all things upon which
> the name of end is bestowed accompaniments of
> privilege, while the name of utility becomes
> an apologetic justification for things that
> are not portions of a good and reasonable life.[87]

What Dewey suggests as remedy is the alliance of man with
his environment and life-work. He is, by no means, saying that
it is possible to find joy in every activity. What he is advocating is to make means and ends meet. For, it is in this junc-
tion that man can overcome alienation and find satisfaction and
aesthetic significance in what he does. This prescription for
happiness cannot be taken lightly. It lends not only a psychological backing to labor, but it also points to its true value.
For, if everyone is happy in what he does, productivity would
be natural consequence. And when activity is treated as art,
i. e., as simultaneously productive and aesthetic, instrumental
and consummatory, it will become at once a natural event and a
completion of nature. As Dewey expresses it:

> Thought, intelligence, science is the inten-
> tional direction of natural events to meanings
> capable of immediate possession and enjoyment;
> this direction - which is operative art - is
> itself a natural event in which nature other-
> wise partial and incomplete comes fully to it-
> self; so that objects of conscious experience,
> when reflectively chosen, form the "end" of
> nature.[88]

The new perspective regarding the connection of means and
ends provides now a different meaning to the term 'useful.' To
point this out is particularly important because Dewey has often
been charged of being a sheer utilitarian. The notion 'utilitarian' has the usual reference to one who measures things in terms
of their efficacy in bringing into existence certain commodities.
He would not be slighted to be so called, it can be suspected,
if the term would be understood in his sense. But ordinary language invokes the word 'useful' to refer to those activities that
have no immediately enjoyed meaning, such as labors at home, in
the factory, in a laboratory, in school. These are coercive because they require attentive recognition. Thus, they are noncha-

lantly called useful because of the commodities they bring about.
And, in so doing, their occurrence are thought to be thereby justified and explained.

This attitude is, in Dewey's appraisal, cutting short from
consideration the importance of consequences. For, the effect
of such works upon the quality of human life and experience is
simply ignored. To dispel the popular misconception of (his brand
of) pragmatism or (as some would want to call it) utilitarianism
as lacking interest in higher values, Dewey has some ready explanation:

> To be useful is to fulfill a need. A characteris-
> tic human need is for possession and appreciation
> of the meaning of things, and this need is ignored
> and unsatisfied in the traditional notion of the
> useful. We identify utility with the external re-
> lationship that some events and acts bear to other
> things that are their products, ansd thus leave
> out the only thing that is essential to the idea
> of utility, inherent place and bearing in expe-
> rience.[89]

That every activity can become genuine experience, that is, artistic, make this quality immediately available. The idea bears
the social implication that art is a common possession of humanity insofar as everyone is in one way or another involved in
activities. Thus, even "the intelligent mechanic engaged in his
job, interested in doing well and finding satisfaction in his
handiwork, caring for his materials and tools with genuine affec-
tion is artistically engaged."[90]

Dewey mourns the fact that art through history has been regarded as a private possession of the privileged class. As he
looks back in history, the artists, for the same reason, were
isolated from the general mass of men and his profession is bra-
cketed in a distinct compartment. Art works were then confined
within the walls of museums and galleries which, by that process,
became the 'beauty parlors' of civilization. He advocates an end
to this distressing situation. Art, he advocates, must be re-
turned to its natural setting, the human conditions under which,
to begin with, it was brought into being. And it must regain
continuity with those humanizing consequences it engenders in
actual life experiences. He is convinced that progress can take
place only in the restoration of continuity between everyday
events, doings, and sufferings that are universally recognized
to constitute experience and the refined and intensified forms
that are works of art.

The second main thrust in Dewey's writings on arts is its
consummatory quality described as experience-carried-to-the-full.
But, it must be quickly pointed out, here, as in all levels of
human experience, an instrumental value is simultaneously in-

64

volved. This is to be expected, since in Dewey's world, nothing is definitively final. Thus, an activity, any activity, may become so suffused with meaning that it is desired to endure and be a condition of respite. This is not simply 'instrumental' but truly 'consummatory'; it is 'having'; and it is 'being.' "The instrumentation is gathered up into it," says Dewey, "is achieved or fulfilled in it, but is neither arrested nor ended by achievement."[91] Yet, it may be directed to further values because living is becoming (and is, therefore, a continuum). If it were not, it would turn into dust and ashes of boredom. This is what he calls the eternal quality of art, its renewed instrumentality for further consummatory experiences.[92]

In the specific case of art, the value described as both intermediate and final is best expressed in the word 'communication' - communication with nature and communion with humans. Art depicts the live participation of man with nature because he can transform it and create new relationships with it. Indeed, it is "a process of production in which natural materials are reshaped in a projection toward consummatory fulfillment through regulation of trains of events that occur in a less regulated way on lower levels of nature."[91]

Art also functions as a medium of unification among men better than speech can because it is the most universal and freest form of communication. It transcends national boundaries and sectarian biases. Says Kallen in support of Dewey:

> Art is a language that different peoples of different speeches and cultures participate in and enjoy together; the antidote to their parochialism, the communication and sharing of differences which makes of their multitude a unity of their diversity a common bond.[94]

It is to Dewey, "the extension of the power of rites and ceremonies to unite men, through shared celebration, to all the incidents and scenes of life."[95] Art, therefore, must be expected not only to express beauty but also to influence human relationships. How art can function in this way is dealt with in his celebrated work entitled **Art as Experience**.

His theory of art is evidently consistent with his metaphysics. But the substance of the former is not simply drawn by logical deduction from the latter. Rather, his conception of art is (in the same way that his metaphysics is) directly drawn from real experience - man's actual transaction with nature. Thus, his data include not only the permanent and universal, the settled and uniform, but also the perilous and uncertain, process and particulars. The metaphysical categories are embodied here. Thus, the opposing qualities are not to be taken as separate realms but as phases of continuous processes. With this approach, he intends to eliminate the idealization of beauty and its localization in some transcendental world. He is in radical opposition to doctrines similar to that of Santayana for whom "the most material thing in as far as it is felt to be beautiful is instantly immaterialized, raised above external personal relations, concentrated and deepended in its proper being, in a world sublimated into an essence."[96] To these doctrines, because it is viewed as sublime, fugitive, impalpable, the beautiful is regarded as homeless in a material world. It may, they allow, visit time, but it truly belongs to eternity.

While it cannot be denied that there is a quality of intense aesthetic experience that is so immediate as to be ineffable and mystical (such as the ones described by Santayana) an intellectualized rendering of that immediate quality transfers it to a dream metaphysics that is so repugnant to Dewey. Such a rendering would easily be found unjustified when tested against concrete experience, he is certain. The fact is is, concrete experience is directly qualitative. This is why life experience is immediately precious. To get behind that immediacy, to neglect the qualitative setting as it is found, in his judgment, is escapism.

What an actual encounter with works of art tells is that an art object is the "impregnation of sensuous material with imaginative values." But the term 'imaginative value' is not just another expression for the traditional notion of ultimate essence with all its metaphysical denotations. the similarity, if there is any, is purely accidental. Here, the meaning is brought down to earth, where the reality referred to is, to begin with, located. The term stands for the 'gist' of things - that which is retained as indispensable after all irrelevances are eliminated. This is a more realistic signification because every expression leads toward 'essence,' i. e., to an organization of meanings that have been dispersed, and more or less obscured by, incidents attending to a variety of experiences. A work of art would, then, be an expression, not of some eternal essence (as Plato and Bosanquet believed) but of the accumulation of a multitude of experiences in a condensed and striking way. Success in this expression is the true measure of a work of art.

In Dewey's interpretation, a work of art is seen to be nothing less than the subject-matter of heightened and intensified experiences. The artistic function is, then, specified to the formation of experience 'qua' experience. The latter occurs when the material of common experiences is so rendered that it becomes the pregnant matter of a new experience that is greater in magnitude. The consummations which art affords can now be understood in the rhythm of experience as that phase of experience departing from the conflicts and problems towards fulfillment, but still within the continuity of the same experience. That these consummations are natural endings shows that there is no need to flee to any transcendental region.

The fruit of Dewey's reflection here is that essence (or the essential characteristics of persons and objects) is largely the consequence of art, not its cause, and never prior to it.

As a matter of fact, the forms that Plato thought were models of things actually had their source in Greek art, he declares. The process being in fact reversed, the artists should really have been given a more favored place in society, rather than the so-called 'wise men.' As far as Dewey is concerned, ignoring the contribution of artists to society is a clear instance of intellectual ingratitude.

Another corrolary of his reflection on the theme of art is expressed in his criticism of the elevation of cognitive or contemplative pursuits over the practical and the menial. Those who make such a claim reason that objects of rational thought are the only things that meet the specification of freedom from need, labor, and matter. Objects of rational thought alone are, for them, self-sufficient, self-explanatory. Dewey judges this reasoning as faulty. For, it breaks off the continuity between science and production. He sides with Hegel in maintaining that art can be (if not yet so in this period of history), better expressions of genuine freedom and self-sufficiency than pure contemplation. For, in life, the man who proves himself in practical situations is a better person because he has fuller experiences. This is what Dewey sees as the eason why Hegel lauds ancient epics in making use of heroes who formed or make their own implements, weapons, tools, and even food and drink. Their art issues from their own freedom and their own acts. Amid all types of vicissitudes, he proves master of himself.[97]

The elevation of the merits of practical pursuits does not imply the degradation of cognitive activities. They are only made continuous with one another. Knowing or thinking is instrumental and can be artistic. "Scientific method or the art of constructing true perceptions is ascertained in the course of experience to occupy a privileged position in undertaking other arts."[98] Moreover, thinking is, in its own right, an art.

> ...knowledge and propositions which are products
> of thinking, are works of art, as much so as
> statuary and symphonies. Every successive stage
> of thinking is a conclusion in which the meaning
> of what has produced it is condensed; and it is
> no sooner stated than it is a light radiating to
> othere things - unless it be a fog which obscures
> them.[99]

Thus, the instrumental character of thinking secures its place all the more as art, rather that sets it apart from its product (knowledge).

Dewey is convinced that the dilemma which confronted those who maintained the priority of the cognitive over the practical was how to account for the deepened intelligibility concerning man and the world afforded by works of art and artistic activities, outside the usual enjoyment these provide. They escape

the problem by treating art as a mode of knowing. Aristotle, for
one, stated that poetry was more philosophical than history. This
conclusion was based on the opinion that art was seen to reveal
the inner structures of things that cannot be had in any other
way than by speculative contemplation.

Dewey would not deny that easthetic experience sometimes
results in increased understanding. But, he is quick to add,

> The alleged knowledge can hardly be at the same
> time that of fixed species, as with Aristotle;
> of Platonic ideas, as with Schopenhauer; of the
> rational structure of the universe, as with Hegel;
> and of states of mind, as with Croce; of sensa-
> tions with associated images, as with the sensa-
> tional school...[100]

Rather, what transpires is, cognitive elements enter deeply and
intimately into the production of a work of art. This is due to
the part played bv mind. And mind, in Dewey's conception, is
meanings funded from prior experiences actively incorporated in
perception and production. As he says, "past experience and present perception become one in any aroused and full aesthetic
response. Not only are the senses stirred and engaged but also
those funded meanings we call mind."[101]

But the knoweldge factor does not enter pure and unchanged.
It receives a transformation effected in imaginative and emotional vision. Shelley's statement that "poetry awakens and enlarges the the mind by rendering it the receptacle of a thousand
unapprehended combinations of thought" does not bear the implication that eaesthetic experience is to be defined as a mode of
knowledge. What it is saying is, in both production and aesthetic perception of works of art, knowledge is transformed into
something more than knowledge, because it is merged with some
non-intellectual elements to form an experience worthwhile being
an experience.

In this transformation, the intelligibility, say, of tangled
scenes of life, appear not by reduction to conceptual form in the
way that reflection and science make things intelligible. Instead,
this is accomplished by presenting their meanings as the matter
of a clarified, coherent, and impassioned experience. Hence, the
work of art neither predicts nor interprets the world, in the
manner that science does. It reveals the world! The meaning of
art, says Kallen, "is quite another than the meaning of thought
and its essence is this otherness, ineffably beyond the power of
words to communicate.[102]

In simpler terms, the meanings and values imbued in an art
work are expressed, not merely stated or said. Thus, they can
only be captured aesthetically. This means that the criteria of
scientific inquiry cannot be equally applied to art. And in so
saying, the previous observation that scientific inquiry can

68

also become art is not thereby contradicted. When science starts
expressing meanings rather than pronouncements, it can become an
art. But, for this to take place, the transformation Dewey described must be realized - that transformation of knowledge effected in imaginative and emotional vision.

That art is expression, therefore, means that it is an imaginative adventure. Imagination operates when there is the fusion of the previously encountered and the currently perceived.
This occurs, according to Dewey, through an object rendered a-
cutely and coherently vivid to sense. This fusion is a subtle
set of internal relations constituting a new as well as a whole
experience. The old is merged with the new. This is why the poet
or the painter may deliver to the observer "the light that never
was on sea or land," but it is a light related to light on sea or
land once experienced. The newness appears as the old is bathed
in a new luminosity and in an unprecedented light.

That art can express and communicate successfuly depends on
how it invokes and evokes, not only old experiences, but the common ones as well. These common experiences are achieved, according to some Aristotelian like Sir Joshua Reynolds, by exhibiting the general forms of things. The belief is, for each class
of things, there is one common and central form which which is
the abstract of the various individual forms belonging to the
class. This general form, antecedently found in nature, is produced to be imitated in art.[103] The whole beauty and grandeur
of art thus consists in being able to be above all the singular
forms, local customs, particularities and details.

Dewey does not discourage the pursuit of epxressing general
forms or 'universals' in art, provided the term is understood
as the embodiment of what belongs to expreriences common to many
individuals. The difference can be clarified. In Reynolds, the
'universal' (or the terms 'general' and 'common') refers to a
species of objects, and a species that is already existent by
the very constitution of nature. Whereas, for Dewey, the 'common'
is that which is found in the experience of a number of persons.
Conversely, anything in which a number of persons participate
is, by that fact, common. And the more deep-seated it is in the
doings and the undergoings that form experience, the more common
it is. The 'common' or the 'universal' is not, therefore, something metaphysically prior to all experiences. On the contrary,
it is a way in which things function in experience as a bond of
union among particular events and scenes.

In Dewey's scheme, it is easy to see that anything in nature
or in human associations is 'common,' at least potentially. What
is actually common attains the status because of certain conditions, specially those that affect the process of communication.
He believes that it is by activities that are shared and by language and other means of intercourse that qualities and values
become common to the experience of a group of mankind. And, since
art is the most effective mode of communication, the presence
of common or general factors in conscious experience is an effect

of art.

What makes art such an effective form of communication is
the fact that it is able to transmit the values of a culture in
which it is begotten. More than this, it is itself culturally
engendered. Its origin, says Bertram Morris, is the activities
of men, practical and culturally entrenched. It figures in the
continuities of life and is carried over into the formative aspects of culture. Says Dewey:

> Aesthetic experience is a manifestation, a record
> and celebration of the life of a civilization, a
> means of promoting its development, and is also
> the ultimate judgment upon the quality of a civi-
> lization. For while it is produced and enjoyed by
> individuals, those individuals are what they are
> in the content of their experience because of the
> cultures in which they participate.[104]

The intimate connection between art and culture is a historical fact, he observes. The arts, through the ages, embody ways
of life, feeling, and thought in delightful expressions - like
the cathedral of Rheims, the pagodas of Buddha, or the cupolas
of arabian mosques. These are intimations of memorable transactions among men, transactions that may be qualified as religious,
social, domestic, etc. Furthermore, they determine the current
direction of ideas and endeavors in a community, so that they
can be seen as supplying the meanings in terms of which life is
criticized or esteemed; they supply materials for evaluating the
life led in that community.

Dewey admits that the artists may be critical of their societies and times, and so impress marks of defiance in their
works. But their criticisms are always given from a standpoint
within that culture in which they participate. Otherwise, these
would not be relevant. The point is, art can depict the collective individuality of a community and culture, both its passive
face and its rebellious moods. This is why the good works of art
are 'realistic' in the sense that they are so revealing of the
stark poverty of spirit that thrives in some societies; thus
they haunt because they penetrate so deeply. In their popular
or 'fine' forms, they are also comprehensive in dimension, en-
compassing all levels of life. Finally, they are bold and are
able to face the challenge of social ills, because they are free
from convention.

But works of art are idealistic, too. Hence, they transcend
locales and project suggestions for the future. They are, in a
subtle way, the "measure of success in civilization and in life
and in wisdom;" they offer "a myriad examples of what an undis-
torted experience would be and should be;" they serve as models
"of what society and life might approximate, ordered vitality,
patterned energy, and immediate delight."[105] For its vital role,

then, of informing and reforming a community, art must be promoted. Dewey's prescription (as Kallen reads it) is: "to provide
aesthetic experience abundantly is the first and last task of
civilization."[106] The transmission and perfection of the arts
of life and its values and the participation in them by the imagination seems to be the only sure way of saving civilization.

There is indeed a striking relation between art and (at least)
the possibility of a community. It is when boundaries are set
up, when prohibitions imposed, when men cut themselves off from
one another, that censorship rules and art degraded to a cult.
These also signal the deterioration of mankind to the state of
uncivility. This point was already discussed above. Art conspicuously serves the task of compounding the world's heritage
from the past and its present knowledge into a coherent and integrated imaginative union – a task reminiscent of the scientific enterprise.

That art is an exemplar of shared life, shared experience,
and free communication, shows why it is essential to or is the
heart of democracy. It can help break the barriers created by
industrialism, sectarianism, and other types of interests which
choke off the free give and take of the democratic process.
Kallen states:

> In the degree that the liberty of the artist pas-
> ses livingly into, and as livingly grows out of,
> the liberty of communication wherein democracy
> lives and moves and has its being, art integrates
> anew, and in a new way, with life; esthetic expe-
> rience becomes the easy portent, the secure pro-
> mise, of that which every other experience ful-
> fills itself in.[107]

#

CHAPTER III

SOCIETY: THE MATRIX OF INDIVIDUALITY AND FREEDOM

As was shown in the preceding chapters, the course of human development follows a pattern which includes bionatural and socio-
cultural phases. The former is established in the first two levels of transactions; the latter is attained in the third level.
The conclusions arrived at in those deliberations are as follows.
1) man is rooted in nature from the crudest manifestation of sensitivity in his interaction with the physical environment to the
most sophisticated manifestations of his aesthetic sensibility;
2) he is a social product, in the sense that he takes the con-
tours of his community's culture as he imbibes the language of
the region where he lives, the values of its elders, and the artistic expressions of its people.

It, therefore, appears that Dewey's philosophy of man is radically aligned with theories reducing the human person to a mass
of social relations. It even carries a deterministic undertone
quite capable of lending philosophical backbone to a social psychology similar to that which B. F. Skinner espouses. This is not
a forced interpretation considering that even some of Dewey's
ardent sympathizers regard his thoughts to be, at least, moving
in that direction. Horace M. Kallen, for one, criticises him for
the inadequacy of his account of individuality in terms of causal
sequences and necessary connections.[1] More bluntly, George Santayana charges that Dewey manifests "a quasi-Hegelian tendency to
dissolve the individual into his social functions, as well as
everything substantial or actual into something relative and
transitional."[2]

Indeed, Dewey's own expressions warrant such charges. For
instance, in his psychology, he describes the seat of mind as
"the qualities of organic action as far as these qualities have
been conditioned by language and its consequences."[3] The mind
that emerges is not as such an individual mind, he declares. It
is rather "a system of belief, recognitions, and ignorances, of
acceptances and rejections, of expectancies and appraisals of
meanings which have been instituted under the influence of custom and tradition."[4] The "self" absorbs both natural and cultural elements in its environment. And, from all indications, its
dependence on that environment is total, since the latter's action is so subtle and pervasive that "it affects every fiber of
character and mind."[5] According to Levi, Dewey's private self
"grows in an environment of social interactions which defines
its limit and mirrors its qualities, so that it finally comes
to resemble the image that it sees refelcted in others."[6] Thus,
social arrangements, institutions, and laws are agencies of human welfare. But these are so not only in being able to provide
some things for individuals (happiness not excluded); they are
so in a much stronger sense - they serve as means for creating
individuals![7]

Fortunately (for opponents of social determinism), however, a deterministic reading is not contextually accurate. For, this would place Dewey's position outside the perspective of his favored category of transaction. It is quite true that he insists on the creative role of society in forming mental, psychological, and moral dispositions. But he is equally emphatic in the assertion that the same society is simultaneously the matrix of individuality and freedom. The former aspect of his overall view of the human condition is explicitly affirmed in practically all of his writings. The latter aspect f his theory can be discerned contextually from: 1) his metaphysics introducing 'preferential behavior' as the root of individuality, 2) his advocacy of the educational function of society, 3) his social psychology describing the development of character through habits, and 4) his definition of human freedom in terms of choice, power, and intelligence. The following section will be devoted to elucidating each point in succession.

A. The concept of 'Social-Individuals'

The continuity of Dewey's development from metaphysics to psychology is easily traceable. What is not readily visible is the consistency of the latter with the former. It will be the aim here to demonstrate that consistency, i. e., that his concept of 'community' is framed on a metaphysical base that attempts not only to guarantee real individuality but also to provide the ground for a social psychology that can account for the moral growth of (what may be termed for the present purpose as) 'social-individuals.'[8]

1. The Root of 'Social-Individuality'

The discussion on the three levels of interaction in Dewey's metaphysical works includes a concept central to the issue of social-individuality. That is the concept of 'preferential behavior.' Experience and Nature presents it as a full-blown metaphysical notion. The article entitled "Philosophies of Freedom," originally published in 1928 in Freedom in the Modern World,[9] makes explicit its connection with the ideas of freedom and individuality. "Context and Thought" offers an application of it to the problem of thinking.[10]

To succeed in relating to Dewey's sense here, the description of Dewey's world reviewed in Chapter II must be recalled. It is, in his view, a realm that is contingent, unsettled, and unfinished, although its movements also have traceable patterns. These patterns mark differences among things such that these things can be graded according to the degree of complexity of (natural) transactions in which they are engaged. In the lowest level of relations, there are inanimate things which exhibit recognizable characteristics of bias or selective responses. Far from being an abstraction, the phenomena, Dewey declares, are a commonplace. "Existences are cold and indifferent in the presence of some things and react energetically in either negative or positive ways to other things."[11] This marks, in his observation, the distinctive contribution of things to what takes place; "it sets a peculiar direction and gives certain quality to the changes that come about."[12]

In higher forms, the selectivity thus described achieves more stability. Lower kinds show selective reactions in a transitory manner. Iron, for instance, does not keep itself simple iron. As it interacts with, say water, it it turns into iron oxide. But, in plants, some identity is maintained, though parts may completely change in the course of (vegetative) development. Interactions of various parts take place in a fashion that tend to continue a characteristically organized activity. The identity is traceable in the way that their lives take a historical course; they utilize, as far as they are able, conserved consequences of past activities in order to adapt to changes that may follow.

In animals, the organic parts are even more developed, attaining a condition conducive to the perpetuation of patterned activities. It is here that Dewey finds the basis of 'sensitivity.'

> Each "part" of an organism is itself organized,
> and so of the "parts" of the part. Hence its
> selective bias in interactions with environing
> things is exercised so as to maintain itself,
> while also maintaining the whole of which it is
> a member.[13]

The operative presence of the whole in the parts, and vice versa, constitutes susceptibility - the capacity of feeling - where responses are not only selective but also discriminatory. This capacity, which is not realized in plants, appears in animals as genuine sensitivity and interest. This sensitivity, in turn, as they become more developed, are expressed as feeling. This takes place when "susceptibility to the useful and harmful in surroundings becomes premonitory, an occasion of eventual consequences within life."[14]

As sensitive discriminatory reactions to different environmental forces multiply and as motor organs increase in scope, in delicacy, and in intricacy of movements, feelings begin to vary more and more in quality and intensity. And when it reaches a certain level of transaction, communication is arrived at. This is identifiable because here "the qualities of feelings become significant of objective differences in external things and episodes past and to come."[15] At this stage, feelings are not just had but become significant of objective differences. Preferential behavior attains a "mental" status, and thus can be more aptly called 'choice.'

In "Context and Thought," Dewey employs the term 'selective interest' to apply to the phenomenon of bias in thinking. It is, he declares, present in all operations of thought. Curiously, he identifies it with the 'subjective.' "The organism, self, ego, subject, give it whatever name you choose, is implicated in all thinking as in all eating, business, or play."[16] Also, it is equivalent to individuality, for it is a unique manner of entering into interaction with other things. It is, however, not opposed to the objective 'per se' but to the mechanical, where thinking is not original but merely repetitive.

In this account, Dewey does not mean to undermine the depth and 'sanctity' of subjectivity. Selective interest, he is certain, is present not only in conscious thought. He gives the assurance that some inner underlying elements of selection surface even when a thinker does turn upon himself, inquire into, and attempt to discount his in dividual attitudes. At times, it may be noted, his concession is almost embarrasing. For, his language sounds like a disguised resurrection of the Aristotelian lexicon (and its later development in medieval philosophy), particularly that set of terms applied to the "substantial soul." He states, for instance, that if there is what can be called the 'subconscious' of human thinking, it is definable in terms of those deeper interests.

> Apart from language, from imputed and inferred meaning, we continually engage in an immense multitude of immediate organic selections, rejections, welcomings, expulsions, appropriations, withdrawals, shrinkings, expansions, elations and dejections, attacks, wardings off, of the most minute vibratingly delicate nature. We are not aware of the qualities of many or most of these acts; we do not objectively distinguish and identify them. Yet they exist as feeling qualities, and have an enormous directive effect in our behavior.[17]

In "Time and Individuality," preferential behavior in the human level (i. e., where communication occurs) takes a historical (or temporal) course. Individuality, in this context, is manifested and measured according to the distinctiveness of the ways of responding to various conditions in the life history of a man.

> The career which is his unique individuality is the series of interactions in which he was created to be what he was by the ways in which he responded to the occasions with which he was presented.[18]

At the start, it is like a malleable material; it is spontaneous and unformed being a mere capacity for development. Then, environing conditions are met along the way. The unique ways of responding to them render them constituents of an ongoing unique history. Actual conditions, therefore, serve as opportunities for shaping up an individuality.

> Since individuality is a distinctive way of
> feeling the impacts of the world and of showing
> a preferential bias in response to these impacts,
> it develops only through (transaction) with actual
> conditions.[19]

By actual conditions, Dewey is referring to both nature and culture as factors that shape the human form. The self emerges from the complexities of organic and social transactions. Unlike the cartesians and the existentialists, Dewey neither presumes that subjectivity is an original quality only awaiting its time to unfold nor takes for granted that mind is predisposed to be an independent creative source. Even more sharply, he differs from them by dispensing altogether with the notion itself of 'subject' (of experience) or permanent 'ego' hiding behind a physical veil. He finds neither evidence nor justification in confirming the view that mind is an enclosure where resides the formal capacity of apprehension, devising and believing -- free to entertain any thought or belief whatsoever. On the contrary, what he finds at every turn are experiences corroborating the conclusion that communication is a condition of thought and mind. If there is a sense in which 'subject,' ego or 'mind' denotes a substantial reality, it has to be conceived behavioristically as a **system** of beliefs, desires, and purposes which are formed in the interaction of biological aptitudes with a social environment.

That actual social conditions stand as the complement of preferential behavior in the formation of individuality makes it plain why, for Dewey, the 'social' is neither an extension of what is meant by 'individual' nor an additive accumulation of the latter. He explains:

> The individual and the social are not names for
> any actual existences. Their relation indicates
> the ways of interaction between human nature
> and cultural conditions. The problem involved
> here is not to determine the relation of one
> entity with another but to ascertain the effects
> of interactions between different components of
> different human beings and different customs,
> rules, traditions, institutions - things called
> "social."[20]

Thus, human beings are simultaneously individual and social! And

Dewey unabashedly proclaims so:

> At the very best, individual and social stand
> for traits of unitary human beings; traits, more-
> over, which are so integral that they are but two
> aspects of man in his actual existence... "Social"
> ties do not inhere in "individuals;" they inhere
> integrally in human beings in their very humanity...
> "Individual" is as truly but an adjective as is
> "social."[21]

The error he sees in the view that there lies a residual self
beneath acts and appearances starts from the observation that a
man carries a number of arbitrary relationships, say as a member
of a church, of a business organization, of a political party.
And because an individual can be dissociated from any of these
groupings, there grows the opinion that man can be isolated and
be as it were a 'pure self.' From this premise, the unreal question of how individuals come to be united in societies or groups
develops. The individual and the social are then set opposed to
each other. What emerges thereafter is the problem of reconciling
them. [22]

Conclusively, in Dewey's mind, the term 'social' describes
the fact of man's continuity with his environment; 'individual'
qualifies his "distinctive way of behaving in conjunction and
'connection' with other distinctive ways of acting, not a self-
enclosed way of acting independent of everything else..."[23] The
latter is achieved within the context of the former such that man
becomes more individual as he becomes more social. Becoming social does not, therefore, necessarily entail becoming passive
conformists - creatures whose preferences and responses are effectively controlled by alien forces. It rather means to a distinctive way of belonging to a community without dissolving individuality. For, in the process, neither personal bias and intelligent choice are surrendered nor responses are exercised
without responsibility.

The theory evidently involves both preferential behavior and
plasticity, not as opposed terms but as complementary ones. But,
Dewey will argue, there is no incoherence in accepting both. The
point is to present the ambivalent character of nature, specifically human nature, in a most faithful manner.

> Existentially speaking, a human individual is
> distinctive opacity of bias and preference con-
> joined with plasticity and permeability of needs
> and likings. One trait tends to isolation, dis-
> creteness; the other trait is connection, conti-
> nuity. This ambivalent character is rooted in
> nature, whose events have their own distinctive
> indifferences, resistances, arbitrary closures

and intolerances, and also their peculiar openness, warm responsiveness, greedy seekings and
transforming unions. The conjunction in nature
of whimsical contingency and lawful uniformity
is the result of these two characters of events.
They persist upon the human plane, and as ultimate characters are ineradicable.[24]

Concretely, Dewey explains 'plasticity' as the specific a-
daptability of an immature creature for growth. This means that
humans, particularly in younger years, are receptive of stimuli
in their environment. But this state or (better still) capacity
is not a purely passive one. It is both able to retain and carry
over from prior experiences factors capable of modifying subsequent activities. This is how habits are, in fact, acquired or
definite dispositions developed. But the case is not like the
passive plasticity of wax which takes a form solely according
to external pressure. Rather, it is like the way a thing takes
on the "color" of its surroundings, the way it assimilates the
character of its environment while retaining its own bent. Still,
the quality means more.

It is essentially the ability to learn from
experience; the power to retain from one experience something which is of avail in coping
with the difficulties of a later situation.
This means power to modify actions on the basis
of the results of prior experiences, the power
to "develop dispositions." Without it, the acquisition of habit is impossible.[25]

It is, therefore, simultaneously passive and active.

Dewey's solution to the concomitant problem on the psychological plane is based on the same thoughts. To be sure, he was
aware of the celebrated case of 'fragmented individuals' or of
the so-called 'split personality.' On this, he says:

We arrive at true conception of motivation and
interest only by the recognition that selfhood
(except as it has encased itself in a shell of
routine) is in process of making, and that any
self is capable of including within itself a
number of inconsistent selves, or unharmonized
dispositions.[26]

This is why, as he describes the development of the social person, he also directs attention to that which stands up as the
counter-balance to what could be, in most occasions, a dominant
social force. This counter-factor is the movement inward, toward
subjectivity and independence.

78

> The human individual in his opacity of bias is
> in so far doomed to a blind solitariness. He
> hugs himself in isolation and fights against
> disclosure, the give and take of communication,
> as for the very integrity of existence. Even
> communicable meanings are tinged with color of
> the uncommunicated; there is a quality of reserve
> in every publicity.[27]

Dewey does not, however, favor an exaggerated type of independence, i. e., without some connectedness. He believes that from
the social standpoint, dependence is a power rather than a weak-
ness. It actually signifies 'interdependence.' This means that
the more a man is self-reliant, the more he is aloof and indifferent.[28] Just as extreme transparency of self can cause a man-
gled personality, so also exaggerated isolation from the environment with which it is naturally connected can bring about psychological solipsism.

> Psychologists have made us familiar with dis-
> turbances labeled "withdrawal from reality" ...
> What are these withdrawals but case of the inter-
> ruption or cessation of "the active operative
> presence of environing conditions in the acti-
> vities of human being"? What are the resulting
> psychological phenomena but evidences that the
> self loses its integrity within itself when it
> loses integration with the medium in which it
> lives?[29]

From the side of subjectivity, the self emerges as the central organization of thought and action. But this admission does
not constitute a return to the old Aristotelian view. Dewey is
careful to reiterate that the 'self' is to be conceived not substantially, as the carrier of experience, the source of consciousness, or permanent ego. Instead, the concept is to be understood
functionally, i. e., as a quality of behavior. As such, it stands
as the integration of all the different qualities of transactions.
Thus, the self or mind would not appear as a transcendental being
regulating in some mysterious manner those transactions and con-
ferring rationality upon them. Rather, it would emerge as a distinctive manner of participation in events such that the "significant distinction is no longer between the knower and the world
(but among) the different ways of being in and of the movement of
things; between a brute physical way and a purposive intelligent
way..."[30]

The self, Dewey continues, shows itself in the conduct of
the individual when outcomes are predicted and anticipated. Those
predicted and and anticipated outcomes become controlling factors
in the present ordering of activities. If there, he concedes, a
need to give sense to regarding individuality as an inner dimen-

sion, it is only by signifying that man "is not a mere property
of nature, set in place according to a scheme independent of him,
as an article is put in its place in a cabinet, but that he adds
something, that he marks a contribution."[31] He insists that there
must always be the understanding that such a world of inner experience is dependent upon an extension of language which is a social product.

    In Dewey's context, then, the normal personality is one cha-
racterized by a balanced complementation (not a dualism) in the
dual direction of selfhood. It consists in the "oscillation between surrender and assertion of the inner."[32] The individual, he
says, is indeed not a divided being, but he has a double status
and import. There is the individual who, in one aspect, is at
peace with its environment because of the reinforcement it provides his activities and the satisfaction it gives to the requirement of his preferences. And there is the same individual
who, in another aspect, has his bias set at odds with the operations of the things through which its needs can be satisfied.
In the first consideration, the self is more yielding. But this
is only because it is secure in its home. The situation is actually a fulfillment. Thus, the mind, in this case, expresses
itself through appropriation and enjoyment of the world of which
it is a part.

    Pursued further, this theme is developed by Dewey into a
full-blown theory of religious experience in A Common Faith. In
this work, as is the anticipation in Experience and Nature, the
unification of self throughout the ceaseless flux of what it
does, suffers, and achieves is said to be unattainable by itself alone. For, it "is always directed toward something beyond itself and so its own unification depends upon the idea of
the integration of the shifting scenes of the world into that
imaginative totality we call the universe."[33]

    In the second consideration, the self is more pronounced in
its individuality. If its odds with the world become overwhelming, it may indeed succumb to 'egotistical solitude' or suffer
psychological disorientation. But, ordinarily, it enforces its
desires by remaking conditions. If it does not, it regains unity
as the dominating energies of community life become incorporated
to form his mind.[34] The problem with a notion of individuality
set in the context of Dewey's transactional framework may be discerned here. His treatment of the relation between sociality and
individuality, by his own recognizance, may be seen as suffering
from ambivalence.[35] But this point may only be noted here. A fuller discussion of the issue will be included in the concluding
chapter.

    In the meantime, the condition of the social-individual may
be clearly described. In all departments of human life - from
education to politics - the balance of selfhood must be sustained
to allow for both stability and renewal. That Dewey's world is
never finished only shows that man cannot be completely at home
in it. Yet, this is no admission of the reality of the afterlife.

It is merely a presentation of of the obvious fact that there is
always room for improvement. But this is not denying that there
are also aspects of it that may be appropriated and enjoyed, such
as its aesthetic dimension. In all events, the lot of man calls
for giving due importance not only to the need for maintaining a
healthy environment, but also the active effort of bringing about
change in established conditions to make possible the improvement
of self. This is why, as will be seen later, Dewey's community is
engaged in a continuous movement of transactions in which certain
parts influence other parts, which are, in turn, influenced by
the force of activities in the search for better and better order.

2. Society and Conduct

Implicated in the preceding discussion is the question of
human conduct. How can conduct be simultaneously the consequence
of community life and the creative agent of the community in attaining new forms? In Human Nature and Conduct, Dewey develops
a social psychology designed to answer this problem. Briefly,
the position he defends is a third alternative to two opposing
schools of social reform. One, basing itself on the notion of
morality attributed to inner freedom cooped within personality,
proposed that the only solution to improving conditions is to
purify hearts. The other, denying any such power but postulating the malleability of human nature to the forces of environment, endorses changes that can be accomplished only in the conditions and institutions themselves.

Both, in Dewey's judgment, are self-defeating proposals. The
first freezes aims to an unattainable ideal and imprisons morality to an unreal inner world. The second provides no genuine
leverage for change; it throws men back upon accident disguised
as a necessary law and puts trust on some violent change.[36] To
regard conduct as an interaction between the two terms - human
nature and environment - is Dewey's way of avoiding being penned
in by the controls of the two theories. Progress, in his alternative program, may be observed to proceed from both directions.
Freedom itself is available only in that kind of interaction in
which human desire and choice count.

Dewey's interpretation of human nature and conduct revolves
around the ideas of 'habit,' 'impulse,' and 'intelligence.' While
distinct, the three are not regarded as separate forces in man.
No marked line divides one from the others. They compenetrate and
are coterminous with social factors. The concepts of 'habit' and
'impulse' may be dealt with presently. Treatment of the notion of
'intelligence,' being central in Dewey's theory of freedom, may
be postponed for that section.

Broadly speaking, habits are acquired attitudes and dispositions. Like any physiological act, they require the cooperation
of organism and environment. The idea (of habits) can be better
understood if they are regarded, in their developed form, as art.

As such, "they involve skill of sensory and motor organs, cunning or craft, and objective environment."[37] To stress the importance of surrounding factors, Dewey points out that moral dispositions do not belong exclusively to self and are, therefore, not subjective. Virtues and vices, as forms of habits are working adaptations of personal capacities and outside elements.

The reference to personal capacities does not reduce them to some inner or potential faculties requiring only positive stimulus from the outside to be activated. In saying that habits are dispositions or attitudes, Dewey is pointing to their condition of operativeness or actuality.

> The word disposition means predisposition, rea-
> diness to act overtly in a specific fashion when-
> ever opportunity is presented, this opportunity
> consisting in removal of the presssure due to the
> dominance of some overt habit; and that attitude
> means some special case of a predisposition, the
> disposition waiting as it were to spring through
> an open door.[38]

Habits are, therefore, active means rather than mechanical abilities. They do not exist apart from preferences; they are not lacking in urgent impulsion. On the contrary, they are tendencies to action. They constitute the self or what may be called 'will.' As means, they are not just tools; they project themselves by energetic ways of acting. In both physical and moral acts, they mediate between wish and execution. Thus, a wish takes form only in conjunction with an idea, in the same manner that an idea takes shape and consistency only in connection with a habit (behind it). This manifests that reason is not prior to habit. As a matter of fact, the latter influences the former.

Dewey is making it clear that the execution of an idea is dependent upon habit. Thus, the formation and texture of that idea are similarly channelled on the grooves of habit. This is so because an idea can be carried out only with a mechanism already present. If the mechanism is deficient, no intention in the world is capable of producing effective results. In all cases, the design and structure of the agency employed indicates directly the outcome.

That habits are indicative of character means that the latter is no more than the interpenetration of the former, i. e., the continued operation of all habits in every act. This explains the unity of character and conduct and, by the same token, of motive and act - elements that have been severed by other theories. In Dewey's use of the term, 'will' represents something moving and practical. It is not something separate from consequences, much less opposed to them. In fact, it is the cause of consequences: "it is causation in its personal aspect, the aspect immediately preceding action."[40] He finds it hard to conceive

82

of will as something which can be complete without reference to
deeds prompted and results obtained. Much less is it cut off
from environing conditions!

> If we surrender preconceived theories as to the
> nature of "will," if we extend the meaning of
> character to include the whole body of desires,
> purposes, conviction, manifested in deliberation
> and choice, then surrounding conditions which
> arouse desires; which direct wants toward one
> object rather than another for satisfaction;
> which confirm certain purposes and weaken others;
> which lead to prizing some objects and disparaging
> others, have intrinsic meaning.[41]

Dewey's position does not entail the denial of the possibility of deeds being judged properly without taking into account
the disposition as well as their concrete consequences. But the
justification of the procedure lies not in isolating disposition
from deeds nor consquences. Rather, it consists in viewing the
total scene. A single act is only one of a multitude of acts.
Hence, there is need to take into account the disposition. Deeds
and consequences fix the moral quality of an act. Disposition
shapes deeds and consequences according to its form.

Dewey shows more sharply the role of habits as dispositions
effecting and affecting deeds in the case of the so-called virtues. Virtues are desired not for themselves but insofar as they
are significant means. For example, honesty, courage, kindness,
etc. are ways of producing specific natural goods or fulfill-
ments. Dewey admits the danger of oversimplification in appro-
aching virtues in this manner. The fact is, there is, oftentimes
a need to distinguish virtue as resident in character alone from
objective conditions. A desirable trait does not always produce
a desirable result. Similarly, good things happen with no assistance from goodwill. Because luck plays a part, Dewey advises
that one must refrain from taking the notion of goodness in character and in consequences in too fixed a manner.

The role of social conditions in the formation of personal
habits can be seen in the experience that these are set by prior
and established customs. The individual usually acquires the morality of his social group in the same way that he inherits its
speech. This is also how customs persist. But, Dewey is careful
to note, this fact does not make men automatons. Although habit
is an ability and an art formed in the course of previous experiences, it is not merely repetitive in its exercise. On the
contrary, as experience shows, it is available for new emergen-
cies. He is convinced that a habit which is no more than "ens-
lavement to old rut" is bad. [42] The proper attitude is to take
mastery of the conditions which enter into action. This is saying that habits must be intelligent, i. e., not confined to
tedious uniformity.

The social complicity involved in conduct widens the area
of individual responsibility. Only in a situation like that of
Robinson Crusoe would habits be formed in a moral vacuum. Thus,
Dewey maintains, no social element is morally indifferent. If
it is a question of crime, he calls for reform rather than re-
tribution. And reform should take place not only in the criminal
but more importantly in the social conditions that occasioned
the crime. For Dewey, guilt is a social phenomenon; crime is a
social partnership; conduct is always shared. To transform the
willful criminals would require changing the objective conditions that enter into their habits. In this regard, he observes
that the best we can do for future generation is "to transmit
unimpaired and with some increment of meaning the environment
that makes it possible to maintain the habits of decent and refined life."[43]

From the standpoint of conduct, the emphasis on objective
arrangements is complemented by giving due attention to the "subjective" factor in habit. The concept 'preferential behavior' re-
appears in this context. Its import is maintained with equal vigor. Dewey is convinced that even the simple taste for flowers
may be an initial step in building reservoirs and irrigation ca-
nals. For, this taste can mature into full individuality when
conflict of habits releases impulsive activities to modify a habit, custom or convention. What was, at first, the individualized quality of habitual activity is abstracted and

> becomes a center of activity aiming to recons-
> truct customs in accord with some desire which
> is rejected by the immediate situation and which
> therefore is felt to belong to one's self, to be
> the mark and possession of an individual in par-
> tial and temporary opposition to his environment.[44]

The connection of habits with intelligence is hinted at in
the present discussion. Dewey states that the former are conditions of intellectual efficiency. They operate on the intellect
in a two-fold manner: Firstly, they restrict its reach and fix
its limit. This signifies that habits confine attention to a present problem and prevent the mind from straying. Unconnected
with habits, thoughts tend to grope and fall into uncertainty. At
times, though, habits become routine. When this happens, thought
is no longer possible or necessary. Habits become rigid manne-
risms leading to thoughtless action. This dull efficiency of action is, fortunately, not a frequent occurrence. This is because
habits are constantly encountering new circumstances. Secondly,
habits operate upon intellectual activity in a positive way. The
wider the range of a person's habits, the greater the extent of
his field of observation, the more flexible would be his ability
to discriminate.

The other element in conduct is impulse. Like habit, this
is not an innate tendency. It may, however, be regarded as a na-

tive activity. In itself, it lacks meaning. It becomes definite only when it interacts with a social environment. Dewey admits that there may be a capital stock of native instincts. But each one of them is modified in the process of living, of engaging in various transactions.

The complex interplay between native instincts and objective conditions shows that native impulses have the capacity to reorganize habits, change their qualities, and lead them to new directions. This assertion may, at first glance, appear incoherent with a point discussed above. For, there, it was stated that native activities are themselves directed by acquired habits, and habits, in turn, can only be modified when impulses are redirected. But the two statements are not discontinuous and the reasoning from one to the other is only apparently circular.

The difficulty may be resolved by looking at this issue through the question of how it is possible to change institutions while habits dominate native activities. On this matter, Dewey suggests two ways. The first is to take advantage of the education of the young in order to modify prevailing types of thought and desire. An educational atmosphere should be fostered in which habits can be made more intelligent and sensitivity can be made more percipient. When so fostered, the gain may be observed in many ways. Habits and sensitivity would be informed with foresight, would be aware of actual conditions, would be sincere, direct, and flexibly responsive than those now current. Only then can they squarely meet their own problems and propose their own improvements.[45]

Dewey is implying here that educators should, to some extent, have already broken off from the domination of a given social institution. For, this liberation is precisely what they are supposed to achieve in others. In the Problems of Men, speaking on the duty of educators, counsels that they become aware of the kind of world in which we live and discover for themselves what specific things are needed to execute decisions arrived at. He further advocates that "one great business of the schools at present is to develop immunity against the propaganda influence of press and radio."[46] Educators should teach people to discount the unconscious prejudices that their social environment impresses upon them.

The second way that habits are reorganized and redirected can occur independently of deliberation and control. It, oftentimes, happens in a complex culture where habits are formed on differing and even conflicting patterns. And when they do rub and wear upon each other, the resulting attrition may release impulses for new adventures. The problem that surfaces in this situation concerns the uncertain direction of these changes. What the social scientist can do is to analyze the possible direction of such changes and forearm society of the eventual outcome.

For Dewey, the reorganizing capacity of impulses manifests

that they are originally flexible and that they show themselves
in diversified activities according to the way in which they interact with their surroundings. This explains the constant process of renewal in society. The old claim that native tendencies
are forever the same confuses the performance and rigidity of
custom for that of native impulses. The fact is, instincts are
easily modifiable through use and are susceptible to educative
direction. Paradoxically, custom is a great inertia in guiding
impulses. But, in turn, the native stock of impulses can result
in a great diversity of customs.

Evidently, Dewey is not saying that phenomena like war be
attributed to instincts, say, the tendency of pugnacity. Instincts are meaningless and ineffective if detached from social
conditioning. War, like any other social phenomena, is generated
by conditions affecting native activities. "The ineradicable impulses that are utilized in them are capable of being drafted
into many other channels."[47] The view that impulses have a direct causal effect is simply uninformed. The truth is, there is
a diversity of customs and institutions which the same human nature produces and employs. Thus, Dewey suggests that we should
not start with direct causative power in explaining something.
We should not, for example, look for state-forming forces; we
should not explain the origin of the state by saying that man
is a political animal, as some classical theories do. Such an
account is a logically circular.

> And at worst, the alleged instinct and natural
> endowment appealed to as a causal force them-
> selves represent physiological tendencies which
> have previously been shaped into habits of ac-
> tion and expectations by means of the very so-
> cial conditions they are supposed to explain.[48]

The procedure of numbering and classifying native impulses is
also rejected for the same reason. It makes thinking artificially
rigid, in opposition to events which are fluid. It is also a mis-
take to define human nature in terms of a set of primary instincts, such as love, egoism and altruism, greed, fear, etc. For,
"in fact there are as many specific reactions to differing stimulating conditions as there is time for, and our lists are only
classification for a purpose."[49] Theories that depend on such a
classification, Dewey would insist, wrongly presuppose that
there is a ready-made self behind human activities, a position
already dismissed for not being consistent with the nature of
self as an on-going process.

The doctrine of separate psychic forces with direct manifestation in human behavior, such as hunger and sex, is similarly
untenable. It fails to recognize that, in each act, the whole
organism is involved in some way, that the environment is never
identical for any two acts. Separate-impulse theories are based
on oversimplification. They transform visible social effects into

impulsive causes. In Dewey's analysis, impulsive energy is seen indeed to find some kind of outlet. But this can only be carried forward to a satisfactory conclusion with the aid of prevailing custom and convention. Yet, custom and convention can also be rigid. For that reason, there is a constant need to rejuvenate them by the release of new impulses. And thus continues the inward and outward oscillation of selfhood, the complementation of subjective bias and objective factors in the growth of man and his community.

B. The Educational Function of Community

The preceding section has identified those relevant elements in Dewey's theory of 'social-individuality' which are inconsistent with a purely deterministic perspective. It argued that 1) social agencies relate to beings endowed with the capacity for selective response such that social intercourse brings about not automatons but social-individuals; and that 2) the psychological import of social environment in shaping conduct includes or should include the possibility of both redirection of habits and social reconstruction. The following section will show that 'freedom' for Dewey, if it has any real and functional meaning at all, is a condition actualized only within a context of sharing, i. e., within a genuine community.

What is, therefore, demanded, as a condition of moral growth and of the actualization of freedom, is an effectively educative social milieu. This is why Dewey insists on promoting the educational value of social communications. His program in this regard is again full of assurances that social existence is not necessarily opposed to the development of individuality. On the contrary, society as a whole, if it is going to be a community, has to provide the educational atmosphere for it. The key is always in what kind of atmosphere is available. How such an appropriate atmosphere can be established remains to be seen.

It does not need to be restated that the term 'social environment' bears for Dewey an intrinsic connection with social-individuals engaged in the third level of transaction. It denotes more than the physical surrounding that encompasses an individual person. It expresses the specific continuity of that surrounding with his active tendencies. The difference is quite sharp. In a physical relation, the connection is mostly external - as in the case of inorganic beings and the locale in which it exists. In a social relation, the interaction is dominantly internal to the ralation; there is what Dewey refers to as the element of concern.[50] The concept stands for the active role social environment takes in the transaction. The case is, for example, depicted in the care with which parents have with their children, particularly in their younger years.

What constitutes man's distinctive environment is that with which he 'varies.' This means that the human environment consists

of those conditions that promote or hinder, stimulate or inhibit
the characteristic activities of human beings. The adjective
'characteristic' implies that there are native tendencies in
man - those that Dewey calls 'behavioral preference' in his metaphysical works and 'impulse' and 'instincts' in his psychological
writings. The activities and dispositions arising from these tendencies are conditioned by what enters into them. This may be
in the manner of either a sustaining or a frustrating influence.

In the context of the present issue, the educational function of society or the community refers to the various ways social environment forms the dispositions of human beings living
in the fold. These ways can best be observed in the process of
nurturing immature members of society. In the same way that animals are trained, children, says Dewey, are directed by controlling natural stimuli that affect them, by modifying their spontaneous actions through the formation of some desirable habits.
They are disciplined to conform to the overt behavior and moral
counsels of their elders. But, unlike animals, the changes that
result take place not only in their outer actions but also in
their mental and emotional dispositions. As he points out, ordinarily, "altering the external habit of action by changing the
environment to affect the stimuli to action will also alter the
mental disposition concerned in the action."[51]

An animal, say a horse, follows its master's cue because
of the benefits derived from doing so; it gets food or avoids
being punished. Its attention is limited to the pleasurable or
painful consequences of actions. It gains no new interest, not
even in the service it may be rendering. In man, the interest
becomes common with those he is learning from and living with.
He is able to share in their ideas and emotion and, hence, in
their interests. He participates not only in the performance of
acts but also in the accomplishments that arise from those acts.
He becomes, in a word, a true 'partner.'

There is, of course, the possibility that, in some instances, a youth's immature instincts may remain attached to
their original objects of pleasure and pain, as they do in animals. If this were the case, the youth obtains satisfaction and
avoids the pain of failure by eliciting overt actions which are
agreeable to others. But he also (and often he does) really engages in a conjoint activity with the capacity of sharer. Then,
his original impulses are modified into the way of his elders
insofar as the same ideas and emotions that animate them are
also aroused in him.

Social forces, Dewey claims, do not actually implant certain
desires in a direct way nor establish certain purely muscular habits of action. They first stand as conditions which stimulate
certain visible and tangible ways of acting, and which then make
the individual a sharer in the associated activity. As sharers,
he feels the success or failure of such activity as his. By pos-
sessing the emotional attitude of the group, he becomes alert
to recognize the ends at which it aims and the means to secure

those ends. In the process, he will also achieve much of the same stock of knowledge inasmuch as that knowledge is an ingredient of his habitual activities.[52] Conclusively, affirms Dewey, "social environment forms the mental and emotional disposition of behavior in individuals by engaging them in activities that arouse and strengthen certain impulses that have certain purposes and entail certain consequences."[53]

At times, Dewey refers to social forces affecting individuals as the "unconscious influence of the environment."[54] This is opposed to the direct or "conscious" method employed in formal schooling. But, though unconscious, environmental influence can be discovered by inference from observations. First, it is apparent in the habits of language insofar as children are seen to adhere to their mother tounge even when they intentionally acquire other modes of speech. Second, it is observed in the examples of others that effectively modify habits and dispositions. And, third, it is experienced in taste and aesthetic appreciation which are never spontaneous and personally engrained until the current of social habit and custom make them so. (It may be recalled that these are the same media of communication discussed in Chapter II.)

In Dewey's appraisal, this unconscious level of education provided by the social medium is more critical than schooling itself. For, it is more widely shared, being available to everyone. Moreover, it is easily assimilated, being attainable by sheer imitation. Its effect is often deeper and more lasting, the stimuli being constantly present. He also believes that the social influence is an effective method of nurturing growing minds to achieve order in society. To be preferred, he declares, is the use of the nature of the situation basic control. In this way, the young simply has to refer to what others are doing to have a pattern for their actions. In so doing, their actions are directed to a common result and are productive of an understanding common to all participants.[55] He points to that common understanding of the means and end of action as the essence of social control.

But there is a more significant reason for the preference. In a summary passage, he states: the social environment "is indirect, or emotional and intellectual, not direct or personal. Moreover it is intrinsic to the disposition of the person, not external or coercive."[56] Beliefs, he says, cannot simply be hammered nor attitudes plastered.[57] They are communicated by means of the action of the environment in calling out certain responses. It is in this way that a transformation of the quality of experience of the young can be initiated until it partakes in the interests and ideals current in the community.

Dewey is making two vital points. In the first place, he is announcing his non-alignment with the deterministic school in the issue of education. In the second place, he is declaring his view on the aims of education. The former statement is consistent with his negative posture against any absolutistic type of philosophy, specifically that which set ready-made or original instincts and fixed ends for human nature. The latter one is an expression of his aspiration for the ideal community.

In the Public and Its Problems, Dewey criticises John Stuart Mill for postulating a social theory based on a mistaken analysis of human nature. It was Mill's belief, as Dewey sees it, that there was a certain fixed and standardized individual from whose assumed traits social phenomena could be deduced.[58] Conversely, the laws of social phenomena were thought to be nothing more than the laws of actions and passions of men united together in the social state. The assumption was that human actions and passions were, because they had to be, obedient to the laws of individual human nature. This carried the expectation that there were certain social laws, whether normative or regulative, applicable to all times and under all circumstances.

This form of (social) determinism is radically opposed to a naturalistic metaphysics which admits of no predestined course of fixed stops or ends toward which social development will or should proceed. There can be no such laws of individual human nature in a view that regards men as "influenced throughout by contemporary and transmitted culture, whether in conformity or in protest."[59] There may be some generic elements in man, Dewey would admit; but these are at best what are constitutive of his organic or biological make-up. Actions and passions, beliefs and purposed are results of social transactions. Mill's error, therefore, consists in the identification of social with physical uniformities. This is why Dewey, while insistent on the need to apply the method of science in human affairs, vacillates on the question of whether or not science would ever achieve perfect control of human behavior.

> It is absurd to suppose that an adequate psychological science would flower in a control of human activities similar to the control which physical science has procured of physical energies. To imagine it would is simply to reduce human beings to the plane of inanimate things mechanically manipulated from without, it makes human education something like the training of fleas, dogs and horses.[60]

He admits, however, that the possibility that "physiological chemistry, increased knowledge of the nervous system, of the processes and functions of glandular secretions, may in time enable us to deal with phenomena of emotional and intellectual disturbances before which mankind has been helpless."[61] Still, he is equally confident that the control of these conditions will not determine the uses to which human beings will put their normalized potentialities. It has been his observation that men of varied background, even in the presence of remedial or preventive measures, remain to have their experiences and the direction of

90

their restored energies "affected by the objects and instrumentalities of the human environment and by what men at the time
currently prize and hold dear."[62]

Dewey is careful to note that he is not reverting to the admission of the discarded concept of 'free will.' He is merely
pointing out the defect of a purely behavioristic approach. He
is certain that a change in the educational method similar to
what is being proposed in a deterministic program would not be
successful. What it will do is "release new potentialities capable of all kinds of permutations and combinations which would
in turn affect human nature and its education transformation in
a continuous and endless procession."[63]

The conclusion expressed in the last statement coincides
with the second point indicated above, namely, Dewey's view on
the specific aims of education. Among these aims is the construc-
tion and reconstruction of experience which add to the meaning
of that experience, and which increase the ability to direct the
course of subsequent experiences.[64] For Dewey, education is a social process. For, it means securing a sound direction and development for the immature through participation in community life.
This means, in effect, that education varies with the quality
of life which prevails in a group. If that quality is directed
toward change, so will education be. If it favors perpetuation
of its own customs, education will, likewise, be stagnant. "Any
education given by a group tends to socialize its members, but
the quality and value of socialization depends upon the habits
and aims of the group."[65]

For Dewey, social education must be geared to providing the
atmosphere for the release of various forms of individualities.
To this end, he advocates the use of experimental social method.
This method surrenders pre-conceived specific goals but takes
every care "to surround the young with the physical and social
conditions which best conduce, as far as freed knowledge extends,
to release of personal potentialities."[66] This is the only way
to meet future social requirements and the development of society. For, this would ensure continuous readjustment through effectively and productively meeting new situations produced by
varied intercourse.

The aims of education thus spelled out have direct bearing
to the pursuit and attainment of community life. And if the latter is a moral end, the former, which develop the power to share
effectively in social life is likewise moral.[67] It is in accordance with this aim for community that any social enterprise
should be gauged, Dewey declares.

The two points selected by which to measure the
worth of a form of social life are the extent in
which the interests of a group are shared by all
its members, and the fullness and freedom with
which it interacts with other groups. An undesi-

rable society, in other words, is one which internally and externally sets up barriers to free intercourse and communication of experience. A society which makes prevision for participation in
the good of all its members on equal terms, and
which secures flexible readjustment of its institutions through interaction of the different
form of associated life is in so far democratic.
Such a society must have a type of education which
gives individual and personal interest in social
relationship and control, and the habits of mind
which secure social changes without introducing
disorder.[68]

But the mode of free association is only good insofar as it
elevates the quality of experience.[69] Free association is not
an end in itself! It cannot be cut off from the moral and aesthetic values it is expected to engender and promote. In this
statement, Dewey clarifies the difference between his own brand
of instrumentalism and forms of either utilitarianism or pragmatism.

Dewey's sympathy is evidently directed toward the progres-
sivists. He is convinced that a society based solely on custom
does not and cannot fully utilize variations. Only a community
open to progress counts individual differences as means to its
growth. Such a community is necessarily democratic. It is a form
of association allowing for intellectual freedom and the play
of diverse gifts in its education programs.[70] All indications
show that, for Dewey, the relation between democracy and education is reciprocal. "Democracy," he says, "is itself an educational principle, an educational measure and policy. There is
nothing novel in saying that even an election campaign has a
greater value in educating the citizen of the country who take
any part in it than it has in its immediate external results."[71]

On the occasion of his ninetieth birthday, he reiterates the
same sentiment during a dinner in his honor. He expresses concordance with the statement that it is not majority rule which constitutes the heart of democracy but the process by which a given
group, having a specific kind of policies in view, becomes a majority. He favors the statement because it recognizes precisely
the educative value of democratic methods. The act of voting, he
declares, is a culmination of a continued process of open and
public communication in which prejudices can erase each other
and sound ideas come out of the interchange of facts and ideas.

Thus far, Dewey has been calling attention to the unconscious influence of social forces. But he does not mean to limit
to this means the promotion of education. It is true that social
media of communication such as tradition, linguistic habits and
artistic expressions are educative, but there are institutions
formally established for the purpose, namely, the schools. In
emphasizing the importance of the former, he does not thereby

downplay the role of the latter. The two are meant to complement
each other. The fact is, schools, in his view, are (or are meant)
to be miniature societies. That is, it is required of them to
reflect social realities.

The need for schools is as old as mankind. But it is never
more vital than in modern society. He believes that "as societies
become more complex in structure and resources, the need of formal or intentional teaching and learning increases."[72] The meanings contributed to present activities by past collective experiences are what supply content to social life. And because these
grow in number and import, proportionate to social life, "there
is need of special selection, formulation and organization in
order that they may be adequately transmitted to the new generation."[73]

Likewise, there are unrefined elements in any social environment. It is the aim of schools to eliminate as far as possible
those unworthy features to prevent them from deeply influencing
mental habitudes. If they are not totally unsuitable, conscious
teaching can free them of some of their grossness.There is also
the demand for balancing the various elements in the environment
to make them more productive of meaning. For this end, Dewey suggests, schools are supposed to give individuals the opportunity
to escape from the limitations of the social group in which they
are and come into contact with a broader environment. The expected result is the liberation of the young from confinement not
only within the locale of their birth but also within the time-
situation controlling the ways of life of the group they happen
to exist with. In this manner, they can take advantage of the experiences of alien cultures, learn from the lessons of the past,
and obtain resources for developing the future.

Dewey fears that, in attempting to realize these aims, there
may arise an undesirable split between the experiences gained in
more direct associations and what is acquired in schools. This is
why he proposes that schools take the form of their communities,
that they be, in structure, embryonic communities. In subject-
matter, they must be socially representative, "so as to make
skills and knowledge gained transferable to out-of-school situations."[74] He urges that they be integrated with social life,
i. e., with the forces that are producing social changes and
with the needs that arise from these changes. For, it is only
from such an understanding that an attitude of intelligent actions can be formed.[75]

Especially in a democratic society, keeping with the times
is an essential requirement for survival.

It is because the conditions of life change
that the problem of maintaining a democracy
becomes new, and that the burden that is put
upon the school, upon the educational system
is not that of stating merely the ideas of the

93

man who made this country, their hopes and their
intentions, but of teaching what a democratic
society means under existing conditions.[76]

How this can be accomplished is contained in what may be
called Dewey's program-of-education-with-a-social-purpose. Such
a program would, at least, include two features. The first is
setting the objective of education as attitude-formation rather
than transmission of barren information. Specifically, it would
require "the substitution of methods of inquiry and mutual consultation and discussion for the methods of imposition and incul-
cation."[77] The difference consists in the fact that the method
of inquiry is that "a kind of education that connects the materials and methods by which knowledge is acquired with a sense
of how things are done and of how they might be done."[78] In simpler terms, he is endorsing a kind of approach to learning where
the theoretical is merged with the practical.

Second, the program should also include formulating a curriculum made up of a balanced combination of humanistic and scientific subject-matters. This is a measure to bridge the gap between the two worlds created by specialization. Pure humanistic
disciplines, those that separate theory from practice, are as
inadequate as technical courses not supported by humane perspectives. The training of the statesmen and men of letters provides
no knowledge of the technical forces that shape the social structure. Similarly, the training of the scientists and technicians
leaves them ignorant of the social consequences of their craft.[79]
It is with this understanding that Dewey sums up the purpose of
a liberal arts college:

The problem of securing to the liberal arts college due function in democratic society is that
of seeing to it that the technical subjects which
are now socially necessary acquire a humane direction.[80]

Furthermore, if schools are supposed to keep up with the
times, they must be future-oriented. For, education involves
not only the reconstruction of experience as stated above, but
also the increase of the ability to direct subsequent experiences. Such an ability must first be a possession of teachers before they can impart it. Thus, on the question of whether or
not teachers should be ahead of their times, Dewey replies in
the strong affirmative. He advocates taking part in directing
social changes as one of their basic duties.

C. Freedom, A Consequence of Community Life

Dewey's metaphysics and psychology have already demonstrated

that no man exists isolated and insulated from his environment.
In his political works, he sustains the same view. For that matter, the classic socio-political problem of the relation between
or of individuals to society is a meaningless one in his context.
We might as well, he says, make a problem of the relation of the
letters of an alphabet with the alphabet itself. "An alphabet
'is' letters, and 'society' is individuals in their connection
with one another."[81] To speak of individuals apart from such a
connection is to speak of an abstraction. Man is born, exists,
and realizes his selfhood in and through social transactions.

It is, therefore, understandable why Dewey is quite unwilling to talk of the problem of freedom as a metaphysical issue,
i. e., as concerned with the search for the ultimate cause or
first principle of choice. As he declares in his contribution
to Monroe's Cyclopedia, "in certain of its aspects, the problem
of freedom of will has become so encumbered with the refuse and
debris of all kinds of other matters as to be best 'solved' by
letting alone."[82] The intent is not to skirt the issue. His philosophy is sufficiently equipped with applicable categories to
pursue the problem along that line. The previous section has, in
fact, already shown the possibility of constructing a solid theory of freedom based on the notion of 'preferential behavior.'
It is also not the case that Dewey lacks a clear stand on the
matter. In the same Cyclopedia, he enumerates unambiguously his
opinions: 1) he rejects the idea of choice without motive and
asserts that motives truly originate from self; 2) he recognizes
that plasticity, tendency to variation, growth, and readjustment
of habits are native to the self; 3) he attests that preference,
selective activity in a specific direction, is a concrete trait
of human actions; 4) he assigns to reflection the function of
presenting and weighing alternatives in choice.

But these statements are nonsensical and valueless if detached from concrete facts, concrete facts as Dewey perceives
them. These show that freedom is not a natural endowment but a
social achievement. Thus, "liberty is always a social question
not an individual one."[83] Obviously, He strongly opposes the
traditional notion of an original causal force known as instinct
or 'will.' In his judgment, such a conception negates the social
and temporal characters of man's nature and, hence, his authentic
freedom. In positive terms, it assumes that freedom is an absolute right such that man can exercise freedom independently of
others.

As was mentioned earlier, he does allow the use of the term
'will.' But this is with the understanding that it be taken to
denote "certain empirically detectable and specifiable consequences, and not a force or entity, psychological or metaphysical."[84] Similarly, he sometimes speaks of 'natural' freedom.
But this means nothing more than the adaptedness of man to his
earthly environment. At best, it could refer to the harmony existing between a man's energies and his surroundings. It is a spontaneous type of freedom, and it is freedom in the weakest sense
of the word. It is a condition that cannot be trusted because

if unguided, it is at the mercy of accident. Moreover, there is in it and about it nothing distinctively human. Even in the lowest forms of life, a natural coordination of the sort can be found.

Human freedom, as a fact, means, then, more than that basic and insecure harmony of things in nature with nature. Essentially, it is a power, the power to control the manifold of man's environment according to his deliberate purposes. Such a power, Dewey emphasizes, is attainable only through cooperative activity. It can only come out of conscious agreements among men, and, for that matter, supplements or supplants to some degree that freedom of action which is nature's gift.[85] This saying that there can be no objective and effective freedom without organization. This conclusion, he points out, can be gathered from the experiences of past societies. The failure of the early nineteenth century "individualism" was due precisely in misunderstanding that reality of freedom. It wrongly misplaced its hope for the restoration of harmony between man and nature on liberation from oppressive legal and political measures. The basis of the hope is, of course, the metaphysical doctrine of free-will coupled with an unreasonable confidence in natural harmony.

For practical purposes, Dewey advises that the followers of that doctrine rethink their view and adopt

a philosophy that recognizes the objective character of freedom and its dependence upon a congruity of environment with human wants, an agreement which can be obtained only by profound thought and unremitting application. For freedom as a fact depends upon conditions of work which are socially and scientifically buttressed. Since industry covers the most pervasive relations of man with his environment, freedom is unreal which does not have as its basis an economic command of environment.[86]

To bring about the conditions described, various social forces have to be consolidated. The natural condition of interconnectedness already supplies the foundation. But, in the complex world of human transactions, a more dependable source of control and organization is called for. As will be seen in the next chapter, this is the occasion in which the entry of political authority is justified.

But that justification does not mean awarding absolute power to political authority. Its power extends or is confined only to the functions that promote freedom. And it is for this end that such an authority should be established to begin with. For, human freedom is not a given; it is a social phenomenon and, hence, requiring social institutions which political authority can help establish. Dewey elucidates on the social character of freedom in his discussion of its threefold aspect.

1. Freedom as Choice

In his psychology and social philosophy, Dewey is quite ready to
acknowledge and even promote the qualitative difference of human
actions. This is where his metaphysics has led him. But, in spe-
cifying the nature of that difference, he is not too secure. "if
man's nature, original or acquired makes him do what he does, how
does his action differ from that of a stone or tree?"[87] It is
easy to say that in man "a power called will lies back of choice
as its author, and is the ground of liability and the essence of
freedom."[88] But this, in his judgment, is more of an escape than
a solution. How can something which has already been there before
a person becomes and is, therefore, not his own making be the
ground of his liability? The thought suffers from the defect of
tracing responsibility to a ready-made power outside of the individual person. In fact, a man is what he is because the make-up
of his habits, desires, and purposes are, in their content and
meaning, provided by association.

Expectedly, Dewey reverses the order of relation and locates
in future consequences the ground of liability. This is precisely
why in practice, infants, idiots, and insane people are not held
responsible for their actions. It is absurd to do so because it
would have no effect on their consequent behavior. Similarly, the
reason that a growing child is not imputed with responsibility
is simply that he does not have it yet. The case is not that
free-will is suddenly thrust upon him, but that this takes form
in the process of growth and then becomes a necessary factor in
further growth.

The acquisition or assumption of responsibility, while not
possible without "external" factors provided by association, is
never complete without some active, practical participation from
within to make the change that is effected significantly individualized. If left to purely external factors, the outcome would
be mechanical individuals who would not be different from puppets
manipulated on strings. Dewey fears this danger to be more threatening in a modern society where technological advancement tends
to reduce men to passive, submissive and pliant creatures without
identity. He calls this social phenomenon the tragedy of "lost
individuals." Its occurrence he attributes to "the fact that
while individuals are now caught up in a vast complex of associations, there is no harmonious and coherent reflection of the
import of these connections into the imaginative and emotional
outlook on life."[89] Thus, just as much as he insists that social
ties which holds individuals together are not merely external but
react to mentality and character, so also does he emphasize that
it is the singular beings who, in their singularity, think, want,
and decide.

The section on social individuality has alrady shown that

"participation from within" does not coincide with the traditional concept of 'free will.' Dewey's move is not, therefore, a
reversal to the same error attributing individuality expressed
by choice to some native spiritual principle. This he has already
vehemently rejected and continues to reject. Rather, he is refe-
ring to 'selective response.' This idea is further developed in
an article entitled "Philosophies of Freedom." Preferential behavior, he contends, takes a historical course; it is a function
of an entire history. Understanding a man requires understanding
the course of life he lived. But the qualification 'historical'
does not mean fixed or one-directional. Past experiences carry
with them a large set of varied possibilities. And when incorporated with the present, they open up new dimensions. This is
why, for Dewey, a continuing diversification of behavior is always possible. It is a manifestation, too, of man's basic doci-
lity and capacity for moral rehabilitation.

Choice appears in this situation as a preference among and
out of preferences. It takes the form of a new preference out
of a conflict of preferences. In this way, both uniqueness and
the possibility of diversification or novelty are accounted for.
And although selective responses are condtioned by past experiences and present relations, individuality manifests itself
as one's response to opportunities. The historical development
of man, explains Dewey, is not simply the case of "external redistribution, rearrangements in space of what previously existed," but of genuine qualitative changes. Thus, causality is not
ignored. On the contrary, it is considered as entering the scene
as a presupposition of preference and bias.

> In the description of causal sequences, we
> still have to start with and from existences,
> things that are individually and uniquely just
> what they are. The fact that we can state chan-
> ges which occur by certain uniformities and
> regularities does not eliminate this original
> element of individuality, of preference and
> bias. On the contrary, the statement of laws
> presupposes just this capacity.[90]

If indeed individuality is the ground of freedom, then the
issue of man's freedom is not whether or not one's choices have
causes. Dewey insists they do. Instead, it is the question of
what type of cause determines his choices and what he does with
it. If his responses become so routine and mechanical, in effect
he loses his individuality. If he allows himself to be pushed
and pulled, then, for all practical purposes, he has no freedom.
He may still be regarded as an individual, but only spatially
so, insofar as he remains separate from others. But this is not
individuality without qualification.

A thing is one when it stands, lies or moves

> as a unity independently of other things...
> But even vulgal common sense at once intro-
> duces certain qualifications. The tree stands
> only when rooted in the soil...[91]

Dewey is saying that freedom becomes a reality only when deliberation is allowed to enter in choice. Insight and fore-sight provided by experience itself are the elements involved in deliberation. He describes it as a dramatic rehearsal of va-rious possibilities. It occurs when an activity is disintegrated and held up by the confusion of various elements. Its relation to choice can be seen in the fact that choice is the emergence of a unified preference from a host of competing preferences and occurs only after deliberation.

But there is both a reasonable and an unreasonable choice. The former consists in an effective relationship among desires and is not something opposed to desire as such. It is not a force to use against impulse. Its consequence is habit, the achievement of a working harmony among diverse desires. The latter is charac-terized by the absence of such an effective relationship among desires and yields no working harmony among them.

The office of deliberation is to resolve entanglements in acti-vities. Once recovered, it aims to restore continuity and promote harmony. The case is not that man acts consequent to reasoning but that reasoning puts before him possibilities that are not di-rectly or sensibly present. The motive, Dewey makes clear, is not necessarily utilitarian. For, the problem of deliberation is not the calculation of future happenings but the appraisal of present proposed actions. This means that deliberation will continually be called upon in new circumstances and, hence, must be readap-tive.

Aims and principles enter into actions only when delibera-tion takes place. There are, however, no fixed and final ends. Aims are ends-in-view, not things outside of one's self and his circumstances to be sought. Principles are flexible, adaptive, and continuous with actions, never established once and for all. An end is not an end to action, but a means and the pivot of a present activity, stimuli to a present choice. Principles are not rigid norms but methods of inquiry and forecast; they are growing directives to intellectual activity in order that this can be made to cope adequately with uncertain situations in life.

Conclusively, then, for Dewey, selective response becomes real choice only when deliberation is allowed to enter. When in-cluded, choice becomes the capacity for deliberately changing preferences. This is the crucial factor in an individual's par-ticipation in any event. Thus, social-individuals, though recep-tive of certain patterns of conduct and modes of thought, are nevertheless actively free inasmuch as they actually choose, ne-gatively or positively, preferences made available by transac-tions. This view separates Dewey from mechanists, those whose account of human development allows no room for deliberation and, hence, for real individuality. In the absence of deliberation, how can there be anticipation and control of consequences to affect preference? Without deliberation, there can only be determinism.

Evidently, freedom is expressed in choice. Choice, however, is dependent on natural and social transactions that make up the life-history of a man and his intelligent deliberations. It is, like all human capacities, given content within the medium of social intercourse. This is why it is neither antecedent nor fixed; it never has a uniform content. In Dewey's terms, to think otherwise is to ignore the fact that the mental structures of individuals, the pattern of their desires and purposes, change with every change in social constitution. In Freedom and Culture, he explains liberty as relative to time and place, such that the measure of what men do and can do is the description of the kind of culture in which they associate and live.[92]

Summarily, freedom as choice is a possibility rooted in man's capacity to respond uniquely to presented conditions. As a possibility, it can only be realized by actual transactions with objective conditions. Here, Dewey locates the significance of social conditions in fostering creative individuality. In dealing with freedom, he understandably prescribes that a philosophical account, if this is at all necessary, be not separated from concern with the cultural, religious, political, and domestic layers of social life. For, it is within these various levels of human transactions that choice is shaped. If these are enlightened, so also will choice be intelligent. The note on the need for a healthy social atmosphere directly leads to the second aspect of freedom.

2. Freedom as Power

An implication of the view that freedom involves practical participation from within so as to make change without possible is that a transition from choice to action must take place. The meaning of freedom is thereby enlarged to include power to act in accordance with choice. For, what is choice if it cannot be elicited in the form of actual and effective pursuance of the object of choice? Cut from the latter, choice is no better than wistful thinking. This is why Dewey believes that all struggles made in the name of liberty have been declared against institutions and laws that obstruct and interfere with self-determination in action; that is, those that stifle the power-to-act-in-accordance-with-choice. Carrying out of choices always requires a medium. When this is absent, freedom can be no more than an illusion.

Dewey cautions that the power of executing choice should not be identified with the power of carrying wants into effect. Choice, as shown above, involves deliberation. On the one hand,

100

for choice to be genuine, it must be an intelligent desire. On
the other hand, wants are uncontrolled by foresight of consequences and untempered by insight into actual conditions. In
his judgment, it was the confusion between the two functions
that vitiated the program of classical liberalism. Its politics
were built on the philosophy that the more free individuals were,
the better it would be, since free institutions would be the natural or necessary outcome. The followers of the idea wrongly

> thought of individuals as endowed with an equip-
> ment of fixed and ready-made capacities, the ope-
> ration of which if unobstructed by external res-
> trictions would be freedom, and freedom which
> would almost automatically solve political and
> economic problems,[93]

What was maintained, as far as government actions were concerned, was the 'laissez-faire' policy. Positive measures were
regarded as necessarily oppresive so that they were confined to
legal and police matters. The purpose, of course, was to provide
security to the freedom of behavior that one individual enjoyed
against interference arising from the exercise of the same freedom on the part of others.

The political and economic problems that liberalism sought
to remedy were connected with the task of reconciling liberty
and equality. The 'laissez-faire' school claimed to be the only
logical form of liberalism for the following reasons: if, on the
one hand, liberty were the dominant social and political goal,
then the natural diversity and equality of natural endowments
would inevitably work out to produce social inequalities. To give
free rein to natural capacities would certainly produce maked inequalities in cultural, economic, and political statutes. If, on
the other hand, equality were made the goal, there must be important restrictions put upon the exercise of liberty.[94] The only
possible solution was, as stated, to tolerate any amount of actual social inequality, provided this was the necessary result of
the free exercise of natural capacities.

The idea of natural or original capacities in the sense of
fixed instincts and desires has already been dismissed as a stum-
bling block to a realistic solution. Its adherents ignored the
part played by transaction with the surrounding medium in generating impulses and desires. Dewey insists that free institutions
are not the consequences but the cause of free individuals. He
calls on history to bear witness to the failure of the application of the principle of free play. While it was able to supply
inspiration and direction to performing endeavors that modified
institutions, laws, and social arrangements that had become oppressive, the beneficiary was only those liberated individuals
who, to begin with, already enjoyed privileged status. All the
others were left at the mercy of the new conditions where reigned
the freed powers of those advantageously situated. [95]

Similarly, the notion that men would be equally free to act if the same legal arrangements applied equally to all irrespective of differences in education, in command of capital, and the control of social environment furnished by the institution of property is absurd, in Dewey's appraisal. Actual and effective rights and demands are not inherent in the human constitution but pro-ducts of transactions, he would reiterate. The case of economic differences illustrates clearly the principle. If the individual is born to the possession of property and another is not, the difference is due to social laws regulating inheritance and the possession of property.

It can be surmised that Dewey has in mind here the difference in the treatment of properties in a communist regime and that in a democratic system. In any event, for him, the only conceivable conclusion, both intellectually and practically, is to introduce positive and constructive changes in social arrangements - changes wherein inequalities of natural endowment can operate under laws and institutions that do not place permanent handicap upon those of lesser gifts. Upon these measures, he believes, depend the attainment of freedom conceived as power-to-act-in-accord-with-choice.

Dewey's intent is realism, as is apparent in the approach he is taking here. Freedom, he recognizes, involves not only security from the trespasses of one's neighbors. With it alone, man remains powerless. Contrary to John Locke's contention, "not power but impotency, not independence but dependence, not freedom but subjection, is the natural state of man..."[96] Freedom further requires energy in action. This, an individual alone cannot secure. The fact is, he is a part of the whole. And, as a part, his action is limited at different directions by the action and counter-action of others in the whole. Even if there is a power that is native in him to initiate an act, there is no power that is native in him to carry it through. The nature of action explains why. When it is elicited, it is immediately caught up in an infinite and intricate network of interactions. If he acts blindly on private impulse or judgment, he affects the whole, just as much as others affect him.

Attainment of freedom demands without question coordination and harmony with others constituting the whole. For, in acting in accord with the whole, man is reinforced by its structure and momentum.[97] This means that social organization is, in the final analysis, the source of power that makes man free. Dewey clearly anticipates Martin Luther King's now famous insight: "No man is free until all men are free." And he said it first as a philosophical statement: "We are bound together as parts of a whole and only as others are free, can anyone be free."[98]

The implication of "freedom as power" for Dewey's political theory can be drawn without strain. The problem of liberty or freedom is one and the same as the issue of the distribution of powers. The conception is validated in praxis, he is certain. The demand for liberty is truly a demand for power - either for

the possession of powers of action not yet possessed or for re-
tention and expansion of those already possessed. Thus, if one
wants to know what the condition of liberty is at any given time
and place, he only has to examine what persons can and cannot do
in that circumstance. This shows what has already been stated -
the possession of effective power is always a matter of the distribution of power that exists at the time. But, further, it
also shows that there is no such thing as liberty or effective
power belonging to an individual, group, or class except that
which stands in relation with the liberties or effective powers
of other individuals, groups, or classes.

The relativity of liberty to the existing distribution of
powers also necessarily means that wherever there is liberty at
one place, there is restraint in another. For,

> The system of liberties that exists at any time
> is always the system of restraints or controls
> that exists at that time. No one can do anything
> except in relation to what others can do and can-
> not do.[99]

Both the distribution of powers and the system of controls are
identical with the actual social arrangements (legal and political, cultural and economic). This is why the efforts of government and struggles of individuals in society have always been to
make it more even and equitable.

Dewey's opinion here is not an unpopular one. S. I. Benn
and R. S. Peters, among others, would agree with it. Their analysis of social situations bears it out. For instance, if a factory situation is not regulated by a superior power, an employer
may constrain people by threatening their livelihood

> or we may live at the mercy of gangs like Chicago
> in the thirties, or be subject to the terror of a
> Ku Klux Klan, or in fear of a press that can black-
> mail us by threatening our reputation. These are
> arbitrary constraints, springing from power un-
> limited by rules, and we look to rules of law to
> defend us from them.[100]

But the tension in society is not confined solely to the
conflicts among different actual powers that always may rub a-
gainst each other. It includes, according to Dewey, the push and
pull between custom or conventional morality and new directions.
This is, however, not unrelated to the former. The attempt to
define liberty in terms of the existing distribution of powers
is an attempt to maintain in the existing system control of powers, of social restraint and regimentation. Thus, the struggle
is not really between liberty versus restraint and regimentation,

but between one system of control of the social forces upon which
the distribution of liberties depends versus some other system
of social control which would bring about another system of distribution of liberties.[101]

One notable critic who agrees with Dewey on the subject of
freedom conceived as power is F. A. Hayek. He is worth noting because his critique of Dewey gives Dewey an occasion to clarify
his transactional view of freedom which is often attacked for its
behavioristic tone. Hayek concedes on the importance of objective
conditions but takes exception to externalizing the source of
freedom. He believes that individual or personal freedom is that
state in which a man is not subject to coercion by the arbitrary
will of another or others. He cautions, however, that this is an
ideal condition. So, the aim of a policy of freedom must be, at
least, to minimize coercion or its harmful effect wherever it may
exist. But Hayek is careful to distinguish between the question
of how many courses of action are open to a person and the question of how far in acting can he follow his own plans and intentions. He says,

> Whether he is free or not does not depend on
> the range of choice but on whether he can expect
> to shape his course of action in accordance with
> his present intentions or whether somebody else
> has power so to manipulate the conditions as to
> make him act according to that person's will ra-
> ther than his own.[102]

Freedom, then, presupposes that there is some private sphere in
man's environment which is not accessible to the interference
of others.

Hayek points out that it is wrong to identify individual
liberty with the use of liberty. It is wrong to describe individual freedom as the physical ability to do what one wants, the
power to satisfy his wishes, or the extent of alternatives open
to his choice. These misconceptions are entertained by people
with illusions that they can fly or that then can alter their
environment to their liking. Also, continues Hayek, the absence
of restraints is often wrongly confused with influences on human
action that do not come from other men (but from other sources,
such as those from nature itself).

Hayek is afraid that it is only too easy to pass from this
notion to regarding freedom as the absence of obstacles to thinking of it as the realization of desires, or even as the absence
of external impediments. This is unfortunate, because it is not
far from understanding freedom as the effective power to do whatever one wants. Furthermore, liberty defined as power leads to
the identification of liberty with wealth. The appeal of the word
'liberty' will then carry with it the support for a demand for
the redistribution of wealth!

Hayek's point is sufficiently clear. He himself makes sure that he is not misunderstood. The key, he says, to his criticism of such "progressives" as J. R. Commons and John Dewey lies in their inability to make proper distinctions:

> Whether or not I am my own master and can follow
> my own choice and whether the possibilities from
> which I must choose are many or few are two en-
> tire(ly) different positions.[103]

The only problem with this clarification and the criticism as a whole is, they constitute a basic misapprehension of Dewey's view and, hence, do not apply to it. Whether or not Hayek's reading is a case of either misinterpretation or simple misunderstanding is not important. The fact is, Dewey would even concede to Hayek's distinction, although he would be quick to caution that it could not be pressed too hard. Dewey says:

> Regarding freedom, the important thing to bear
> in mind is that it designates a mental attitude
> rather than an external unconstraint of movements,
> but this quality of mind cannot develop without a
> fair leeway of movements in exploration, experi-
> mentation, application, etc.[104]

Dewey's maintains consistency; his point here leads to the the expected conclusion, the same one already cited above. Free-dom as power, like freedom as choice, requires objective condi-tions. Choice and power have meaning only when there are real possibilities - genuine possibilities open in the world, not in the will, as Hayek himself insists. These are the conditions for desire to count as a real factor, as a force, in the strict sense of the term.[105] But to bring them about, the instrumentality for guiding present actions and controlling future possibilities has to be summoned. (This point is what Hayek has missed in reading Dewey.) This is the factor that determines self-mastery which Hayek seems to have thought Dewey ignored in his theory of free-dom. This factor or (in Dewey's language) instrumentality is in-telligence, the third aspect of genuine freedom.

3. Freedom as Intelligence

Both choice and power are aspects involved in the concept of freedom. And these are reciprocally significant. Choice that is not expressed in action hardly counts; action, analogous to the release of energy that falls like an avalanche, merits no prize. Freedom, therefore, neither consists in mere internal assent to certain objectives nor simply in outer movement. It is truly both, simultaneously, and the connecting link is supplied by intelli-

gence. Choice which intelligently manifests individuality enlarges the range of action, and this enlargement, in turn, confers
upon desires a greater insight and foresight, and makes choice
even more intelligent.[106]

Dewey illustrates the idea. On the one hand, an act's success elicited from a blind choice depends upon luck, and, consequently, is not dependable. It will be a case of good fortune if
the resulting action does not get the one who acts into conflict
with surrounding conditions. Situations may go against the realization of his preference in the manner of obstruction or more serious entanglements. He may be on the side of luck or that circumstances may be propitious. He may be endowed with native talent
that enables him to sweep away resistances. For a time, he may
even attain to a certain amount of freedom (judged from the side
of power-to-do). But who is always lucky? Another problematic
thing about luck is, it sometimes brings success that may only
reinforce a foolhardy impulsiveness that renders future subjection all the more probable.

On the other hand, freedom of movement - the external or
physical side of activity - is to be prized, not in itself but
as a means to freedom as choice. It supplies new materials upon
which intellligence may exercise itself and, thereby, becomes a
condition of growth. It is the negative side of freedom because
it is equivalent to freedom from restriction. But it is one of
the prerequisites of the positive aspect: the "power to frame
purposes, to judge wisely, to evaluate desires by the consequences which will result from acting upon them; power to select and
order means to carry chosen ends into operation."[107] Independently, it produces only a semblance of freedom, for it is actually at the mercy of impulses. With intelligent judgment, it
becomes productive of success.

Intelligence, then, is the heart of choice and the key to
freedom-in-act. In **Human Nature and Conduct**, Dewey's emphasis
is on present actions. The duty of intelligence, he says, is to
clarify and liberate impulses. "Intelligence converts desire
into plans, systematic plans based on assembling facts, repor-
ting the events as they happen, keeping tab on them and analy-
zing them."[108] The goal is not set on future events. Intelligence, it is true, may have an effect on the future, but only
as it gives attention to present activities. The improvement of
conditions in the future is a result, not an aim toward which
man works. Humans will not know how much control of future contingencies is possible until they have developed the habit of
using intelligence as a guide to present actions.

In "Philosophies of Freedom," Dewey's outlook is futuristic.
Choice is defined as a preference formed after consideration of
consequences. Its function is to liberate man from the uncertain-
ties of the future. Dewey is not saying that sucess is guaranteed
with deliberate consideration of consequences. "No one can fore-
see all consequences because no one can be aware of all the conditions that enter into their production."[109] Luck, good or bad,

is always present in life. And good luck, or the favorable cooperation of environment, is always necessary. But luck seems to
have a way of favoring the intelligent and showing its back to
the stupid. The improvement of chance for success is not, however, the only advantage of applying intelligence. Even in de-
feat there is something to be learned from its use.

> ...as in a scientific experiment an inquirer may
> learn through his experimentation, his intelli-
> ligently directed action, quite as much or even
> more from a failure than from a success. He finds
> out at least a little as to what was the matter
> with his prior choice. He can choose better and
> do better next time... Such a person forms the
> habit of choosing and acting with conscious re-
> gard to the grain of circumstance, the run of af-
> fairs. And what is more to the point, such a man
> becomes able to turn frustration and failure to
> to account in his further choices and purposes.[110]

He thereby gains freedom or power; everything serves his purpose in being an intelligent human being. It is a gain that can
be nullified by no amount of external defeats.

It must be noticed that Dewey is not prescribing secure control of future consequences by the manipulation of available alternatives according to rigid and mechanical rules. In the first
place, no such rules are possible. The world is not objectively
fixed and settled once and for all to yield them. This situation
does not, however, render choice insignificant. On the contrary,
it is what gives the latter true value. Only if change is genuine, if nature is still in the process of making, if objective
uncertainty is what stimulates reflection, then that variation
in action, novelty and experiment and, hence, freedom in choice
and action have true meaning.

> Variability, initiative, innovation, departure
> from routine, experimentation are empirically the
> manifestation of a genuine nisus in things. At
> all event it is these things that are precious
> to us under the name of freedom. It is their
> elimination from the life of a slave which makes
> his life servile, intolerable, to the freeman
> who has once been on his own, no matter what his
> animal comfort and security. A free man would
> rather take his chance in an open world than be
> guaranteed in a closed world.[111]

In the second place, even if rigid and mechanical rules are possible, they are not subjectively propitious to the growth of
freedom. This is why "in addition to security and energy in ac-

tion, novelty, risk, change are ingredients of the freedom which men desire"[112] more than a prosperous career prepared in advance. No genuine choice can take place without unrealized and precarious possibilities.

Dewey illustrates the last point by taking the case of child devlopment. There are two extreme ways of handling this case. One is to rear a child in a situation where he can do whatever he pleases. In this approach, the environment set by others actually humors all his choices. He meets the minimum of resistance; the help of others brings his preferences to fulfillment. All the appearances of power of action are present. Yet, there is no real freedom here. For, there is no growth in the intelligent exercise of preferences. The child is 'free' only because his surrounding conditions happen to be what they are, an artificial situation dependent on others. What actually transpires is merely a conversion of blind impulse into regular habits. Thus, his autonomy disappears, as he moves into other social conditions.

The other extreme way is to treat a child with rigorous discipline. In every manifestation of spontaneous preference, someone balks at him, hinder him, interfere with his actions. What disciplines him are circumstances adverse to his preferences. In this way, no 'inner' freedom in thoughtful preference and purpose can be expected. Such a type of discipline, says Dewey, is a travesty. It lacks ordination to the production of habits of observation and judgment that ensure intelligent desires. In both this and the first case, there is no blending of check and favor which influences thought and affects action. In the first case, there is no test for preference because it does not rub against resistance. In the second case, there is no room for originality and individuality in preference because choice cannot be asserted within, while action is regulated by external compulsion.

The case is the same with adults in moral, industrial, political, and cultural life. Dewey's words sufficiently explains it:

> When social conditions are such as to prepare a
> prosperous career for a things are made easy by
> institutions and by habits of admiration and
> approval, there is precisely the same kind of
> outward freedom, of relatively unimpeded action,
> as in the case of the spoiled child. But there
> is hardly more of freedom on the side of varied
> and flexible capacity of choice; preferences are
> restricted to the one line laid down, and in the
> end the individual becomes the slave of his suc-
> cesses. Others, vastly more in number, are in the
> state of the "disciplined" child. There is hard
> sledding for their spontaneous preferences; the
> grain of environment, especially of existing
> economic arrangements runs against them. Both
> the check, the inhibition, to the immediate ope-
> ration of their native preferences no more confers

on them the quality of intelligent choice than it
does with the child who never gets a fair chance
to try himself out.[113]

What Dewey is consistently objecting to is the notion of
freedom as static and antecedently given. What he is insistently
proposing is a kind of freedom that grows, one that allows opening for novelties and better possibilities by perception of consequences, as intelligence is applied to present problems. Such
a freedom should consist in a trend of conduct that causes choices to be more diversified and flexible, more cognizant of their
meanings, as it enlarges their range of unimpeded operation. Certainly, intelligence is the key to a freedom of the sort. Again,
this is not a gift from above; it is brought about by social conditions human beings promote as they form their community.

#

CHAPTER IV

THE POLITICAL ORDER AND THE HUMAN COMMUNITY

The ideal human condition, in Dewey's theory of the moral life, is existence in a genuine community. In retrospect, what he has beeing saying in the preceding chapters may be summarized as follows: 1) the metaphysical order of transaction is poised toward the formation of the human community as the culmination of natural evolution; 2) the improvement of organic associations into a field of effectively educative communication is simultaneously the emergence of that community where intellectual, moral, and aesthetic values thrive and where these same values tie commmunity members together; 3) real individuality and freedom take roots and mature only in a communal environment were those specified values are promoted.

In the present chapter, what will be reviewed is Dewey's commentary on what he believes to be the major cancer of the times: the breakdown of communal ties brought about by the advent of technological and economic growth. In his observation, traditional bonds that used to unite men are disappearing. For this reason, he calls for the reorganization of societies to remake and reform them into a Great Community. The process has already began, he believes, with the establishment of democracy as a system providing order in the political life of some people and, more significantly, the adoption of it as a way of life.

To follow Dewey's thoughts on the nature and value of democracy, the proceeding developments will be divided into three sections. The first will explore the various facets of human transactions which, in his judgment contribute to the foundations of human societies in general and of states in particular. It will also identify those forces which, according to him, have corroded traditional communal ties. The second section will attempt to determine the reasons, inspite of some misgivings, for his preference for democracy as a political organization to promote order in modern societies. It will appear that his theory of the function of political authority regards political organization as a structure born of need and, hence, is not an antecedently fixed establishment.

The democratic system of government is one meritorious effort among others designed to resolve conflict of interests and coordinate aims in the complex network of human transactions. He believes that its ethical justification lies in the fact that, in principle, it reconciles human liberty and political authority in order to achieve harmonious relations among people. But, inspite of its advantages, Dewey finds it inadequate to resolve the conflicts in modern societies and, therefore, to bring about that Great Community he envisages. The third section will seek to recapture his vision of democracy more as a way of life than a political system as the ideal community. It will recall his pos-

tulate that the social efficacy of community consists not only
in its alliance with the method and spirit of science but, more
importantly, also in its reliance upon shared moral and social
commitments.

A. The Cultural Foundations of Human Communities

There are two general perspectives that run through Dewey's deliberations on social philosophy. The first, with more negative
message than constructive doctrine, can be found in his arguments
against old liberalism. The second, with positive bearing, but
noticeably without concrete suggestions, is contained in his idea
of the Great Community. The former has a strong economic reference; the latter presupposes a cultural backbone supporting the
constitution of communities. The casual reader who stumbles on a
few essays critical of traditional liberalism like Liberalism and
Social Action, Individualism Old and New, and other small articles of more or less the same intent may, at first glance, gather
the impression that Dewey is an economic determinist. Only a careful analysis, aided by his more comprehensive works on the subject, such as Freedom and Culture, Public and Its Problems, Art
and Experience, Philosophy and Civilization, would yield a balanced interpretation.

In Freedom and Culture, Dewey is most emphatic in his declarations on the importance of culture. The complex social conditions constitutive of the extent or limit of man's freedom also
determine both the need for and the character of the state (or of
any formal social organization for that matter). The reasoning
here is consistent with the theory of freedom already discussed.
Freedom needs objective conditions for its inception, growth,
and sustenance. A slave society ruled by a despot thrives only
in a cultural setting that supports slavery. Similarly, a community of free men finds its nourishment in an environment of free
culture. This is why, Dewey is convinced, "the problem of freedom and of democratic institutions is tied up with the question
of what kind of culture exists; with the necessity of free culture for free political institutions."[1]

Political institutions are, in fact, shaped by the movements
of men in all facets of social life, not only of those within the
political field. Human relations, such as those found in industry, in communication, in science, in art, and in religions,
which affect daily associations simultaneously affect attitudes
and habits expressed in government and rules of law. Dewey explains that this is not a denial of the fact that the political
and legal elements act and react to shape other aspects of community life. Rather, it is an assertion that political institutions
are more an effect than a cause. Moreover, the foundations of
political and other social institutions cannot be limited to any
single factor.

One aspect of culture that he includes as an important de-

terminant of social life is the arts (which have already been explored in Chapter III). Literature, music, drama, architecture
are not mere adornments but "things in whose enjoyment all should
partake, if democracy is to be a reality."[2] They are compelling
means of communication by which emotions are stirred and public
opinion formed. This is why a totalitarian regime, committed to
control the lives of its subjects by controlling their feelings,
has to take over first the channels of communication, prominently
the various media of the arts.

The moral factor is equally important for Dewey. For, he
realizes that human beings hold dear certain things and struggle for those which they prize. From the standpoint of community
life, this is an indispensable element. Community survives only
when some values are prized in common, and it disintgerates into
mechanically enforced connections whey these are lost. Closely
tied to the moral issue is the question of what kinds of social
philosophies appear in a society as competing ideologies. Dewey
thinks that some schools, dazzled by the success of mathematics
and the physical sciences, have considerably affected certain
types of political thinking (conceivably the 'laissez faire' kind
of liberalism) by their denial of the possibility of regulating
ideas and judgments about values. This passing statement may not
be too significant to elaborate on at this point, but it is note-
worthy as an evidence of his effort to divorce himself from extreme libertarians who reject the import of normative morality.

What is momentarily significant is to ask if Dewey maintains
a hierarchy among the enumerated social factors he identifies as
constitutive of political institutions and social movements. Or,
to rephrase the question, is there any one factor that is so pre-
dominant as to be regarded the causal force, and the rest (in relation to it) as secondary ones, if not strictly effects? This is
likely what he means when he asks: Is any one phase so dominant,
productive and regulative of others? Or are economics, arts, morals, science, etc. only so many aspect of the interaction of a
number of factors? His reply is unambiguous. The act of isolating
any single factor, however strong its workings at a given time,
"is fatal to understanding and to intelligent action."[3]

In this declaration, Dewey parts company from exponents of
economic determinism, and from any form of social determinism for
that matter. He concedes that economic relations and habits, such
as the uneven distribution of property, or the increase in the
number of miserably poor people as compared to the number of the
extremely wealthy are indeed important factors in the constitution of political agencies. The extensively ramified conditions
of employment makes political action assume an importance for
workers (employed and unemployed) which it does not have when
conditions are settled and secure.[4] The rise of new economic forces has brought about a strong contender to the authority previously wielded by existing political institutions.[5]

His comments here and other places manifest not only his
sensitivity to, but actual grasp of, contemporary issues which

may indeed, for the greater part, he acknowledges, revolve
around economics. Elsewhere he says,

> In brief, economic developments which could not
> possibly have been anticipated when our political
> forms took place have created confusion and un-
> certainty in the making of the agencies of popular
> government and thereby have subjected the idea of
> democracy to basic strain.[6]

But the importance of economics does not make it the exclusive consideration to be reckoned with. For, it is never sepa-
rable from other aspects of culture. While it plays a significant
part in shaping the qualities of the present culture, it is itself a product of other phases of cultural transition. For instance, the growth of science has affected industry and commerce
- the production and the distribution of goods, regulation of
service related to these activities and similar functions. Thus,
he continues, "unless we take into account the rise of new
science of nature in the seventeenth century and its growth to
its present state, our economic agencies of production and distribution cannot be understood."[7]

In his more critical writings, Dewey maintains the same position. Attacking old individualism, he points out that its
failure consisted in the attempt to subordinate the only creative individuality (that of mind) "to the maintenance of a regime which gives the few an opportunity for being shrewd in the
management of monetary business."[8] He suspects that this mate-
rialistic attitude may not have directly sprung from scientific
and technological advancement. From all appearances, it may have
been the reflection of the philosophy cultivated by the class in
power that the creative capacities of individuals could evolve
only in a struggle for material gain. Dewey vehemently opposes
such a philosophy. For, to him, material advantage is a means,
not an end. "The ultimate place of economic organization in human life is to assure the secure basis for an ordered expression
of individual capacity and for the satisfaction of the needs of
man in non-economic direction."[9]

If there were a grain of truth in economic determinism, he
allows, it could be found in the experience that industry and
commerce are not outside of human life but within it.[10] This
means that they are not remote from, much less contradictory to,
human values honored by communities. In a way, economics can
serve as an instrument for making secure such values. This is
why he prescribes that "we should through organized endeavor
institute the socialized economy of material security and plenty
that will release human energy for pursuit of higher values."[11]

Conclusively, when Dewey emphasizes at times the economic
phase of culture, his objective can be interpreted as an acknow-
ledgment of its impact on the turn of social events, that is,

on the "qualities of the present culture." But, he is quick to
point out, justifying economic emphasis does not prove that the
issues of politics, of freedom, or of community can be settled
by it exclusively. These problems, just as much as the conflicts
within industry and the distribution of income, cannot be resolved except "by the aid of correlative changes in science, morals and other phases of our common experience."[12] What in the
concrete are the problems and conflicts Dewey is referring to
here can be gathered from his reflections on what he so curiously
calls the 'lost community.'

The 'lost community' is precisely the result of overstres-
sing economic advantage. If old communities established prior to
the dramatic scientific and technological inventions of the nineteenth centrury were characterized by mutual interest of citizens
in shared meanings, values, and socials goals, the emerging societies have been shedding off communal concerns. In the industrial world, what mechanization and the concomitant urbanization
of small towns have produced are multiple organizations whose
internal structures simulate the machines they use - aggregates
of member-parts with purely mechanical connections. Functionally,
these organizations are a collectivity where no one member can
execute, perhas even comprehend, the direction of his own operations. Dewey, deploring the situation, describes it thus:

> ...the ratio of impersonal to personal activi-
> ties in determining the course of events has
> enormously increased. The machine as compared
> with hand tool is an impersonal agency. Free
> land and an abundance of unappropriated and
> unused natural resources - things which brought
> man in face-to-face personal connection with
> Nature and which also kept individual persons
> in pretty close contact with one another - have
> been replaced by impersonal forces working on a
> vast scale, with causes and effects so remote as
> not to be perceptible.[13]

In the field of commerce, the corporate bodies are made up
of individuals whose aims are far from being altruistic. The behavior of businessmen is the opposite of the 'neighborly' conduct of their predecessors; it springs from survival imperatives
and status motivations. Antony Jay's conclusion that the modern
individual is outwardly corporate but internally submerged faithfully depicts reality.[14] As in the case of industrial organizations, economic associations are so structured that they effectively exclude employees from taking part in management. The employees cannot but simply execute plans in the making of which
they did not have any share. Their activity is motivated by no
more than the profit for the management and wage for themselves.
And when private gain and material security are the overwhelming
interest, the kind of minds that can be found are warped, frus-
trated, unnourished by their functions. This is to be expected

since their application to their lifework lack the richness that
only the use of intellect, imagination, and emotion could achieve.
Consequently, they are driven to conformity; and conformity has
a a pejorative meaning for Dewey. It

> Is a name for the absence of vital interplay;
> the arrest and benumbing of communication...,
> it is the artificial substitute used to hold
> men together in lack of associations that are
> incorporated into inner dispositions of thought
> and desire.[15]

In the political order, Dewey refers to the same phenomenon
as the 'eclipse of the public.' The rise of new societies has
divided man into fragments of varying objectives. It has created
many publics of different and, oftentimes, conflicting interests.
And because the stronger group with financial or political power
usually prevails, the less privileged masses are hindered from
expressing and executing their wills. The result is a situation
where the real public concerns can hardly be distinguished from
the spurious ones. In Dewey's phraseology, the intensification
and complication of the scope of the indirect consequences of human transactions have brought about a public that cannot identify
and distinguish itself.[16] When this happens, the problems become
not only social but also psychological. If an individual, says
G. W. Allport, commenting on Dewey's psychology, belongs to many
publics, his interests cannot truly be fulfilled by being par-
tially included in multiple groups.

> If a given citizen is, say, a veteran, a "dry,"
> a believer in free trade, a broker, a motorist,
> a home owner, an urbanite, a pacifist, how shall
> he vote to gain total inclusion for his pattern
> of interests? Or what groups shall he join that
> will bring unity into his life?[17]

These, then, are the instances of 'lost communities' in the
different levels of social existence; these are the artificial
conglomerates in cities and suburbs, in factories and offices.
They are all characterized by the almost total lack of personal
or familial ties. They are affected by and infected with the cor-
rosion of religious and cultural affinities. They are all subject
to occupational specialization which respects no traditionally
revered institutions. The appearance of the individual in these
conglomerates is no more encouraging. As this individual is
caught up into a vast complex of associations, he is placed in
a condition where "there is no harmonious and coherent reflection of the import of these connections to the imaginative and
emotional outlook on life."[18] It is this abnormality, Dewey believes, that causes much of the unrest, boredom, and hurry so
depictive of modern life. The analysis of the two terms of the

social scene - the tragic plight of the 'lost individual' is only
a different view of the same phenomenon called 'lost community.'
After all, a community consists of individuals in their relations
to one another.

The collapse of the original status of man as social-indivi-
dual has understandably led to the present awareness of and preoccupation over the problems of disorganization, disintegration,
decline, insecurity, breakdown, instability, alienation, and the
like. Specifically, the lack of cohesiveness that guided past
relationships is what drives men in an age of abundance and political welfare to the quest for community. But Dewey does not locate the problem in the tension between old values and new associations (as those values mediate between man and his larger
world of economic, political and cultural transactions). For,
old values are no longer a factor to contend with. They were, in
fact, already virtually eliminated by the onrush of modernization. Rather, "the lost community," he says, "is the consequence
of the disintegration of familial bonds; ...loyalties which once
held individuals and which gave them support, direction and unity
of outlook in life, have well nigh disappeared."[19]

There are indeed new kinds of ties that have sprung up. But
these have proven to be inadequate to present needs. Even in the
primary level of relationships, new forms of social kinship show
little evidence of offering much psychological and moral meaning
for the modern man. If this were not case, men would not be confused and bewildered. if new ties are effective, the scampering
for new directions in politics, religion, cultural movements
would be no more than a passing frenzy of an insane world. Here,
Dewey's vision can be seen to stretch beyond his time. The political upheavals in South America, Middle East, and parts of South
East Asia, the Fundamentalist Revolution in North America, and
the 'future shock' and 'third wave' (to borrow Alvin Toffler's
apt terms) experienced by men in technologically advanced countries validate his analysis.

So much with the problems, what is or what are the solutions
to these various forms of disintegration? Dewey offers a simple
approach although requiring the arduous task of marshalling the
energies and resources of men in all levels. This consists in the
recovery of the the traditional virtues of community! He would
not concede to the conclusion that associations founded upon kinship, faith, or locality cannot any more be expected to communicate adequately to individuals the psychological and moral grati-
fication of social living.

He would not accept the proposal that the answer can be
found in creating radically new contexts of relations; this has
already been tried and found wanting. He would admit, though,
that the pace of change is so swift that it is practically impossible for underlying traditions to keep step.[20] He is confident,
however, that these traditions could be readjusted to meet the
demands of the times. And the readjustment would include intelligent guidance of the dispersion and intensity of change.

Evidently, his stand is grounded on the perception that modernization is not inherently incompatible with the moral values and social relationships which worked for the extended family, the parish, and the village of earlier generations. He states:

> But we can assert with confidence that there
> is nothing intrinsic in the forces which have
> effected uniform standardization, mobility and
> remote invisible relationships that is fatally
> obstructive to the return movement of their con-
> sequences into the local homes of mankind.[21]

While it is true that he blames technological advancement and economic expansion for demolishing ties that form local communities and substituting impersonal bonds for personal unions, he never regards them as the root of all evil. The harmful effects of growth have entered man's life because of his own doing. Anticipating Alvin Toffler's diagnosis of social stresses as manifestations of 'future shock,' Dewey suggests that man's accountability can be traced to a lacadaisal attitude that made him so rapt with the marvel of change that he felt no awareness of the need to equip himself psychologically and morally for the outcome of the process.

Dewey's disposition is one of mixed emotions. From one side, he is convinced that "unless local communal life can be restored, the public cannot adequately resolve its most urgent problem: "to find and identify itself."[22] From another side, he is hopeful that the new order of things may yet bear its fruits. This disposition can be gathered from his description of his vision of the Great Community. It is, Levi correctly reads, a conception that

> wavers between a fear that without the re-estab-
> lishment of face-to-face relations and without the
> restoration of local communal life, no true democ-
> racy is possible, and a hope that through some re-
> creation of true communication on a broader scale,
> something approximating democractic quality may
> infuse the wider area.[23]

Visibly, there is a nostalgic undertone in this description of the good life. His pathos, though, is not beset by despair - that the intimate community with roots can no longer reappear.

But recovery of the past does not necessarily mean abandonment of the achievements of humanity. Dewey's advise is to keep pace with change and not be overcome by its rapidity in scope and intensity.[24] Advancement through science and technology is a phase of evolutionary development and must be accepted as such. But acceleration in change is not the same as progress. 'Prog-

ress,' for Dewey, means "increase of present meaning which involves multiplication of sensed distinction as well as harmony,
unification."[25] The reasonable approach to growth is, therefore,
a combination of cautious awareness of its direction and prompt
will to guide its course. whenever necessary, in the direction
of progress (the term 'progress' understood in his usage).

In brief, Dewey is espousing a movement toward establishing
the Great Community - a community in which the virtues of the yet
unspoiled relationships of the past enrich the contemporary scene.
His program for social renewal includes, as already mentioned,
recapturing and re-invigorating the old spirit of community so
that it may animate the economic and industrial revolution taking
in modern times. He is certain that such a spirit is still effective, if only it can be adapted to the new setting and dispersed
through the instrumentalities of modern communication. He is optimistic that there can be a merging of old values and new forces. Unfortunately, he offers no more than vague projections on
how this can be realized. In any event, he speaks of the event in
the following cryptic terms:

> Uniformity and standardization may provide an
> underlying basis for differentiation and libe-
> ration of individual potentialities. They may
> sink to the plane of unconscious habituations,
> taken for granted in the mechanical phases of
> life, and deposit a soil from which personal
> susceptibilities and endowments may richly and
> stably flower. Mobility may in the end supply
> the means by which the spoils of remote and in-
> direct interaction and interdependence flow back
> into local life, keeping it flexible, preventing
> the stagnancy which has attended stability in the
> past, and furnishing it with the elements of a
> variegated and many-hued experience. Organization
> may cease to be taken as an end in itself. Then
> it will no longer be mechanical and external...[26]

He does have some clear suggestions, though. Socially, he
advocates a more solid organization of the forces of production,
a measure that calls for voluntary agreement among management
and labor of industry and economics, even outside the boundaries
of direct government control. It must be noted, however, that
this is not a sign of negative regard for government control on
the part of Dewey. For, there are indications that he is aware
of the problems which lack of institutionalized control often
brings, such as the rise of monopolies and oligopolies. Instead,
it may be suggested, his attitude is a reflection of his belief
that the establishment of community must start from the base -
where the people who are actually engaged in the industrial or
business activities may be found. He trusts that a system of cooperative effort, where labor enjoys an increased share in controlling the conditions of its activity, could result in the

liberation of minds and promotion of social responsibility. As
if responding to Karl Marx' critique of capitalism as an environment that breeds alienation, he dclares that there is the
need, for

> securing greater industrial autonomy, that is
> to say, greater ability on the part of the wor-
> kers in any particular trade or occupation to
> control that industry instead of working under
> these conditions of external control where they
> have no interest, no insight into what they are
> doing, and no social outlook upon the consequences
> and meaning of what they are doing.[27]

Politically, he espouses a type of parochialism that advances localism, a plan similar to Jefferson's wards. This, according to Morton and Lucia White's interpretation, is Dewey's solution to his search of a new type of relations to counteract
the overwhelming effect of all big organizations (including
cities).[28] Incidentally, it is their observation that this conception extends to the area of education. Here, Dewey's project,
so they say, is to devise a program in which the qualities of
the new society are retained, while creating schools that would
represent the virtues of pre-industrial, pre-urban America.

Culturally, his theory of aesthetics, as drawn above, is meant
to bring every type of object and activity, including those generally regarded as belonging to pure labor or business, to the
area of consummatory experience. As he says, "making and using
tools may be intrinsically delightful."[29] In assigning to art
the function of making man come to terms with his surroundings
and opening to him a vast and rich field of communication, Dewey
is actually showing an opportunity for sharing interests and
values.

In all the levels mentioned, the merging of traditional
values of intimate community and the complex machineries and
mechanisms of modern life can be realized. But, for it to be so
realized, some effective instrumentality - to organize intelligence, to guide individual motivations, and, more precisely, to
control the indirect consequences of human transactions - may be
required. This brings the development to the question concerning
the necessity for a democratic political organization as a social
superstructure.

B. The Need for a Political Organization

'Freedom' and 'community' are reciprocal concepts in Dewey's
scheme. Community, on the one hand, is constituted of free social-
individuals. Freedom, on the other hand, objective freedom, can
only be fully realized in a community. But community, as has been

shown, is not an immediate achievement. If so, by what means can
it be achieved? Evidently, there must be some form of organization structured to promote the kind of freedom that makes community possible. Natural freedom, which consists in no more and no
less than the harmony existing between a man's energies and his
surroundings is precarious and is always at the mercy of accident. Thus, effective organization is called for to complement
natural freedom. Without it individual powers would be so arbi-
trarily arranged that conflicts of interests would be a common
scene; potentialities would not be released with intelligent guidance capable of bringing them to fruitful conclusions; instrumentalities for a relatively secure life would not be devised to
cope adequately with future contingencies.

The deterioration of communal life and the ever-growing complexity of modern societies described in the preceding section
have even more intensified the demand for a greater organization
- one that is both comprehensive and effective enough to direct
tangled variety of transactions and control the unharnessed impetus for growth. It is not for sheer adoption of the 'American
way,' much less for lack of ingenuity, that Dewey summons the
resources of the democratic idea and practice to meet the problems of the time. Rather, it is for moral and pragmatic reasons.
He believes that democracy, as a political system, is both ethically justifiable and socially effective in achieving the ends
of shared living. More importantly, democracy, as a way of life,
approximates his idea of the 'Great Community.'

It must be noted in passing that the distinction just cited
between political democracy and democracy as a way of life (or
what may be conveniently referred to henceforth as 'communal democracy') is not introduced here to facilitate a coherent reading. It is explicit in Dewey's works. In one passage, he says
that 'democracy' is a word of many meanings.

> But one of the meanings is distinctly political,
> for it denotes a mode of government, a specified
> practice in selecting officials and regulating
> their conduct as officials. This is not the most
> inspiring of the different meanings of democracy;
> it is comparatively special in character. But it
> contains about all that is relevant to "political"
> democracy.[30]

More inspiring is the conception of 'democracy' as a way of life.
He explains:

> Democracy is much broader than a special poli-
> tical form, a method of conducting government,
> of making laws and carrying on governmental
> administration by means of popular suffrage
> and elected officers. It is that, of course.

But it is something broader and deeper than
that. The political and governmental phase of
democracy is a means, the best means so far
found, for realizings ends that lie in the wide
domain of human relationships and development
of human personality.[31]

This is democracy as a way of life - a way motivated by the
necessity for the participation of every mature human being in
the formation of values regulative of men living together. This
is a necessity for attaining general welfare and development of
men as individuals.

Concerning political organization, Dewey identifies the need
for it with the demand for an institutionalized system of authority. He explains both in terms of surrender and exchange. Obviously influenced by Locke, he states that men surrender certain
amounts of natural freedom to arrive at some conscious agreements
and, in return, receive some secure liberties. While not denying
the sacrifices involved, he believes in the fairness of the procedure. The exchange "is not unlike surrendering a portion of
one's income to buy insurance against future contingencies, and
thus to render the future course of life more equably secure."[32]
The reasoning is clearly pragmatic. "The question is to the balance of freedom and security achieved, as compared with practical alternatives."[33]

From the ethical point of view, the position may, at first
glance, appear quite vulnerable. For, it seems to be proceed by
justifying the means by the end. Is freedom an instrument of security? Or, does security exist for freedom. This objection is,
of course, valid if what is at stake is security in place of
freedom. But Dewey has already made clear that in his discussion
on freedom that what organization achieves is not security 'per
se' but objective freedom. Natural freedom, he already stated,
is hardly freedom at all. To give up some of it is not really
much of a loss. To lose some of it and thereby acquire security
is much of a gain. For, security is a state of freedom, that is,
objective freedom. This is a distinction absent in Locke. Dewey
disagrees with him in holding dear that state of nature. If in
Locke, the transition is from a blessed condition to a less precarious one, in Dewey, the exchange is not from the possession
of freedom to the loss of it but from less to more freedom!

At any rate, political organizations, governments, and politics arise from need. In fact, they are later phenomena in the
history of human transactions. For Dewey, this implies that they
are not absolute needs. Indeed, some communiites do not require
them. "immediate contiguity, face-to-face relationships, sharing
of values, too direct and vital to occasion a need for political
organization."[34] Likewise, in social groups separated by natural
barriers and cultural differences and, for that reason unconnected by any common interest, no 'public' can be formed. And, if
there is no public, neither can there be an inclusive state.

The forms that political organizations take are also subject to the requirements of the times and the judgments of leaders. "They do not originate in a once and for all way."[35] The
greatest change that can be accomplished is the outcome of a vast
series of adaptations and responsive accomodations as demanded by
particular situations. In the same way, the movement toward democracy originate neither from a single idea nor from one unbroken
impetus.

> The temperate generalizations to the effect that
> the unity of the democratic movement is found in
> effort to remedy evils experienced in consequence
> of prior political institutions realized that it
> proceeded step by step, and that each step was
> taken without foreknowledge of any ultimate re-
> sult, and, for the most part, under the immediate
> influence of a number of differing impulses and
> slogans.[36]

Dewey observes that the conditions from which arise the
efforts toward the establishment of a political form (including
democracy) were primarily non-political in nature. To trace how
it developed requires consideration of the "distinctive religious, scientific and economic changes which finally took effect
in the political field, being themselves primarily non-political
and innocent of democratic intent."[37] This statement shows Dewey
to be upholding the cultural foundations of political states.
It also argues that (if the conditions that brought about political forms of government were non-political) there were social
arrangements in which no political institutions existed.

The establishment of the state coincides with the emergence
of a public. For, the term 'public' signifies, in Dewey's vocabulary, the proper province of the state. Such a province is located
somewhere between associations that are so narrow (or close) and
those that are so remote. Face-to-face transactions, as already
stated, asks for no intervention; unrelated interests have no common ground upon which they can be organized. Thus, only when the
quantitative scope of the results of conjoint behavior generates
a public with a need of organization can there be a state.

The external mark of such an organization is found in an
authority system embodied in officials. Dewey himself does not
elaborate on this idea. But his view parallels some contemporary
theories and may, perhaps, be understood in the same manner without doing violence to his genuine thought on the matter. For instance, R. Bierstedt has a simple explanation. Writing on the
problem of authority, he describes the process in which an unorganized group is transformed into an organized one in the following manner:

> In the first place, informal procedures and

>   patterns of interaction come to be standardized
>   as norms. In the second place, roles come to be
>   standardized as statuses. It is the institutiona-
>   lization of procedures into norms and roles into
>   statuses which results in the formal organization
>   of the association; they are its organization.[38]

Similarly, Dewey states that the role of leader which one or
several members may play comes to be institutionalized in one
or several statuses (in his word, officials) to which authority
is attached in accordance with norms. The purpose of this is to
make the association stable and to ensure continuity.

The preceding discussion makes two points clear. It defines
the province of the state, i. e., the public; it indicates the
need for authority, a need that is not only sought but is actually generated, as the public requiring organization emerges.
That the public is the domain of the state means that where lies
public concern, there also extends authority. But what precisely
is a public concern? In an obscure statement, Dewey defines it as
that pertaining to the consequences of transactions that affect
others not directly engaged in them.

The problem with this definition and with his attempt to
specify those types of consequences that are to be regarded public will become evident very shortly. In the meantime, it is
worth mentioning that he opposes the public realm from the private sphere. The private sphere applies to those situations or
transactions which affect only the parties directly involved.
Also, he makes it plain that the term 'public' should not be confused with the term 'social.' For, "some social acts, though inclusive of many individuals, are not public if they do not affect
others not involved in said acts. And, as such, they are not subject to state regulation."[39]

1. The Function of Authority in a Democratic State

Dewey proposes that the best way to define the function of authority in relation to the public is to state its aim of protecting
the interests shared by the members constituting the public.[40]
For this reason, authority has to uphold the claims of the organized public as pre-eminent over other interests.[41] The obvious
problem with this general notion is how to determine in precisely
what consists a public claim and how far it extends. If state regulation reaches to where the public interests end, what could
possibly be outside of its control?

Dewey's definition appears to be too broad, especially if
one is to consider that hardly anyone can think of a transaction
which does not bear some consequences to others not involved in
the act. In one way or another, transactions between or among
people will have some effect, however indirect, on non-partici-

pants. This is precisely the problem that infects the theory of 'self-protection' which John Stuart Mill so vigorously defended. Simply, the class of actions that affect no one but the doer or doers would be hard to find. Even marital relations which seem to be a wholly private affair would, if unregulated, bear indirect consequences on family life and the social structure.[42]

Whether he is aware of it or not, Dewey is laboring on this point under the stress of inconsistency. Some passages expressing metaphysical generality and, hence, applicable here, assure his readers that isolated occurrences, like private affairs, never take place.

> Associations in the sense of connection and combination is a "how" of everything known to exist. Singular things act but they act together. Nothing has been discovered which acts in entire isolation. The action of everything is along with the action of other things. The "along with" is of such a kind that the behavior of each is modified by its connection with others.[42]

But the distinction between public and private must be maintained if his political theory is to stand. For, in the final analysis, the basis of the theory lies in the conviction that the source of rights and obligations, and, therefore, of authority and government, is the relationships men sustain with each other.[44] Social problems occur, Dewey maintains, because "men are confronted with situations in which different desires promise opposed good and in which incompatible courses of action seem to be morally justified."[45]

This is why he takes a valiant effort to save the distinctions by making some specifications. He explains that transactions between singular persons and groups, he explains, bring a public into being when their indirect consequences are of importance. There are some factors which enter to make up importance, namely: "the far-reaching character of consequences, whether in space or time; their settled, uniform and recurrent nature, and their irreparableness."[46] But, he himself admits that, even with this qualification, vagueness is not, thereby, eliminated:

> Each one of these matters involves questions of degree. There is no sharp and clear line which draws itself, pointing out beyond itself... just where a public comes into existence which has interests so significant they must be looked after and administered by special agencies, or government officers. Hence, there is often room for dispute.[47]

His final comment by no means saves the case: "The line of demar-
cation between actions left to private initiative and management
and those regulated by the state has to be discovered experimentally."[48] The statement counsels one to look for something. What
it is and how it can be found, he does not tell.

Obviously, it is a difficult matter to determine when exactly is an indirect consequence far-reaching and irreparable. (Are
they not all, in the long run?) The settled, uniform, and recurrent nature of the consequence is also a questionable description. What it may mean is that public interest is usually concerned with modes of behavior which are old and are, therefore,
well-established, whereas new projects are ordinarily undertaken
by private initiative. Public interest also applies to instrumentalities that have come into use as a matter of course and are
prerequisite of other customary pursuits, e. g., the building and
use of highways.[49] But is a public engendered only by old and
well-established modes of behavior? Even new projects, the emergence of which he himself attributes to private initiative and
interest, can also be regarded as public in view of their consequences. This is why the invention, production, and application
of new methods in industry and business are, in practice, subject
to government regulation.

It goes without saying that the matter of sustaining the
distinction in real political and social practice is problematic,
if not controversial. The sad consequences of adopting a position
against keeping the distinction clear are considerable. It can be
speculated that Dewey is aware of this and is, therefore, quite
resolved in keeping the distinction, notwithstanding the difficulty it brings to the effort of maintaining philosophical cohe-
rence. Such being the case, the issue concerning why Dewey adopts
such a vulnerable view is understandable. Unfortunately, as will
be seen later, he would rather erase the distinction, if it can
be conveniently done.

In the meantime, to see the negative consequences of abro-
gating the distinction, consider a position with a conception
of the 'public' and 'private' akin to that of Dewey. The view
of Charles Reich, a contemporary social critic, taking a strong
affirmative stance (that is, for keeping the distinction between
private and public domains sufficiently marked in social and political life) is a useful example. Political experience in the
U. S., he observes, proves that a great number of social ills
springs from its loosening. In his anatomy of the American corporate state, he takes note of the disappearing line. "In the
corporate State, most of the 'public' functions of government
are actually performed by the 'private' sector of the economy.
And most 'government' functions are services performed for the
private sector."[50]

Some instances of the former would be the practice of hiring
private firms by the U. S. government to build the national defense systems, to supply the space program, to construct inter-
state highways, even to do its thinking for it (as in the case

of the so-called 'think-tank' institutes. Of the same kind are
cases resulting from the deputizing system by which a far larger
sector of the private economy is enlisted in government service.
Appropriate examples of the latter would include government ex-
penditure for research and development benefitting private com-
panies, subsidies to industries, credit and financial services
to homeowners, roads to aid develop privately owned resort areas.
Reich explains the danger of this public-private and private-pub-
lic integration:

> Once the line between "public" and "private"
> becomes meaningless and is erased, the various
> units of the Corporate State no longer appear
> to be parts of a diverse and pluralistic system
> in which one kind of power limits another kind
> of power; the various centers of power do not
> limit each other they all weigh in on the same
> side of the scale, with only the individual on
> the other side. With public and private merged,
> we can discern the real monolith of power and
> realize there is nothing at all within the system
> to impose checks and balances, to offer compe-
> tition, to raise even a voice of caution or doubt.
> We are all involuntary members, and there is no
> zone of the private to offer refuge.[51]

Dewey anticipates a similar integration. But contrary to
one's expectation, he seems to welcome its eventual occurrence.
Speaking of the movement in reverse (i. e., as compared with
Reich's description), he states:

> It is possible that the time will come when not
> only railways will have become routine in their
> operation and management, but also existing modes
> of machine production, so that business men ins-
> tead of opposing public ownership will clamor
> for it in order that they may devote their ener-
> gies to affairs which involve more novelty,
> variation and opportunities for risk and gain.[52]

Again, the underlying reason for this attitude can only be speculated upon. It may be that he favors social growth to come more
from the initiative of citizens and less from government sponsor-
ship. Certainly, the reason cannot be the desire to extend government charge and, in the process, widen its authority. For, as the
next section will show, community is not automatically established with the creation of a more powerful state.

In any event, it is important to save the distinction between public and private. For it is, in Dewey's development, the
basis for determining the roles of political authority. As he

believes, the need for organization of the public into a state and the institutionalization of roles of leaders into statuses in form of public offices arise from or is one with the need to protect those who may be affected by private transactions. In this statement, he is citing the negative aspect of government function. Without state regulation, conflicts from various groups with different interests would bring about social chaos, particularly in the modern setting.

He is careful to note that social conflicts are not totally due to man's self-centeredness but rather to the nature of human freedom as power-in-relation-with-others. He would be unwilling to accept the proposition that man is a wolf to another, as the individualistic school would contend. He would postulate in place an account that would attribute the occurrence of conflicts to collision of freedom possessed and exercised by one with that possessed and exercised by another.[53] In this context, the role of government is to make the distribution of liberties or powers more equitable. He would agree with the Hobbesian view that in the the factual scheme of social relationships, one has to rely on the force of sovereign power "to constrain the arbitrary power of individuals and associations, harnessing all lesser arbitrariness by one supreme arbitrariness that spoke through the law."[54]

But the laws that the state upholds in exercising authority are not rigid and unchangeable. The term 'law' means two things for Dewey. First, it is the statement of the conditions of the balance and organization of powers promulgated to avoid conflicts of interests. Second, it is a procedural guideline both in fixing conditions under whch interest groups in society may operate and in introducing new ideas to the existing system. Because interests vary and time calls for different ways of resolving conflicts, law cannot remain stagnant and absolute. Likewise, authority which obtains elegitimacy precisely from the law is not to be regarded fixed once and for all. In operation, it many not be too arbitrary, but it is nonetheless meant to be experimental. Its merit is weighed according to success in practice.[55]

Here, Dewey is setting forth two conditions for a workable type of state organization: 1) firmness and clarity in its constitutions and institutions to provide a quasi-enduring order, that is, one less vulnerable to accidents; 2) flexibility in practice, to allow room for change and novelty. If there is no stable principle of government (ordinarily expressed in the constitutions of the land), if there is no definite structure solidified by laws (understood as procedural guidelines in the operational level), the original system would collapse as soon as the founding fathers pass on. Dewey's perception is not without confirmation in real experience. For instance, the government of troubled Bolivia in the seventies once lacked permanence because the ultimate political decision was left to the sensitivity of the people who, incidentally, was supported by the military. And since that sensitivity was so precarious and unstable, governmental policies changed as often as the people changed their presidents. The turnover in leadership was quite frequent because no one could serve popular demands long enough.

The first condition is also important in handling future contingencies. If there were no stable laws to regulate actions before they are executed, a melee among various interest-factions would likely ensue. If there were no special agencies to take change and control the consequences of different types of trans-actions - consequences which are projected in important ways be-yond the persons and associations directly concerned with them, then there would be no effective organization of powers to render them predictably orderly and useful. This reasoning is based on the experience that men are not always prudent and considerate with regard to the effects of their dealings.

Conclusively, the view that one of the positive functions of political authority is to remedy the inadequacy of non-insti-tutionalized social regulations can be attributed to Dewey. He would agree with the statement that "a society in which every citizen is the censor of his neighbour's morals is likely to be an inharmonious one."[54] Similarly, it is not an arbitrary exten-sion of thought to attribute to him the belief that state autho-rity should emerge as the embodiment of the citizen's moral cons-ciousness. Authority personified in officials of the government should thus express and represent the moral values of the citi-zenry.

This is why authority is binding. It makes men liable for their actions because it makes them aware of their moral duties. In this connection between authority and moral (not only civic) responsibility lies Dewey's reason for claiming that authority does not violate the exercise of individual freedom. Authority only directs freedom to prevent it from degenerating to license. Conversely, the moral consciousness of the people stands as a check to prevent authority from becoming an arbitrary power.

The second requirement or condition in the formulation of a system of political organization, namely, flexibility in prac-tice, is significant to the possibility of change and progress. It implies that state activity should not be monopolistic, in the sense that it should not assume control of all social func-tuions to the point of eliminating private initiative. Likewise, it should not be rigidly authoritarian, in the sense that it should not enforce laws that are unrelenting to shifting condi-tions. That it be not monopolistic follows from the principle that no individual or group, no person or institution can claim for itself the possession of all knowledge. This is why Dewey reacts with repugnance against social arrangements which involve fixed subordination maintained by coercion. That it not be autho-ritarian follows from the logic that to sustain absolute conser-vatism against current change is an exercise in futility. The outcome can only be what has already been experienced by mankind in the unfolding of its history - the constant rivalry between authority and innovative individualism.

A state that excludes the masses from participating in deci-

sions of public concern is despotic, says Dewey; it gives individuals no opportunity to reflect and decide what is good for them.
It is also unwise; for it deprives itself of the potential resources that could and should otherwise be at its service. "The
inidividuals of the submerged mass may not be very wise. But
there is one thing they are wiser about than anybody else can
be, and that is where the shoe pinches, the trouble they suffer
from."[57] Furthermore, an all-embracing state is bound to fail.
For, it ignores the reality that needs and interests of people
vary enormously, and that there is no ideal pattern of the 'good
life' which would be right for everyone.

Because a monolithic organization would certainly collapse
in the face of the complexity and diversity it must cater to,
the political structure must be sufficiently flexible. In this
view, Dewey notes, is his point of contact with what is known
as the pluralistic conception of the state. In praise of that
conception, he says:

> Pluralism is well ordained in present political
> practice and demands a modification of hierar-
> chical and monistic theory. Every combination of
> human forces that adds its own contribution of
> value to life has for that reason its own unique
> and ultimate worth. It cannot be degraded into a
> a means to glorify the state.[58]

But he is careful to observe that he differs from the pluralistic outlook in that his doctrine does not prescribe inherent
limits to state action, either as a positive function (such as
instituting a welfare program) or as a negative one (such as circumscribing its power to merely settling conflicts among diverse
groups).[59]

That the state should not promulgate and enforce laws that
are closed and rigid follows from that reasoning based on the
fact that life involves risk, situations change, new problems
arise calling for new arrangements, new directions open up pointing to progress in culture. And, because novelty springs generally from individual minds, laws should not only be complai-
sant but also encouraging by including provisions for aiding
private initiatives.[60] Also, this second condition flows from
the premise that the presence of unrealized and precarious possibilities is a necessary ingredient of human freedom. In actual
experience, it is only in confronting them that choice acquires
value.

> Invariant virtue appears to be as mechanical
> as uninterrupted vice, for true excellence
> changes with conditions. Unless character ri-
> ses to to overcome some new difficulty or con-
> quer some temptation from an unexpected quar-

ter, we suspect its grain is only a veneer.[61]

It must be emphasized at this point that Dewey's arguments against monolithic and authoritarian rule do not support the conclusion that he favors a state that governs least. Similarly, these must not be construed as indicating his preference for the dissolution of the positive role for the state.[62] There may not have been emphatic assertions on the matter, but his view is sufficiently clear. He prescribes that the state provide efficient means to guide, harness, and expand individual energies. Hence, he affirms that "a measure of the goodness of a state is the degree in which it relieves individuals from the waste of negative struggle and needless conflict and confers upon him positive assurance and reinforcement in what he undertakes."[63]

However, Dewey postulates no concrete policy on how this objective of aiding individual initiative can or is to be realized. He is neutral on the the question of how far state activity might extend. Its scope, he believes, is something to be critically and experimentally determined. Its value is to be measured according to the soundness of its consequences - consequences that promote the enhancement of objective freedom and develop men's intellectual, moral, and artistic capacities. Dewey's attitude is, again, cognizant of the precarious character of reality. "Just as publics and states vary with conditions of time and place, so do the concrete functions which should be carried on by states."[64] Hence, at one time and place, a large measure of state activity may be called for and, at another, a policy of quiescence and 'laissez faire' may be sufficient. This attitude is also consistent with the view that freedom and individuality are potential qualities, dependent upon social conditions for their actualization.

2. The Ethical Justification of Political Democracy

In view of the distinction Dewey makes between political and communal democracy, it seems unfair to criticize his political theory as having made the state disappear, as its moral reference was proposed to be too indirect.[65] It is true that his thoughts on communal democracy center on the many associations and relations constitutive of community. But, by this, he does not mean to diminish the importance of the state. His intention is to locate it in its apprpriate sphere, which is outside the confines of these associations and relations. Thus, one cannot expect to find an elaborate discussion of state functions in the context of communal concerns just as he cannot anticipate meeting the issue of shared values in the tretment of political aims.

The distinction between political and communal democracy must not, however, be construed as indicating real separation. The political order, while functionally (i. e., for the purpose of exposition, of analysis, or simply of understanding) distinct, cannot be separated apart from the communal realm. The reason is the purpose of analysis, of exposition, or simply of understanding) presented as a distinct order, is not thereby proposed as a separate realm. This can be gathered from the sort of aims Dewey assigns to the political establishment. These aims concern the need for and the need of community. Hence, the moral reference of the state is hardly indirect; it is, on the contrary, directly related to the formation and conservation of community!

The last statement undrscores the moral status of the state. But this does not mean that, in Dewey's estimation, all types of governments are equally justified. This interpretation can be arrived at from implicit remarks rather than open declarations. For, unfortunately, He does not spend much time discussing systems other than political democracy. Thus, when he speaks of the state, he means first and foremost a democratically constituted state. On whether or not the reason for the silence is his opinion that no other system is justifiable, the texts offer no aid. And, even with respect to the justification of political democracy, he is not sufficiently explicit. Inspite of this limitation, however, the present interpretation is supported by the assurance that the integrity of his theory is tenable only if viewed in its light.

Certainly, the statement that political democracy is morally based is not a self-evident proposition, he would be the first to admit. His argument, which sets the tone of this section, rests in principle on the belief that the end-in-view of human associations and organizations of any kind has to be the attainment of communal ends. These ends chiefly include freedom in the context of communal existence and self-enrichment through cooperation in promoting cultural progress. Since these are not given in man's original condition, the instrumentality of a form of government adapted to said aims is required. The key word is 'adapted.' No political system is adequate to secure communal ends if, in principle, it already involved curtailment of human and cultural freedom. But is there any system of government adapted to serve communal ends?

Before addressing this question, it must be noted that in positing community as the moral referent of the state, Dewey does not thereby declare it to be an absolute end or an 'intrinsic good' (in the Aristotelian sense of the term). Whether or not valid arguments can be presented to prove the contrary inspite of what he says is beside the point. Simply, 'absolute' and 'intrinsic' are not meaningful terms in his context. Categories sharply dividing goods into instrumental and intrinsic are alien, not to say repugnant, to Dewey's taste. A classification of the sort is permissible only if it is useful in serving as a tool of insight. Its importance can only appear in assessing individualized response in an individual situation, not as set of rules to be applied like drug-store prescriptions or kitchen recipes. This is why Dewey can, without being inconsistent, postulate a movement toward community, while simultaneously maintaining an experimental attitude on the issue of the scope of state actions.

Thus, 'tools of insight' may serve as working principles in developing effective methods of resolving problematic situations. In this sense, communal concerns function as working moral principles. Concretely, if the ethical justification of a particular political system is to be sought, freedom and culture are the consequences to look for. In Dewey's evaluation, political democracy is preferable on both counts. His reasons for this contention will be discussed below.

In the meantime, a return to the question posed earlier concerning the justification of the state - is called for. The point is, political democracy, 'qua' political, is an authority system and, hence, requires justification. This issue demands particular attention and inquiry since, in recent political literature, the possibility, not only the need, of such a justification is being challenged. Robert Paul Wolff's statement on political philosophy may be taken as the center of the controversy. His view, although quite radical, is simple enough to understand. He argues: on the ground that any state is inherently an authority system and because authority is in itself quite incompatible with human freedom, the only morally tenable position to maintain is the rejection of any political authority system. He calls this position 'philosophical anarchism.'

The conclusion that authority is incompatible with human freedom is indeed radical. But it is not novel. Dewey has been preaching the same idea a generation earlier. But he makes an important qualification. 'External' authority is never compatible with human freedom. The difference is, Wolff takes all forms of authority as external to the reality of freedom. Dewey does not. In fact, Dewey believes, a political system intrinsic to the operation of a free community is already in process, viz., in the workings of political democracy. Given that claim, what he must show is how such is the case. If he could show that authority in political democracy is indeed consistent with human freedom and a free growing culture, then he would be simultaneously proving that political democracy is morally justified.

His line of argument can be conveniently explored if it were compared with Wolff's premises. Wolff declares that men, on the ground that they are metaphysically free, that they can choose, acquire knowledge and deliberate about their choices, have as a primary duty the preservation of that state of freedom which is a gift of nature. This means that a man who is free is one who takes responsibility for his actions. To be reponsible for one's actions is to, at least, attempt to ascertain what is right (although in the process he may arrive at a wrong judgments). Wolff acknowledges that man is ordinarily bound by constraints. He refers to such a relation to moral constraints 'submission to laws.' But this relation, he emphasizes, must be only to laws that he himself made, if following them were to be justified. He may follow others, but he may justifiably do so not because he has been told to do so but because he himself freely decides to do so.

But, (Wolff continues to explain) 'obedience,' in the strict

sense of the term, connotes the contrary. It consists in following the law because it is the law or a person because he or she
is duly constituted to command. Obedience is, then, an act of
submitting one's will to another; it is doing or forebearing a
command of another when no sufficient reason other than that command exists. Authority, on the other hand, is the correlative
of obedience. It is a demand for obedience and, hence, for submitting one's will to another. Because obedience is tantamount
to forfeiture of one's autonomy, it is a violation of the moral
duty to remain free. Thus, authority demanding such a forfeiture,
has no justification. Anarchism, for that reason, is the only
tenable alternative.[66]

Dewey would disagree with Wolff on various counts. In the
first place, the former's notion of freedom departs from the traditional idea of metaphysical will which the latter obviously re-
tains. Such an idea, Dewey would contend, constitutes a departure
to a separate or an ideal realm. Wolff's conception of freedom
is infected with the same kind of transcendentalism that afflic-
ted the classical theory of 'free will.' The key to freedom, realistically understood, lies in knowledge, knowledge of the facts
which enable men to employ them in connection with desires and
aims. The case is similar to the manner a physician or an engi-
neer is free in his thoughts and actions according to the degree
in which he knows what he deals with. 'Freedom,' in this sense,
is brought to the realm of actual events. Here, Dewey is quite
convinced, it emerges as power. And 'power' means efficiency in
action, ability to carry out plans, capacity to vary courses of
action and experience novelties, power of desire and choice to be
factors in events.

In the second place, Dewey's metaphysics that sustains both
atomicity and continuity (Cf. Chapter I, p. 13) posits freedom
not as a ready made faculty but as a potential trait realizable
only within the context of social transaction. In this sense,
freedom cannot be opposed to authority. If freedom means or implies knowledge and efficiency in action, and such cannot be attained without organization, then freedom depends on authority.
For, organization implies the assumption of the role of leaders
by some persons in relationship with others.

Authority, in this scheme, appears as the support of freedom rather than its enemy. But, this is true only when authority
does not present itself as an external force, i. e., as an order
separate from the citizenry.[67] This is why Dewey prefers the democratic system. For, in such a system, the cause of liberty and
equality are both served. The employment of general suffrage and
of majority and representative rules is, in principle, a manner
of giving practical recognition to the moral belief that every
man is a source of claims or, in the language of Kant, belongs to
the kingdom of ends.

The democratic rule "one man, one vote" is, in his judgment,
an expression of equality basic to the notion of life where interests are, though not the same for all, shared by all in terms of

133

consequences, as these interests act upon one another. The freedom of discussion and association ensures that claims are given
the chance of being stated and impartially heard. There are, then,
two sides to authority in a democratic state. There is the negative side, insofar as it is a system of control and restraint
over indirect consequences of (private) transactions among citizens. There is the positive side, insofar as it sponsors private
incentives and extend their individual powers. The government,
through which the public is organized, Dewey declares, must serve
both ends, if it were to remain morally justified. To do otherwise is to lose its claim to loyalty and obedience - factors
which in the first place permit governments to rule.[68]

The assignment to the people of ultimate authority is a concrete translation into the political order of the moral value
that individuals are ends-in-view and institutions are instrumentalities. Stressing the importance of adhering to this moral
precept, Dewey says:

> Democracy has many meanings, but if it has a moral
> meaning it is found in resolving that the the su-
> preme test of all political institions and indus-
> trial arrangements shall be the contribution they
> make to the all-round growth of every member of
> society.[69]

Again, the "all-round growth" of men in society is to be understood in a communal sense, i. e., growth of individuals as related with others. This is why the source of rights, obligations
and authority is (not in the individual, taken in isolation from
others but) in the relationship men sustain with one another.[70]
Conflicts of interest can be resolved to community advantage only
by considering the consequences of alternative outcomes on all
concerned. "Right expresses the way in which the good of a number
of persons, held together by intrinsic ties, becomes efficacious
in the regulation of the members of a community."[71] Also, rights
and obligations express the relationships which is established
among men. "It is a parent not just an isolated individual, that
a man or woman imposes obligations on children; these grow out of
the office or function the parent sustains, not out of mere personal will."[72]

The reasoning can be easily be applied to state authority.
For, political powers and obligations grow out of the functions
members of a community bear in relation to one another. This is
why such powers and obligations cannot stand opposed to the individual relations constituting the community. They start and flow
back to the members of the community.

> The two facts that each one is influenced in what
> he does and enjoys in what he becomes by the ins-
> titutions under which he lives that therefore he

shall have, in a democracy, a voice in shaping
them are the passive and active sides of the same
fact.[73]

Because authority in a democratic state is elected through
popular mandate, it is a system of public governance. There is
no power that is absolute or that exist on its own right. Political power is always a delegated power. This claim is, again, a
rejection of the concept of external authority. Such a concept
is, in Dewey's judgment, equivalent to the surrender of the potentialities of human nature. The only legitimate authority is
that which is intrinsic to the community. A person who is offi-
cially invested is not acting on private capacity but "as the
representative of relations which many share."[74] The people from
which power originally comes is committed to it as an act of
self-obedience.

Insistently, Dewey rejects any form of authority, any species of rights and obligations which are privately established,
issued, or judged.[75] He believes that the approach in which acts
are tested by principle and principle by the acts it promotes
is most efficacious. For, it can alter with no violence, those
relations which are not conducive to the good of each individual.
This is why he deplores those public officials who misrepresent
their constituents. He obviously does not imagine that universal
consensus can be obtained at all times and under any condition.
But, he suggests, the consequences must, at least, be carefully
studied. And when these are seen to be advantageous to all or to
most, there is sufficient ground to assume that those affected
would desire an enactment or policy that would bring them about
and, hence, obey it. The disadavantaged minority would expectedly
be unhappy with it, but they, nevertheless, have the same duty
toward it (contrary to what Wolff would think in the case). Dewey
explains why:

> Citizens in a just state respond at their personal
> inconvenience to the demands of the state, not be-
> cause the latter may bring physical pressure or
> mental coercion to bear upon them, but because they
> are members of (an) organized society; members in
> such an intimate sense that the demands are not
> external impositions even when they run counter
> to the good which a present desire calls for.[76]

He does not, however, expect or want all to be moral conformists
to the rule (much less the tyranny) of the majority. For, he sees
equally a justification for non-conformism.

> The justification of the moral nonconformist is
> that when he denies the rightfulness of a parti-
> cular claim, he is doing so not for the sake of

private advantage, but for the sake of an object
which will serve more amply and consistently the
welfare of all.[77]

The authority of law stands in similar relationship with
individual freedom as the officials or institutions that enforce
that law. For a law expresses the condition of a certain ordered
relationships. It is never formulated for individuals in isolation but for the relations they bear with one another.[78] Law is,
therefore, the statement of the conditions of organization of
energies, energies which conflict and result in violence if left
unorganized.[79] Law is a rule which turns independent, and even
contradictory powers, into a scheme which not only avoids waste
but allows their maximum utilization. "Law," he says. "however
imperfect and poor, is at least a recognition of the universal,
of the interconnection of parts, and hence operates as a school-
master to bring men to reason, power and freedom"[80]

He is implying that to obey the law that organizes human
powers is not to surrender freedom but make it possible. To render allegiance to the law that provides support to intelligent
desires so that these desires may make a difference is not to
give up any choice but to make it effective. This point leads to
the conclusion that

> freedom is not obtained by mere abolition of law
> and institutions, but by the progressive satura-
> tion of all laws and institutions with greater
> and greater acknowledgement of the necessary laws
> governing the constitution of things.[81]

Positively, if the government is to serve the cause of freedom, Dewey prescribes that it must create a conditon where effective release of intelligence, necessary to direct and warrant
freedom of action, can take place. He proposes that this end-in-
view can be achieved by promoting liberal education and cultural
programs, by guaranteeing free inquiry and discussion, by allowing the existence of private associations with the conditions,
of course, that they do not subvert the laws of the land. It is
through these means that government can become an instrument of
rationality.[82] Also, it must reinforce choice by providing alternatives to citizens, such as making schools available even (or
should it be said especially?) to the poor. Finally, it must en-
large individual powers by strengthening the economic base of
society in the effort to maintain harmony of environment with
human wants.[83]

What, then, does Dewey make out of the so-called conflicts
between the individual and the social? between autonomy and authority? That there are social conflicts, he would be the last
to deny. But these conflicts are not really found where they are
ordinarily thought to be located. Dewey consistently rejects bi-

furcations not only in nature but also in society. There can be
no real conflict between the 'individual' and the 'social' because these terms are pure abstractions and, hence, have no real
reference. What do exist are conflicts between some individuals
and some arrangements in social life, between groups and classes
of individuals;[84] between old traditions embedded in institutions
and new ways of thinking and acting which spring from those who
depart from and who attack what is socially accepted;[85] between
a dominant class and a rising class; between accomplishing results by voluntary private effort and by organized action invol-
ving the use of public agencies.[86]

To resolve these conflicts, a separation between authority
and freedom cannot be insisted upon. In the first place, Dewey
reiterates, there is no real and inherent opposition between
these two designated terms. Such an arbitrary separation is harmful because, in practice, it is applied by the use of coercive
force, i. e., by overturning existing authority. Dewey's stance
on the employment of this measure is firm. The use of force is
not an evil in itself. In fact, he says, no ends are ever accomplished without it. It is, therefore, not a good argument against
a measure (be it political, international, jural, economic, etc.)
to reject it because it involves the use of force. What, instead,
may be an appropriate criticism against a state is not the charge
that it uses force but that it does not use it wisely and effectively. Confusion between the two (the use of force and the manner of its use), he says, explains why "penal measures are still
largely upon the level which would convince a man by knocking him
down instead of by instructing him."[87]

Dewey sees a necessary relation between law and the use of
force. In fact, according to him, law is essentially a formulation of the use of force. The justification of this use depends
upon its comparative efficiency and economy. Violence is a different matter. It has no justification in his moral scheme and no
place in his political theory. Violence is a wasteful and unorganized use of energy and, hence, attains no constructive results.
Coercion is but a form of violence and must be treated as such.
It is usually employed to compel obedience. History, he observes,
is witness to the fact that the use of it is symptomatic of the
eventual breakdown of the reigning authority that adopts it. But
inspite of this firmness, he offers no clear-cut line by which
proper use of force and improper reliance on violence may be distinguished. In fact, he admits,

> There is always a possibility that what passes as
> a legitimate use of force may be so wasteful as to
> be really a use of violence; and per contra that
> measures condemned as recourse to mere violence
> may, under the given circumstances, represent an
> intelligent utilization of energy.[88]

The use of force specifically serves as an extra device to

assure the attainment of an end-in-view. Dewey states: "It is an incident of a situation under certain conditions - namely, where the means for the realization of an end are not naturally at hand, so that energy has to be spent in order to make some power into a means for the end in hand."[89] A recourse to direct force is a supplementation to existent efficient resources of effective energy under some circumstances. The question of its justification is a question on the efficiency of means to accomplish the end. Thus,

> If the social end at stake can be more effectively subserved by the existing legal and economic machinery, resort to physical action of a more direct kind has no standing. If, however, they represent an ineffective organization of means to the ends in question, then recourse to extra-legal means may be indicated; provided it really serves the ends in question - a very large qualification be it noted.[90]

Dewey points to a specific instance where the use of non-democratic means is justified. When society through an authorized majority is engaged in a social experimentation that, with assurance, will lead to great social changes but is being prevented from doing so by a minority using force to permit the method of intelligent action to go into effect, "then force may be intelligently employed to subdue and disarm the recalcitrant minority."[91]

Because Dewey considers coercive power only as an extra device to supplement the deficiency of the available resources, it is never the most agreeable means of social direction and control. "Discontent with democracy as it operates under conditions of exploitation by special intersts has justification. But the notion that the remedy is violence and a civil war between classes is a counsel of despair."[92] A recent commentary by Ramsey Clark on the false conflict between liberty and security lends clarity and support to Dewey's insight. Clark maintains that mere words of prohibition, with force and the threat of force as their only sanction, cannot shape human conduct, much less deter crime in a mass society. Experience, he says, tells us that the result of repressiveness is more repressiveness and more crime. A public that believes that police force alone is reponsible for crime control and, hence, no other effort is needed, is gravely mistaken. Excessive reliance on the system of criminal justice is terribly dangerous; it separates the people from their government; it divides the nation.

> It puts institutions of government in which people must have confidence in direct confrontation with dynamics they cannot control. When the system is abusive, society itself is unfair and government demeans human dignity. Then there

> is a contest of cunning between the people and
> the state. The people can never win.[93]

Clark' view, reminiscent of Dewey's perspective, concludes that
the major contribution of law is moral leadership and that it
alone can influence the conduct of its citizens.

As can be anticipated, Dewey's response, if asked for an alternative to violence and coercion is the employment of intelligence and sound education measures.

> It is not pleasant to face the extent to which,
> as a matter of fact, coercive and violent force
> is relied upon in the present social system as
> means of social control... But unless the fact is
> acknowledged as a fact in its full depth and
> breadth, the meaning of dependence upon intelli-
> gence as the alternative method of social direc-
> tion will not be grasped.[94]

He is talking here not of intelligence that is appropriated by
one individual or group in society. Knowledge is never a possession of a superior few,[95] and, hence, no individual or group
can make the determination for himself in everything, much less
for anyone else.[96] Rather, he is referring to scientific or organized intelligence - the method of mutual consultation and voluntary agreement. Such is opposed to the method of fixed subordination of the many to the few, enforced from above and maintained
by coercion.

The utilization of organized intelligence, Dewey believes,
is the only resource that has not yet been tried on any large
scale in the field of human or social relationships. It must be
immediately noted here that his faith in the power of the scientific method is indeed based on the experience that it has been
used and found successful in the practice of science. But such a
faith in its achievements is preceded by the recognition of what
is inherent in the nature of the process itself - the realization
of the union of freedom and authority.

Thus, as has been in the past, its promise for the future is
bright. Science has made its way by releasing (not suppressing)
the elements of variation, of invention and innovation, of creativity in individuals. But inspite of its dependence for development upon free intiative of individual inquirers, it is able to
reach a height where conclusions are held with authority. This
occurs particularly when divergent theories come to agreement by
testing, either to the collapse of one and the confirmation of
the other. But whichever is confirmed becomes a public possession,
thereby enriching the fund of human knowledge. Is only then, that
individual knowledge becomes social, that it becomes true knowledge.

In sponsoring the method of organized intelligence, Dewey does not thereby allow special privilege to experts either in science or in politics. He would say that a class of experts may, at some point, become so removed from common interests as to become a class with private interests and private knowledge. In social matters, that is not knowledge at all. Experts can discover and make known their discoveries, but it is only as an embodied intelligence that their discoveries have true relevance. "No social modification, slight and revolutionary, can endure except as it enters into the action of a people through their desires and purposes."[97] Hence, the seat of authority remains to be in the citizenry, as it makes communal use of the findings of those who are trained and the educated. Of course, it goes without saying that the latter have greater obligation because of their far reaching influence.

Conclusively, Dewey's espousal of organized intelligence in resolving social problems rests on his great confidence in the application of the scientific method. If directed to human relations, such a method can, at least, answer problems concerning the connection between freedom and authority. He does not, however, ignore the enormous obstacle that stands in the way.

> There is the weight of the past history on the side of those who are pessimistic about the possibility of achieving this humanly desirable and humanly necessary task. I do not predict that the extension will ever be effectively actualized. But I do claim that the problem of the relation of authority and freedom, of stability and change, if it can be solved, will be solved this way.[38]

Here lies finally the synthesis of autonomy and authority and, hence, the justification of political democracy. If freedom is intelligence; and if organized intelligence is more authoritative and effective than individual deliberations, as amply demonstrated in the scientific enterprise, then collective intelligence can be taken as synonymous to collective authority. Collective authority is, in turn, but another name for political democracy. As Dewey states: "What is pertinent, what is deeply significant to the relation between collective authority and freedom, is that the progress of intelligence... exhibits their organic effective union."[99]

What is attained at this juncture of social life is freedom that is general and shared, that has the backing and guidance of a socially organized control. At the same time, this is authority that is capable of directing and utilizing change. Such a synthesis is obviously consistent with the notes of freedom and individuality described above as originally unshaped and dependent upon social conditions. It i is also compatible with the kind of authority system Dewey prescribes in his theory of the state which emphasizes experimentalism in practice.

But Dewey's prescription for organized intelligence leading
to the establishment of a human community is not fully within the
scope and capacity of political authority to achieve by itself.
He is very much aware of the inherent weaknesses and limitations
of political power. A more reliable social control and direction
can only arise, he believes, from mutual agreement where freedom
instead of submission is the abiding principle. This requires a
full-blown cultural revolution which call for all segments of society and all phases of human transactions to be involved. As he
puts it: "Control of individual is effected by the whole situation in which individuals are involved, in which they share and
of which they are co-operative or interacting parts."[100] This
idea brings into focus the following section on commununal democracy.

C. Democracy: The Ideal Community

The flow of Dewey's deliberations that were followed up to this
point leads directly to his concept of 'ideal community.' It is,
therefore, quite expected that he would declare in his most important work on the subject, the Public and Its Problems, that
"democracy is not a concept, except perhaps verbally, distinct
from that of 'community.'" It is not, he says, an alternative to
other principles of associated life; it is the idea of community
itself.[101]

But what democracy is he referring to? In view of the distinction between political and communal kinds of democracy, this
question is in order. Is the ideal community one that is founded
on a well-structured system of government where institutions
function according to defined limits and where popularly elected
officials genuinely represent their constituents? Or, is it the
unspoiled association of men based on kindship and/or common
concerns? Perhaps, it is a combination of both. Dewey is not himself clear on the subject. But he does say that both are, in effect, ingredients of that Great Community which is in the process
of making.

He acknowledges that, just as there will always be some form
of political relations and activities even within the closest possible community, a political machinery - some contrived system of
authority based on some defined constitutions and laws, such as
the state - is, in general and at times, indispensable. In so saying, it is implied that it is not always indispensable. But even
when the occasion makes it indispensable, no specific structure
or arrangement is stipulated as necessary and none is deemed to
be permanent. Political institutions, at any given, time are but
crude beginnings of a more adequate relating of parts to the
whole human enterprise. Levi captures the sense of Dewey's comments as follows:

It is clear that for Dewey the idea of democracy

> is defined less by political machinery than by
> the right of the individual to have a responsible
> share in forming and directing the activities of
> the groups to which he belongs, and in participa-
> ting genuinely in the values which the groups pro-
> mote.[102]

He is indicating that, for Dewey, what constitutes a genuine
community is not a particular political structure, however democratic it may be. There are no restrictions as to what kind of
means is to be employed provided it is commensurate to the end-
in-view.

This interpretation may have been based on Dewey's own statements. His advocacy of the objective appraisal of social planning
as a method of stabilizing society in a period of instability or
turmoil includes the prescription that all forms of knowledge and
skill should be applied to a social problem without regard of the
fact that a specific procedure is in use in an anti-democratic
country.[103] In **Philosophy and Civilization**, he declares that society should be free to experiment with the technique of organized planning, even if such a technique is associated with So-
viet Russia. To hold otherwise is to surrender the case to communism.[104] He reasons that what is at stake is not really a
choice between capitalism and communism but one between chaos
and order, chance and control.

His thoughts here are not new; they have been stated before.
He already affirmed that the state is never a permanent order.
Society is individuals in their relations to each other. And because relations vary, so also must the system organizing the relations change. Geiger aptly reads Dewey as saying that the "connection of the state with more elementary social organizations
indicates that states come into existence as they are required;
they grow and develop. They themselves are the consequences of
specific needs."[105]

The reasoning is consistent with the idea of experimentalism.
Dewey believes it is the only realistic outlook in the face of the
inherent instability and problematic nature of societies, particularly of the contemporary ones. Political democracy is an effective means because, in theory, it is compatible with free inquiry and, in practice, employs organized intelligence.

Significantly, in lauding political democracy, Dewey is, at
the same time, depicting in broad strokes the features of the
ideal community. It is, in his vision, an association constituted of beings whose combined actions bear consequences that are
perceived by all and become objects of desire and effort for all.
His words are not precise on this theme, perhaps because of the
elusiveness of the idea he wants to convey. Yet, his purpose is
sufficiently clear. He wishes to define the ideal community not
meerely as the sum-total of some choice associated activities.
It is that, but more than that. The qualitative characteristics

142

of community include participation in collective action and sharing in the results derived therefrom. The aim of community is
understanding and consensus through mutual consultation. There
may not be full agreement, but intelligence is promoted as the
method action so that in cases of differences there may be agreement to differ, tolerance and sympathy until the time when more
adequate knowledge and method of judging are available.[106]

Evidently, 'organized intelligence,' 'experimentalism,'
'scientific method,' 'collective authority' are concepts connected with Dewey's notion of communal democracy. He is, in effect,
asserting the alliance of science and democracy. The point that
the two have qualities in common is indeed a new addition to the
understanding of democracy.[107]

> I would not claim that any existing democracy has
> ever made complete or adequate use of scientific
> method in deciding upon its policies. But freedom
> of communication, the distribution of what is
> found out to every individual as the ultimate
> intellectual consumer, are involved in the demo-
> cratic as in the scientific method.[108]

The scientific enterprize and democracy meet in the point of
their common commitment to the supremacy of method in the resolution of problems. Both involve the activities of sharing, self-
criticism, self-correction, self-direction in dealing with specific issues, emancipation from particular and rigid boundaries
of experience. It is because of this parallelism that Dewey rests
his philosophy of education on the way the scientific outlook and
the democratic way of life come together and manifest themselves
in the best of human bevavior.

Two points are salient in the preceding deliberation. First,
in affirming the scientific as the method of democracy, Dewey is
not only espousing an alternative to other known methods in the
practice of democracy. The democratic process cannot but be experimental. Intuition and external authority, in whatever form they
appear, are procedures that are essentially incompatible with
democracy both in its appearance in the political environment and
in the communal setting. The rationale for holding the supremacy
of method is implicit in the statement. The quality of life takes
its character from the method adopted. Thus, on the one hand, in
a dictatorial system, authority is not controllable because it is
not shared, it is not public, and it is not popular, in any sense
of the term. On the other hand, in a democratic system, the case
is the opposite; it brings, or is capable of bringing, about a
free and moving social life.

Second, in indicating the alliance of science and democracy,
Dewey does not intend to identify one with the other. For, democracy is not simply the experimental method in operation - addressing itself to the problems of human affairs, resolving conflicts

or effecting harmony. It is not reducible to the procedure by which change is controlled and directed to some desirable ends. It is not merely the process concerned with means and ends in a continuum, which of itself has no content. Dewey admits that it, indeed, holds means and ends to be in a continuum. For, ends are never impervious to further inquiry when taken as means for later tests. Also, what arises as end in a situation does not endure as an impregnable permanent belief. The method of science comes from and depends upon beliefs which, though never removed from inquiry, provide the base that allows inquiry to continue.

But the preceding comment does not stand as an argument proving that beliefs can be equated with their tests. The very fact that beliefs are confirmed or rejected in the process of inquiry shows that they are distinct from the inquiry itself. Dewey must, therefore, mean here that democracy is more than a procedural concept; it also has substantive elements which simultaneously define its positive traits. These elements are those beliefs arrived at or validated through inquiry.

Marc Belth suggests a distinction applicable to the issue at hand. Some beliefs, he declares, are always subject open to examination. This kind of beliefs is one that permits action to be executed and sustained. In its absence, there can only be complete doubt and, hence, inactivity. But other beliefs are solidified into and saturated as values as they enter the lives of persons in the community. He explains that the former are beliefs about realities and, as such, are testable as true or false. The latter are values that have meanings far richer than being truths or falisities.[109] The former gives information; the latter are prescriptive of behavior and actions.

Prescriptive values, in Belth's interpretation, are the substance of community. The are comprised of the collected and shared experiences of a particular group. They are begotten of and grow with that group and serve as the soil from which springs further experiences in just the character they come to have. This is an interesting point, especially in Dewey's framework. Stretched to its logical implication, the idea means that no democracy (either as a political system or as a mode of social life) can succeed in a culturally divided society. This can easily serve as an explanation for the collapse of many democratic governments in Asia and America.

Belth's point has another significant implication. It suggests that communal democracy bears a specific moral character. It rests in the commitment to liberate people to the the extent that they are not only free but are capable of making the choices by which their lives may be guided. In other words, it rests in the devotion to uphold the shared values of a free society. Among other things, in this consists Dewey's ideal community.

One vital question looms unanswered. Does Dewey's view extend to denying the necessity of the state in the constitution of communal democracy (or, of what he calls in the Public and

Its Problems the 'Great Community')? Unfortunately, he gives no
clear response to this question. But his sentiment can be drawn
from some related passages. If a mode of associated life which
parallels the traditional communities in intimacy and possession
of civic virtues would be formed, a self-governing community with
no political superstructure may indeed be established. But the
sentiment is, he would be the first to acknowledge, sheer idealism. In theory, the state is only established when it is needed.
In practice, the need is need is perennial. Sometimes, the need
is for a forceful government. At other times, a minimal form of
power may be adequate.

Dewey's feeling is not really one of pathos for the lost
communities of the past, as Levi believes it to be,[110] Rather,
it is a mixture of confidence in man's power and virtue to move
toward that direction and of realism that his dream community
can only be approximated, not fully achieved. The Great Community, he laments, "can never possess the qualities which mark a
local community. It will do its final work in ordering the relations and enriching the experience of local associations."[111]
His confidence has a twofold basis. The first is the perception
that "new forms of human association and communication were being
invented which... gave the promise of meaningful participation
in policy determination, despite the size of organization."[112]
The second is the knowledge that "there is something deep within
human nature itself which pulls toward settled relationships.[113]
The realism is the fruit of his awareness of political history
 bearing witness to what man can achieve and what he can only
idealize. thus, he declares in solemn resignation, democracy is
"not a fact and never will be."[114]

But fact or fancy, Dewey believes that democracy "is more
than a form of government; it is primarily a mode of associated
life, of conjoint communicated experience."[115] Its core ingredient is not, therefore, political but moral. For, while associated or joint activity is a condition of the creation of a community, it is itself merely physical or organic. In his own words:
"communal life is moral, that is emotionally, intellectually,
consciously sustained."[116]

In qualifying it as moral, Dewey is signifying not only the
presence of interaction and interdependence. Close contact alone
does not break down barriers, does not do away with classes and,
hence, with inequality. History reveals many cases of groups and
individuals who are in contact with each other at many points but
are nevertheless kept fixed by arbitrary relations. Contact is
necessary. But it alone, Dewey is convinced, cannot produce communities, unless one believes that human nature yields to the
warmth of physical proximity by inevitably stimulating deeper
response.

So, contact is needed, but it is not enough. What is further
required is participation in collective action and sharing in the
results to be derived therefrom. This entails cultivation of the
sense of social awareness and responsibility. This, in turn, con-

sists in the unification of mind with others in the same fold. Thus, Dewey calls for organized integration of desires and purposes leading to activities with consequences and satisfaction common to all.[117] Equality, in this context, is enhanced through personal participation in a shared culture.[118]

Social responsibility and cohesiveness are possible only when values are prized in common and jointly pursued. It is here where the heart of Dewey's community is located. What makes any social group, class, people, or nation tend to fall apart into associations with merely mechanical connection is precisely the lack of values prized and enjoyed communally. Values are essential, says Dewey, because they are not only enduring principles of social intercourse but are also effective guides of conduct. But because values are shared and pursued jointly only when there is a vehicle for a full and moving communication, there must also exist a strong public opinion. This can be attained by the distribution of the results of social inquiry. Thus, his prescription for a democratic society is that its special values and its special purposes and aims must receive such a mode of distribution so that they can become part of the mind and will of the members of society. He goes farther, to the extent of advocating full publicity of the results of social inquiry with no reservations!

In resume, Dewey's Great Community consists of the following elements: physical proximity, organized intelligence sustained by an informed citizenry, shared values. The first is the proper setting, the second is the powerhouse that moves a dynamic society, the third is the principle of cohesion that turns a mere aggrupation into a close-knit society. The member of such a society is identifiable by the virtue of being one who "understands and appreciates its belief, desires and methods, and who contributes to a further conversion of organic powers into human resources and values.[119]

The emphasis on shared values is a focal point. To overlook it is to miss an essential part of Dewey's notion of community. And this is too easy to overlook. Such is the omission, for instance, in some popular criticisms levelled against Dewey. These criticisms appear in many guises. Levi, for one, objects to his commitment to the scientific method on the ground that it represents an over-estimation of the role which scientific knowledge can play in resolving problems in and of society. The reduction of social issues to the problematic situation, as it is done in science, implies, he claims, "both an unambiguous and scientifically reasonable assessment of the evidence after it is assembled."[120] The problem is, a scientific assessment is possible to experts but not for society at large; an unambiguous evaluation assumes "the kind of agreement upon values and coincidence of interests which a heterogeneous society (however democratic) seems to lack."[121]

What Levi misses in Dewey's intent is precisely the role of value sharing which Dewey insists upon besides the employment of organized intelligence or scientific method. He never assumes that men agree on values. This is why Dewey advocates that this be established, too, perhaps, before anything else. More importantly, he never claims that scientific inquiry is the only means to create harmony among varied interests in society. This is why he proposes a return to the traditional values of small communities to serve as backbone of organized planning. Dewey has always remained committed to the face-to-face community of inquirers. "Systematic and continuous inquiry into all the conditions which effect association and their dissemination in print is a precondition of the creation of a fine public."[122] While he does say that organized social planning is the "sole method of social action by which liberalism can realize its professed aims,"[123] he does not say that it is the only method of establishing a communal democracy.

There is, then, no inherent conflict in Dewey's notion of 'intelligence' and 'community.'[124] It is a fact that the use of the method of intelligence does not of itself lead to community, i. e., to the recognition of and concern for the problems of one and all. It is also not the case that such problems would then be accepted as commonly held and jointly resolvable for the benefit of all concerned. For this reason, Dewey prescribes the complementary proposal of sharing values and sustaining conscious effort to promote those values. These can be achieved principally by education and, if need be, by a cultural revolution. This is why there is, according to Dewey, a constant demand that "the young have to be brought within the traditions, outlook and interests which characterize a community by means of education."[123]

It must be noted that, according to common usage, the term 'community' may not connote the elements Dewey includes in his use of it. For him, however, community necessarily involves communication. communication is sharing interests, that kind of sharing which gives life to the community. This, he declares involves "something which engages the desires and aims of each contributing member."[126] In partaking with others, there is afforded the opportunity of increasing the store of beliefs about reality. But, more significantly, it makes possible the modification, not only of the aims and desires which arise in the course of interchange, but also the individual's ways of behaving. The same can be said of the community as a unit. For, it comprises the organized ways of behavior which the members agreed to live by. Hence, to describe the particular acts of sharing is to describe the ways of living which produce the distinctive character of that certain community in which people live.[127]

Conclusively, Dewey's ideal human situation is life in a democratic community. This conviction is based on the perception that democracy, both as a political arrangement and a way of conjoint living, rests on the faith in human intelligence and trust in the power of pooled and cooperative inquiry and shared values. He is assured that democracy is supported by the belief that each individual has rightful claims and has something to contribute. Although the value of such a contribution can be assessed only as it enters into the final pooled intelligence comprised of the contributions of all. He is confident that it rests on the hope that things, though not complete, will grow and be able to gene-rate progressively the wisdom and virtues needed to guide collec-tive action in the direction of establishing the Great Community.

###

CHAPTER V

CONCLUSION: THE PROSPECT OF A GREAT COMMUNITY

The preceding chapters attempted to show that a careful reconstruction of Dewey's thoughts is capable of yielding a unified and
coherent philosophy. The original stages of development (i. e.,
the phases Dewey himself followed), though not completely mapped
out, were traced closely and faithfully. The sequence flowed
without stalls from the ontological to the physical, to the logical, to the psychological, to the social and, finally, to the
political. The biological framework was adhered to in all areas
of discussion. In metaphysics, it appeared in the category of
transaction - in the description of the universe of reality as
the scene of innumerarable interactions of varying complexities.
In logic, it served as the pattern of inquiry exemplified by
scientific exchange. In psychology, it appeared as the model of
human behavior and is expressed in a theory of individuality set
against the background of the physical and cultural environment.
In politics, it was proposed as the pattern of association and
conjoint activity, demonstrated as the natural or given state
of human existence.

     This chapter will now review some vital points of John
Dewey's thoughts that constitute what has been referred to here
as his theory of community. The process will involve looking
back at significant posts met along the way for the purpose of
gaining a unified whole. A critical stance will be taken not to
destroy what Dewey so laboriously built but to stimulate further
reflection. The intent is, therefore, to continue the growth of
creative intelligence - an aim that Dewey would not only approve
of but pursue himself.

     On the subject of metaphysics, Dewey's approach is a depar-
ture from the traditional inquiry on what constitutes reality
that was initiated by the Pre-Socratics and systematized by Plato
and Aristotle. And, in a world of thought dominated by these two
intellectual giants, a revolutionary scheme that may be called
'process naturalism' cannot but prompt suspicion. Only Alfred
North Whitehead, with his more speculatively developed description of reality as process, could have made heads turn more visibly. But what Dewey lacked in conceptual sophistication, he amply makes up in experiential realism. It is also in this latter
level and not in the former that his forceful response to his
critics may be found. His defense lies in his very objection to
the traditional conception of ontology as ordained to the inquiry of 'being-as-being' or the search for the stable and the
permanent. Such a venture, he believes, is quite futile from the
very start. For, it ignores the brute fact that reality is process or change. To transcend the given order of things by taking
recourse to some supra-natural order of being is, therefore, to
take an illegitimate leap into the realm of the ideal. This constitutes, in his judgment, an instance of what may be called (to

borrow Whitehead's term) the 'fallacy of misplaced concreteness.'

But it must immediately be pointed out that such a closed
form of naturalism is not the necessary outcome of adopting process as the ultimate reality and, hence, as the subject-matter
of metaphysics. Whitehead, pursuing the same non-substantialist
track, breaks through nature's barrier and, in so doing, is able
to philosophize on the nature of God! Perhaps, Dewey suffers
from the same dubious constraint that plagued the British empiricists. Having taken realism to be synonymous with fidelity to
the testimony of empirical apprehensions, the role of reason in
in philosophical reflection has to be unduly minimized.

His critique of tradition is not, however, merely aimed to
replace what he regards as an archaic approach. His primary concern is not to supplant past achievements but to establish an ontology of nature and experience which, because of its realism,
however limited this may be, could be the basis and framework of
humane and practical concerns. In this endeavor, it can easily be
shown, Dewey has succeeded. His metaphysical outlook truly provides a logical ground for a philosophy that articulates (what
he calls) the real 'problems of men' and offers workable solutions, however general these may be. His prescriptions for moral,
educational, social, and political order would be senseless if
not interpreted within the context of naturalism.

Specifically, the categories of unity, continuity, transaction, temporality, and growth describe the human situation
quite vividly and circumscribe the possible extent and limit of
contrived instrumentalities to promote human welfare. These categories are anticipatory of the marks that identify the human community, as can be found in Dewey's later works. The ambivalence,
noted earlier (on pages 72ff.), between individualistic and col-
lectivistic tendencies demonstrates not a doctrinal uncertainty
but an honest effort to capture the real features of the engage-
ment of nature and experience. The observation that individual
organisms are partial but never separate developments within the
universal process of growth and life is arguable and that this
condition expresses the finality of existence is questionable.
But the clarity of Dewey's vision is difficult to ignore. The
term 'community' may have appeared in full vigor with all its
derivable implications only in his later works, but it was an underlying thought even in early reflections - one that would determine the character of his entire philosophy.

The sum-total of the categories illustrates the environment
of the emergent mind. The process involved follows the evolutio-
nistic pattern. Again, this is a point that can be subjected to
endless debate. One salient criticism that deserves to be reviewed here is the charge against Dewey's inability to explain
how the mind, in its exercise of deliberation and choice, transcends mere mechanical selection without being, in essence, outside of nature. To say that humans 'breathe' an air radically
different from that 'inhaled' by lower forms of beings because
the human environment is cultural is to beg the question. For, it

can still be asked, why is it and how did it become cultural?
The evolutionist principle of natural selection reflected in
Dewey's levels of transaction falls short of accounting for how
lower levels advance to a higher plane.

He could have easily adopted any or both of the two usual
mechanistic accounts. One states that nature contains the seed of
life and consciousness. Such a potentiality is inherent in every
element in nature and these properties are revealed as atoms combined into organic molecules of greater and greater complexities.
And it is precisely through the constitution of some appropriate
structures that the elemental particles are able to manifest mental qualities. Another, referred to as 'biogenesis', explains
that at some point in the evolutionary process, a completely new
and unpredicatable quality emerged unexpectedly. But, for Dewey,
these accounts are purely speculative and quite simplistic. The
fact, as he sees it, is given in experience: humans become humans
because of human associations.

But, it must be admitted, Deweys reply to the question of
how a versatile mind is begotten of purely physical materials is,
to say the least, interesting. Its merit needs further consideration. Two important aspects of the same theory deserve review.
The first is the claim that only in transacting with others do
men become human. This, as already stated, is saying that only
in association can distinctively human powers (i. e., the aesthetic, moral, creatively imaginative, emotive, intelllectual capacities) emerge. Such an account (which, incidentally, is also
espoused by other philosophers and psychologists) is a significant postulate. Its influence on the method and content of psychological and social sciences has been far-reaching.

Paradoxically, it is in his insistence on the biological
roots of mind that Dewey is often subjected to barrage. The common charge is, of course, reductionism. This is rather surprising, considering his avowed dissociation from mechanists and
materialists. It is a fact that he does take into account the
differential and purposive qualities exhibited by living beings.
The problem in this instance, however, lies not in what he accepts but in what he fails to accept. While recognizing the presence of differential qualities, he takes them neither as an
aberration of nature or a gift from above. They are to be expected, given the necessary causes and conditions. And all these can
be fully accounted for by the powers in nature.

This is the critical point where he parts company from traditionalists of the Aristotelian and Platonic casts. He is convinced that distinctive human powers are products of natural
transaction, and that is all there is to be said about them. To
go any further is unwarranted, both logically and scientifically.
He cannot find any single justification for the leap to a non-
material source or principle taken by traditionalists to explain
the differential qualities characterizing those powers. He cannot
see the difficulty in admitting that natural agents suffice to
bring them about.

Whether or not Dewey misunderstood the traditional thesis on the nature of mind and the spiritual dimension of man along substantialist lines is difficult to say. What is obvious is that, he was rather swift in his rejection of it. This attitude can be expected considering that the method and perspective of naturalism rules out 'a priori' recourse to any non-natural causes. Thus, his posture can be recognized as an effort to stay consistent with the principles of a closed type of naturalism which he has adopted from the start.

But, it may also have been that, in his estimation, the traditional position dismisses the communal setting of human development which he vigorously advocates. If this were the case, Dewey is mistaken. For, besides the postulate of 'potency' and 'essence,' the educative role of the social environment has always been a part of the official doctrine of the traditionalist camp, though not often explicitly stated to be so. In any event, social stimuli alone are not sufficient, the traditionalists would maintain. For, how can mental quality arise in beings which, from the beginning, are not endowed with the inherent capacity to develop it?

The second significant aspect of Dewey's account of the emergent mind, but which may well be left unquestioned, is the statement on the universality of transaction. Evidently, transaction pervades nature. It appears dramatically in the human order. Humans live in a moving whole called humanity, and each is an interacting part. Such is the inalterable trait of the human condition. Humans, physically dispersed in numerous aggrupations, are divided as to language, race, creed, abilities, economic condition. But diversification does not cut across interconnections. On the contrary, it enriches the substance of communication. (The rise of the north american society is a notable illustration. Its phenomenal growth in almost all aspects of culture can easily be attributed to the wealthy mixture of talents and beliefs of various ethnic groups constituting its citizenry.)

Conclusively, the view that each is so connected with others, that everyone affects (or is affected by) others in some subtle but real way is incontrovertible. Nevertheless, Dewey's account of how that subtle way takes place is what needs further scrutiny. As an epistemological explanation, it is a novel theory; as a psychological claim, it is an unfamiliarstatement. The general conclusion is that mind and all human powers are acquired qualities. The basis of the argument is indicated to be experiential and, at the root, what is given in nature.

The epistemological account is as follows. Speech or verbal communication is always a result of shared experience. this is demonstrated by the fact that speech is in itself (i. e., externally considered) nonsignificant. The term 'meaning' has a referential value. This signifies that they are meanings of and meanings for. They are inherently communal. They are always contextual because they are begotten of culture. When conversants lack a common point of reference, conversation halts. Simply, verbal language can only be communicative (in the sense of transmitting meaning or signification) when there is participation in experience.

Knowledge goes hand in hand with language. For, knowledge occurs only when meanings are absorbed in that system called 'mind.' The implication is provocative. The occurrence of language is simultaneous with the occurrence of knowledge! How can this be when language is acquired and, hence, posterior to thinking! Yet the theory is really not as presumptuous as it appears at a distance. The process of acquiring knowledge (or inquiry) is, he explains, simultaneous with the process of formulating such a knowledge into language. It could be that what is usually taken for language is the articulate verbal expressions learned some years after birth when it could be extended to some subvocal expressions already present as early as the first days of infancy.

The import of the discussion of language and knowledge is not purely academic. Dewey's intent is to establish the extent of social influence and the impact of participation. If participation brings man to the attainment of knowledge, and knowledge elevates man to the level of humanity, then it is through participation that humanity is achieved. Again, the conclusions here reinforces the doctrine that there is a necessary connection between communication and community.

The field of communication is the foundation and the lifeline of community. This can be gathered from the analysis of various orders of human interchange. The first order takes place in the locale of ordinary conversations of day-to-day living. Being the most widespread and accessible, it is an effective medium of education. Dewey regards its role in nurturing the young into the customs and mores of the older generation as indispensable. The second order takes place in the field of scientific study. Being more deliberate and analytic, it provides a more refined and dependable result. Both orders of common inquiry are, however, important in their respective spheres. the former supply guides for practical problems and moral conflicts, the latter makes truth and verification possible.

The last statement is an explicit endorsement of the functional relation between truth and community of men. In fact, for Dewey, the whole import of the term 'truth' is provided by social determination. "To represent things as they are is to represent them in ways that tend to maintain a common understanding... and understanding is a social necessity because it is a prerequisite of all community action,"[1] Dewey declares.

Experience seems to confirm the validity of the preceding thought. Social and political practices in democratic societies such as free press, announcement of governmental programs and activities, participation of citizens through lobbys, unions, and civic organizations in modifying and directing policies and laws have a way of bringing about the greater good for the greater number of people. It seems that dessemination of facts and

154

exchange of views are cathartic. This is, perhaps, why Dewey espouses full publicity of the result of social inquiry. He appears
not to be bothered by the possible conflict between the requirement of full publicity and the necessity of protecting personal
privacy or even national security. In any event, he may think of
cases of this sort to be more in the category of exception than
of general rule.

An important problem connected with the process of social
inquiry is the matter of determining how criteria are to discovered and which criteria are to be adopted and applied. Dewey
proposes that the source of rules governing inquiries in process
and solutions to be preferred is the social context itself. These
rules or criteria represent, according to him, beliefs arrived
at after inquiry and traditions sutained after continued re-evaluation. He does not, however, say what rules were initially used
to establish beliefs and traditions presently regulating conditions. To insist that these (beliefs and traditions) were arrived
at according to previous inquiries is to beg the question. One
could refer to prior beliefs and traditions 'ad infinitum' to
explain away the propriety of any communal solution at any given
time.

Dewey leaves no definitive statement on the subject. On occasions, he maintains that successful consequences of past experiences is a secure rule of action. Yet, he cautions that his is
not a utilitarian position. To illustrate, in discussing the problem of deliberation, he contends that the act is not the calculation of future happenings but the appraisal of present proposed
actions. He means that deliberation will continually be called
upon in new circumstances and, hence, must be readaptive.

Deliberation, he continues to say, results in the conception
of the good as a quality of activity. It is not something to be
quantitatively measured.

> ...good consists in the meaning that is expe-
> rienced to belong to an activity when conflict
> and entanglement of various incompatible impulses
> and habits terminate in a unified orderly release
> in action.[2]

The difficulty is not thereby resolved. He continues to explain
that an action which truly possesses the quality of good is the
outcome of coordination; and its goodness will show in its satisfactory consequences. What these consequence are, he does not
say in precise terms.

The fact is, he would reassert, there are no pre-established
ends in the moral realm. In relation to actions arising from impulse, not even the amount of consequent pleasure should be taken
as the gauge of goodness. In situations that require reflection,
the meanings of the tendencies that are pressing are not actually

known and, hence, can offer no help to choice. It is t
of deliberation to search and experiment in order to
the meanings of conflicting habits and impulses. What
covered are the differences in quality, he advises, not in
ferences in quantity. For, what is at stake is not the issue
quantity but "what kind of person one is to become, what sort of
self is in the making, what kind of person or world is (in the)
making."[3] Again, he does not say precisely what kind of person
or world ought to become.

Admittedly, Dewey's moral theory is more complex than what
can be treated and evaluated here and now. But the point must be
addressed, since it is intimately tied up with the problem of making social and political decisions. Dewey himself would be the
first to admit such a connection. His own critique of other forms
of association is based upon some kind of criteria. For example,
in his appraisal of communism, he points out that he dislikes com-
munists "for their apparent conviction that what they take to be
the end justifies the use of any means if only those means promise to be successful."[4] the content of the text is itself concerned about the problem of justification. It obviously rejects
the utilitarian view.

In few other places, particularly in Experience and Nature,
Democracy and Education, and Human Nature and Conduct, he endorses growth as the first and last criterion of all meaning. The
idea is consistent with the rejection of ultimate end and full
determination. In the absence of more precise articulation, this
criterion seems to be the closest to Dewey's view on what should
regulate social (and individual) endeavors. But, then, growth
carries its own deficiency. As Hart observes, in Dewey's world

> ...nothing reaches full control. For complete con-
> trol is determination, is lack of freedom and there-
> fore Dewey clings to contingency as the source of
> life. The universe must be contingent. The stand-
> point dictates it. Therefore Dewey is forced when
> pointing to intelligence as the only source of cer-
> tainty and to verification as the only source of
> authority, to give certainty and inescapable doubt
> as its eternal partner and to let verification be
> eternally accompanied by further fasification. What
> else can he do.[5]

Growth as a social goal is bothersome in another respect.
What is its precise meaning? Does it apply to the expansion of
intellectual horizon? To the extension of political power? To
the dissemination of a favored set of values (moral or otherwise)? Who or what is going to determine its direction? What
possible justification can be given in electing one direction
over another? What about the growth of a specific culture or
race. Should it be permitted, if not encouraged, to dominate
others in its propulsion for growth?

It is particularly bothersome in the economic field. The thrust toward economic growth propelled by unrestrained free market system is alarming. It has produced, in the same field, the rise of oligopolies and monopolies that have been suffocating the very same spirit that gave them existence. It has created artificial needs and uncontrollable wants. In the process, it has been producing grand-scale pollution. It has already succeeded in disturbing ecological balance; it has rendered extinct a long list of living species and is beginning to exhaust depletable resources. If conservation of natural resources and maintenance of ecological balance are wise measures, how can these be aimed at without controlling the propensity for indefinite growth.

'Growth' may, perhaps, be understood as the development of distinctively human qualities. For, after all, Dewey's instrumentalism is not pragmatism. In it, not everything is means; there are also ends-in view. Work and effort are meant to bring about consummatory experience. Such a level of experience may be what is supposed to be the culmination of growth. Yet, even here, there is no full achievement. Experience does not improve when realized in isolation. It becomes truly consummatory only when shared. And sharing has no boundaries. Growth may, then, mean the indefinite expansion of shared experience, an event that would take place when all people become one great community.

A further difficulty involved in a society that is regulated by its established customs and traditions is how to foster or simply allow room for real novelty and change. The problem is well-articulated in a recent book on the subject of community.

> On the one hand, the idea of a community may suggest exclusivity and conformity. In this sort of community there will likely be a well-established and pervasive set of customs and mores which define both belief and a mode of life. These customs and mores will be enforceable without extensive use of legal coercion although likely, they will be reinforced and mediated by the mechanism of authority. In consequence of the pervasiveness of the mores, the degree of commonality will be high and the bonds of membership strong. But commonality and membership resting on these presuppositions will inevitably militate against the expression, let alone the cultivation, of individuality.[6]

It appears that Dewey's theory can become tenable only if a different source of criteria can be found. These criteria must transcend, and, hence, be independent of, current customs and traditions in such a way that even these can be freely judged through such criteria. It also appears that the only way out of the predicament is to resort to some innate faculty that can intuit the 'good' in the same manner that the Platonic soul is able to discern by recollection the idea of 'the good as such.' But this is incompatible with Dewey's epistemology and cognitive psychology, as was earlier shown. Thus, the difficulty remains.

Yet, it seems not to present itself as a difficulty in Dewey's thinking on the matter. He is emphatic about change and novelty as true ingredients characterizing his community. In fact, these are conceived as the bedrock of freedom and individuality. And this, it may be recalled, is one reason for his insistence on free inquiry. This is supposed to promote change and novelty. But, once again, it may be asked, how can there be free inquiry when social behavior is dominated by customs and traditions? Could it be that any human society, by virtue of its being human, already possesses the native propensity, if not the intuition, for change and that this native propensity is exactly what grows into free expression, which, in turn, inspire novelty?

Dewey rests in his faith in the effective workings of community, however placid this community may be for being controlled by traditional and customary ways. It may, however, not be only faith but also the testimony of experience that as long as there are humans in communication with one another, there will always be an opportunity for new ideas. As long as humans are human, there will also be differences in talents, in desires, in needs. Such differences often grow into conflicting views and interests. And, where there are conflicts, can change and novelty be far behind?

The marvel of human communication is that it takes so many varied forms and occurs in so many levels and situations. Any single form and level is an occasion for expressing differences. Ordinary conversation is a mode of communication where new information is exchanged. Science is a mode of communication that brings about new knowledge and understanding. Politics is a mode of communication where new types of relationships are conceived and instituted. Education is a mode of communication where ideas are transmitted and re-evaluated. All these manifest the liberating power of communication. For Dewey, perhaps the most liberating of all forms and levels of communication is art. It truly promotes freedom and, hence, inspires novelty.

The notion of art leads to the third order of communication which is aesthetics. It is curious that this aspect of his philosophy has not been adequately given prominence. Edman's statement that, for Dewey, art stands as the illustration 'par excellence' of the ultimate meaning of intelligence, moral, democracy, and, ultimately, of the nature of things is an accurate commentary. Art occupies such an important place in Dewey's philosophy because it is such an effective medium of communication. Its contribution to the refinement of culture is paramount. Its value to the growth of commonality (or of the common good) is incalculable. His many statements express his belief that its

social significance, in spite of its long history, has not yet
been fully explored, much less fully understood.

He now shows that aesthetics has no independent and privileged status. The fact is, any experience can be aesthetic. With
this understanding, art becomes universal, not only in the sense
that all expressions can be brought to the level of art, but also
that it is now made accessible to everyone. With this revision,
art can serve both as an object and a medium of sharing. Thus, it
is essential to the establishment and promotion of community.

Dewey's criticism of Kant and sympathy for Schiller are not
meant to be an exercise in dialectic. His rejection of social
dualisms (labor and play, ranks and occupations, laws and customs) is actually a plea for unity, cooperation, and community,
among the various elements in society. The abrogation of the barrier separating means and ends is a move toward overcoming the
alienation that plagues persons employed in labor. It is, unwittingly or not, a fitting response to the Marxist critique that
free enterprise makes proletariats of some people and bourgeoisie
of others as it divides society into a class of workers and a
class of enterpreneurs. In a setting where leisure and work are
not separated, no rigid social stratification can be formed.

What is established here is an essential connection between
art and community. And it is manifested by the fact that art cuts
(or should cut) through social classifications. When recognized,
The industrial men would be released from the feeling that, compared to men of leisure (occupied with entertainment and sports),
they are in bondage. Conversely, artists would be freed from the
guilt that arise from accepting as valid the public injunction
that they are unprodjuctive members of society. Furthermore, as
the people of labor recognize the aesthetic import of their occupation, they would have less envy of people of leisure. By the
same token, as the people of leisure become aware of the limitation of their activities, they would have less pride in exhibiting their indulgences.

Beyond this process of declassification of people in society, art also serves the search for community by compounding past
heritage with present knowledge into a coherent imaginative union.
This is why art could be such an effective medium of communication. And since it is culturally engendered, it is able to transmit the values of the culture in which it is begotten. Thus, art
may be quite depictive of past and actual conditions. But, it is
also revolutionary because it is able to project consequences of
present endeavors.

In a deeper sense, Dewey has brought into clear focus the
ability of art to cause sharing. The successful art, he says, is
that which invokes and evokes common experiences, i. e., those
found in the experiences of a number of persons. The 'common' or
'universal' in art is not something metaphysically prior to all
experiences. Rather, it is the way in which things function in
experience as a bond of union among particular events and scenes

in life. But art does not only recall; it actually causes the presence of common and general factors in conscious experience. For, it is able to bring all men to that higher phase of being which, in Dewey's term constitutes 'consummatory' experience. It is in this sense that he calls aesthetic experience "a record and celebration of the life of a civilization."[7]

But art can only liberate if there is, in fact, a capacity in people to be free. In this respects, Dewey's theory is not wanting. In spite of his refusal to accept a metaphysical realm where 'self' and' will' reside, in spite of the emphasis on human relatedness and the formative role of natural and social environment in the emergence of the 'social individual', he does not leave himself widely open to the charge to the determinism. His concept of preferential behavior provides a metaphysical basis for individuality and allows for a threefold description of freedom as choice, power, and intelligence. Whether or not such a complex conception is thoroughly sound is another question. This is an issue that needs to be settled; but it is such a large one that cannot be fairly treated in this context.

Some passing comments on choice issues on freedom in society may be useful, particularly if the effort is to locate Dewey's position on classical debates. The deliberation on art calls to mind the problem of the role of culture in the development of freedom. From one side, it appears that humans achieved true liberation through culture (and civilization). For, it has changed and uplifted them from the limited capacities of their animal nature to the versatile powers of human artists and artificers. The hunter and the food gatherer cannot be the symbol of freedom in contemporary society. He is, instead, one who has appropriated the skills and talents currently available to move about, obtain goods, and live in ease and comfort. One who does not do so becomes incapacitated and disabled to satisfy neither needs nor wants. As B. Malinowski says, culture is a necessary condition of freedom:

> Culture implies directly and immediately an initial
> installment in freedom. For culture can be defined
> as the artificial, secondary, self-made environ-
> ment which gives man an additional control of cer-
> tain natural forces. It also allows him to adjust
> his own responses in a manner which makes the new
> readaptation by habit and organization more elas-
> tic and efficient thant the adaptation by reflex
> and instinct.[8]

From another side, it seems that culture (and civilization), as it becomes complex and advanced restricts freedom as people get entangled in a network of conditions modern society imposes. It is an encumbrance that covers all facets of life - from the economic to the legal spheres. As Sigmund Freud declares:

The liberty of the individual is not a benefit of
culture. It was greatest before any culture, though
indeed it had little value at that time, because
the individual was hardly in a position to defend
it. Liberty has undergone restrictions through the
evolution of civilization, and justice demands
that these restrictions shall apply to all... Thus
the cry for freedom is directed either against
particular forms or demands of culture or else
against culture itself.[9]

Dewey, of course, can be expected to side with the exponents
of culture. He cannot accept the notion of freedom in the purely
negative sense of 'absence of contraints.' Freedom as power ne-
cesarily involves the assistance of others and the attainment of
quaities proportionate to the demand of actual conditions. In the
first place, to conceive of humans as better of in a primitive
setting is unacceptable. Human development has greatly improved.
Not to take advantage of present resources would foolish pride;
it would be a choice to reverse the course of the evolution toward growth. In the second place, The notion of individuality
outside a cultural context is unrealistic. There never has been
nor will ever be an individual outside the environment of family,
tribe, social associations. And where such an environment exists,
there also will culture be. The cry for freedom, he would proclaim in rebuttal of the enemies of culture, is not against culture itself but for a favored form of culture to take the place
of another.

On another score, it may be recalled that a number of his
critics has brought out some salient problems with Dewey's account of individuality. Horace M. Kallen presents Dewey's theory
as ambivalent in its simultaneous assertion of sociality and individuality.[10] George Santayana describes it as manifesting "a
quasi Hegelian tendency to dissolve the individual into his social functions, as well as everyting substantial or actual into
something relative or transitional."[11] It may, Robert C. Pollock
suggests, give the impression of a balance between individuality
and relation, but it is a doctrine of individuality that nevertheless remains metaphysically inadequate particularly in the
human level.[12]

In all these commentaries, the charge is pointed to the inherent incongruity between sociality and individuality. To abro-
gate the boundary that separates the two realms inevitably result
in an interpretation that would lack necessary sharpness. The account (such as Dewey's) of an individual that arises via causal
sequences and necessary connections cannot be a genuine individual. Levi's observation brings to light the sad psychological
onsequences of such a socially emergent individual. In the absence of a principle of psychic unity (such as one that the substantialist philosophers posit), the only predictable outcome is
fragmented individuals.[13] For, if, in fact, persons have no substantial roots, then they cannot possibly withstand the vicissi-

tudes of either nature or culture. Each person, states George
Geiger of Dewey's account,"is part of a field rather than a
separate entity, and his behavior and finally his mental health
or disease are affected by whatever goes on in the field."[14]

Yet, while granting the applicability of these criticisms,
there is an important angle in Dewey's thoughts on the subject
that may be missed. This angle may, perhaps, be the reason for
his insistence in maintaining a vulnerable conception of the
reality of individuals in society. This pertains to the unhappy
consequence of falling into either one or the other extreme -
social monism, where the faceless individual is absorbed in the
social group, or rigid individualism, where society is prevented
from affecting the insulated and isolated being. Dewey's compromise appears to be the only happy solution. He recognizes
the impact of social forces without denigrating the role of preferential behavior in the emergence of 'social-individuals.'

The application of the theory can only be hinted at here.
The evils of collectivism (political or otherwise) is quite well-
known. At the same time, the disastrous consequence of radical
individualism is equally predictable - chaos or anarchism of one
sort or another. In a pluralistic society such as the U. S.
Dewey's conception is particularly significant. Law and order,
justice and equality appear to be tenable only if individuals
in their differences are also recognized while they are all go-
verned by laws of general applicablity.

But, notwithstanding the problems connected with Dewey's
view on the metaphysics of individuality and sociality (which
will be further explored later), his deliberations on these two
human traits as social phenomena are illuminating. The declaration that free persons are the consequence of free societies cannot be over-emphasized. The truth is, the power of external forces far out-weighs the dynamism of selfhood (in whatever manner
this dynamism may be explained). But this is not only a statement
of fact. In this thought, Dewey shows quite transparently his
concern for the youth. He seens their growth to depend largely
upon what and how impulses are guided in their early transactions
with the older generation. Their maturity hangs on what habits
they form then. Their attainment of the sense of responsibility
is contingent upon the degree of intelligence they receive from
both the formal and informal educative institutions available to
them.

In short, conduct and achievement are, to a great extent
(perhaps, not fully, owing to the contribution of preferential
behavior), socially induced. A criminal just as much as a patriot
is a social phenomenon. Social conditions are, therefore, one of
the necessary objects of consideration in passing judgment in
each case. The counsel to transform objective conditions that
enter into habits so as to rehabilitate criminals or motivate
good citizens is a very healthy prescription. The fact is, objective conditions nurture impulses, shape conduct, and foster freedom.

This last statement explains why Dewey has to revise the concept of freedom. Traditional discussions on the subject have always been confined to the problem of choice. In indicating the necessary connection of choice with power to act and do with intelligence to discover means to ends-in-view, he has advanced the cause of freedom in the manner that must be realized in the social order. In the face of real problems, the important issue, Dewey declares, is not whether one's choices have causes or not but what type of causes determines his choices and what he does with these causes. This implies that choices that do not present themselves as real options hardly count. This is why a fair distribution of power is a required element in the constitution of community. For, if there is going to be sharing, then privileged status must be eliminated!

Intelligence is also an important element in the notion of freedom. For, choice, without enlightened deliberation, is blind; and action, without reasoned foresight of the possible consequences of that action is foolhardy. The connection between education and free community is indicated here. Education, in his sense of the term, does not only mean improving intellectual aptitude. It means, more significantly, breeding free individuals by promoting common concerns and establishing shared values. For, Dewey believes, the most effective form of intelligence and, hence, of freedom is an organized one.

The idea of organization brings to the fore the question on the need for political organization or, to be more precise, the state. The purpose of its existence has already been underscored. Objective freedom cannot be realized without some form of organization. Also, given that the virtues of community are not natural endowments, there is a need for an effective means of directing a variety of tangled human transactions. In so identifying the function of political authority, he is also circumscribing the province of the state, i. e. the public order.

The word 'public' refers to indirect consequences of transactions affecting others not involved in the act. Dewey provides some important clarifications to limits of state authority. His position permits private actions or even transactions to be engaged in without government intrusion. It also implies that it is not the concern of a government to act as the official censor of people's morality. But, in spite of his useful comments, he succeeds neither in marking the precise line that separates public from private domain nor in eliminating the difficulties involved in the distinction. (Cf. above, p. 122ff.)

Such shortcomings should not, however, be permitted to diminish the signicance of his insights so as to be excluded from consideration in discussions concerning the merits of some political theories or public policies. Notable among these are: first, the prescription to operate within the context of firm and clear laws while allowing a certain degree of flexibility depending on need; and second, the proposal that the state provide efficient means to guide, harness, and expand individual

energies. The former is necessary to sustain both stability and
change. the Latter is essential in relieving individuals of the
waste of negative struggle and needless conflict.

But, some question may be raised concerning the first point.
what is meant by clarity with respect to laws. Does it apply to
the articulation so that ambiguity may not be taken as an excuse
for violations? Does it refer to accuracy in the references and
content of laws so that their applications would not be subject
to question and dispute? Whatever may be in Dewey's mind in writing this prescription is vague. It may, perhaps, be taken as an
ideal that must be sought and approximated as much as possible,
though altogether unattainable. This vagueness could be the result of his desire to promote intelligible legal prescriptions and
his inclination to maintain openness with respect to the range
and limits of legal sanctions.

A question may also be raised concerning the second point.
How far should the government intervene either to arrest abuses
or to assist in preventing failure in the private sector, particularly in a free enterprise system? While the aim of sustaining
stability and change is praiseworthy in the abstract, adopting it
as a policy for government action present enormous difficulties.
Who should decide what private interest requires public support?
What rules can be formulated to determine that assistance is directed to or will guarantee the aim of stability or change? For
example, recalling recent events, was the bail-out of the Chrysler
Corporation beneficial to the workings of a free market competi-
tion? Why only Chrysler? What about other car manufacturers or
other businesses? What about the small enterpreneur? Where should
the funding for bail-outs come from? From taxes? From private
banks? From government assets?

At any rate, Dewey's justification for the state, especifi-
cally the democratic state, is based on the idea of what it is
for, logically enough. He is unambiguous about its purpose. It
is and should be an instrument for establishing community. The
democratic state is such an effective instrumentality because
it contains the ingredients indispensable in harmonizing human
liberty and political authority. This harmony is not an end in
itself but is a crucial step toward the formation of a stateless
community.

The democratic state is, therefore, a moral state because
its authority is public authority. The concept 'authority' should
be understood precisely in that 'public' sense. It does not mean
competence. To follow the former is to obey the common will; to
follow the latter is give tribute to eminence. Similarly, it
('authority') should not be confused with the idea of 'leadership.' Leaders can request; authority can require. Leadership
is a mode of influence; authority is a mode of power. The former
does not have the definite sanction that the latter has. Thus,
competence and leadership are personal attributes; the authority
of government is an official function. It is, of course, desirable that competence, leadership and authority coincide. But

when they, do not, authority is not thereby diminished.

The proposition that the bind of authority in a democratic state is not a personal relationship is significant particularly in view of a conception of authority and obedience similar to that held by R. P. Wolff (cited above, p. 131). In his definition, it may be recalled, 'obedience' is doing what a person tells another for no other reason than the fact that he tells it. On that basis, he concludes that such an act is a form of surrendering one's will to another. The anomaly in this view is easy to identify. While it is true that only persons are obeyed (for, authority is an abstraction if not assumed or exercised by a person or persons), they are obeyed not because they are the persons they are but because they are officials, i. e. individuals given authority by the law. In the final analysis, it is the law that is obeyed. It just so happened that it is through some person that the law is expressed or enforced.

The idea of public authority supports the moral principle that every man is a source of claim, and, as a member of the human community, an end in himself. This claim and this value is expressed in a democracy through suffrage. Whether or not casting a ballot is an adequate way of effectively manifesting that claim is beside the point. Dewey insists on both its real and symbolic significance. He does not, however, limit legitimate expression of claims or participation in public affairs to the act of voting. In this connection, what he believes to be the true worth of the democratic process is insightful:

> ...Majority rule is not the heart of democracy,
> but the process by which a given group having a
> specific kind of policies in view becomes a majo-
> rity... It embodies recognition that democracy is
> an educative process; that the act of voting is
> in a democratic regime a culmination of a conti-
> nued process of open and public communication in
> which prejudices have the opportunity to erase
> each other; that continued interchange of facts
> and ideas express what is unsound and discloses
> what may make for human well-being.[15]

But, in the midst of present-day evaluation of the merits of democracy, it is opportune to ask how the concept of democracy as growth is able to function in the context of current technological and ideological revolutions. In the face of the increasing complexity of modern living, is it possible to derive from experience or from the process of inquiry itself the norms of growth and the meaning of the 'good life' (granted that 'growth' is meaningful only if involves some finality)? In the process of economic, industrial, and even political expansion with no clear direction, can man be trusted to create standards by himself, develop and apply the needed controls? These questions are very often raised and are familiar enough to be left as such - questions for further reflections. As has been shown earlier, Dewey does not offer precise and definitive answers to them.

It was suggested earlier (following Marc Belth's interpretation) that Dewey appears to be relying on some adequately formulated ideals connected with the notion of democracy. These ideals are meant to be enduring values which, for that reason, can be regarded as the substantive elements of democracy both as a political system and a way of social living. Indeed, Dewey has vigorously stressed the normative impact of the terms 'freedom,' 'human dignity,' 'sharing,' and 'cooperation,' 'communication,' and 'community.' But how do these values become common? How do these values attain such general acceptance and enduring character?

That he regards them as values that are generally acceptable and are lasting is quite evident by his own admission. But he does not explain why specifically these values and how they become such. He takes for granted that they are such or that he sees human nature to be inherently endowed with the inclination toward the democratic way of associated life. He also advocates the need to educate the young into the values of community. Yet, even here, he does not identify what specific values are to be upheld and, hence, to be imparted to the young.

Belth suggests that communal values come from the collected experiences of the race or the group, given its own unique formation; they serve as soil for further experiences.[16] The practice of living together may then be taken as a means by which they are assimilated in the ways of the group and carried over from generation to generation. The difficulty, however, is that, from all appearances, Dewey regards them as permanent values. But, in what sense permanent? Are they exempted from the process of re-evaluation he prescribes of norms and values in general? This may not be the case, for, otherwise, how can he be extricated from the inconsistency of promoting permanent normative principles while simultaneously prescribing a thoroughgoing experimentalism in all matters of knowledge and belief?

What is reflected in Dewey's deliberation is the ambiguous character of science itself to which he is wholeheartedly committed. Science does follow certain "professional" rules in its operation in dealing with its subject-matter. But no preconceived ends are supposed to be entertained. This is why, in spite of all his praises for democracy, he sponsors no concrete program of social engineering. His entire social philosophy offers no more than general observations on what ails society and what the good life is or should be. As Cork notes:

> Compared to Marx's analysis of capitalistic society and his program for social change, Dewey's remarks on politics appear as generalities, mostly value judgments as to what constitutes the good society.[17]

Turning to another point, it may be suggested that Dewey's
conclusion on the cultural foundations of societies - that all
social forces (including education and art, not only economics
and government) must be comprehensively considered - is sound.
His unswerving trust in the power of organization and cooperation
deserves emulation. His study of the problems of the public is
enlightening. His hope for the establishment of a great community
is sublime. But all these are weighed down by the lack of a well-
defined social program that a constructive social critique and
theory must endeavor to provide, at least, as an illustration
or a validation of applicability and efficiency.

It may be suspected that Dewey's failure in this regard is
not simply a matter of omission. It may be the case that it is
an inevitable result of his experimental method. Or, it may also
be the case that he honestly sees no clearly defined ways of resolving the complex problems of men in society. This is, perhaps,
why he makes the following admission:

> The problem lies deeper; it is in the first ins-
> tance an intellectual problem: the search for the
> conditions under which the Great Society may be-
> come the Great Community. When these conditions
> are brought into being, they will make their own
> form. [18]

But, in the meantime, no concrete proposals can be antecedently
formulated. What those conditions are in positive terms, no one
can tell beforehand. Some negative indications are, however, available. The political structure known as the state will never be
a fixed sovereign. For, it is not an indispensable ingredient of
community. It is "just an instrumentality for promoting and protecting other and more voluntary forms of association, rather
than a supreme end in itself."[19]

Organization itself is not an absolute end but only a means
of promoting association.[20] Association is the end-in-view. And association is but another name for community. Community, in turn,
is essentially democracy. Democracy entails the dispersion of authority to all community members. The more the power of social
control is participated by many, the better will the prevailing
conditions be. These ideas seems to summarize Dewey's convictions.
But many of these convictions may not be realistic. It seems to
reflect a gross over-estimation of men's ability to arrive at
the best choice - best under any human standard, be it progress
or freedom. It fails to take notice of the experience that giving
authority to all does not guarantee the best outcome for all concerned. As a matter of fact, giving equal opportunity to all can
even multiply conflicts! W. H. Sheldon holds this fear:

> We cannot afford to give equal consideration and
> opportunity to all impulses, all motives, all so-

cial experiments. The higher ends must be recognized to be higher, and must be more favored. they
are, in our poor human nature, weaker than the
lower. Fine art cannot compete with best sellers,
nor the philosopher with the inventor.[21]

And when interests do conflict, what interest shall have
authority to settle the dispute? in favor of which interest?
Why? And, granted that human nature is developed only when its
elements take part in directing an utilizing things which are
common (things for which families, industries, governments, chur-
ches, etc. are formed), does this imply that minors are altogether excluded? If not, in what matters and to what extent, for
example, are minors to take part in community councils? What
about the handicapped, the illiterate, the mentally retarded?
Who shall and should speak for them? What about the minority?
How are their interests, concerns, and claims going to be considered especialy in the face of a recalcitrant majority. Questions
of the sort point to some limitations in the democratic process.

On another score, insofar as organizational measures are
concerned, the general patterns that science offers are not an
adequate model for handling problems of social order. Evidently,
before Dewey's program of communal authority can work and the method of science can be implemented, there must intially be formed
a homogeneous society. But, there is a contradiction in his
deliberations here. On the one hand, he advocates homogeneity in
civic virtues while, on the other hand, he foster heterogeneity
of individual contributions to society.

But, is homogeneity (even only in common concerns) really
the goal being pursued? Or, is it truly a desirable goal. If indeed such is (also) Dewey's proposal, it is difficult to recon-
cile with his (other)preference for a heterogeneous community,
one where there exists a variety of interests and claims. Of
course, it may be suggested, sharing could be the link that can
tie them together. But, how can sharing be realized in the midst
of strong differences if not conflicts. Sharing, he says, can
only result if there are values held in common. But, what if
there none or there are so few to serve as an adequate basis for
conjoint activity? Note the circularity. Differences are important for enrichment and novelty. But these positive results can
only be obtained if there are values held in common. How is acceptance of common values to be achieved? By transcending, if not
eliminating differences!

Sharing is both a means and an end. It is an important means
because great accomplishments are achieved through collective effort. It is an end-in-view because it is, in itself, an achievement. But what Dewey ignores in this view is the fact that, however popular the idea may be, it remains to be an assumption that
some may straightforwardly deny. Privacy, for example, is, to
some, just as, if not more, valuable than sharing. Furthermore,
he fails to explain how to determine what ought to be shared and

what ought not and under what rules. Private property, for one,
is an intrinsic element of western democracy and one of the basis
of the free market system. Must this be abandoned in favor of
communal ownership? What about free enterprise, the economics of
a democratic society? Does it lead to sharing? Free enterprise
and capitalism are two aspect of the same system. But capitalism,
by Dewey's own recognition, encourages not the value of sharing
but self-interest, expressed through profit motive, personal advancement, indefinite growth.

He can, of course, say with Adam Smith that the common good
and self-interest are not mutually exclusive opposites. In fact,
it is the belief of the founders of capitalism that self-interest
should be left in its impulsion, even promoted. For, when individuals are left seek to seek their own interests in a free market
system, the inevitable result is public welfare. Yet, he cannot
do so. The concept of community, both as a regulative ideal and
a social goal is antithetical to the notion of competing self-in-
terested individuals. Furthermore, the idea of the "invisible
hand" of competion that animates the free market system runs counter to the concept of 'organized intelligence' which Dewey so
vigorously advocates.

It may also appear that Dewey would favor social or economic
Darwinism - the view that survivors in a competitive situation
are fittest and, hence, the best. The implication is, that those
individuals whose aggressiveness in business, politics, or social
affairs enable them to succeed are to be lauded and emulated.
They are the genuine heirs of the land; they possess those qualities that advances the cause of growth and progress, as proven
by their achievement. But, such is not the case. While it is true
that Dewey would be first to proclaim the influence of Darwin
not only in philosophy but in in science, culture, and civilization, he would not fall victim to the "naturalistic fallacy" committed by those who confuse fact with value, i. e., who take what
happens (naturally) to be what is best. Again, he would reject
the concept of evolution, particularly in the human order, as a
natural event that must be left on its own without human intervention and moral direction.

But, does Dewey have any effective solution the problems of
men in society, even in one enjoying the blessings of a free market system and democratically constituted political organization?
In the face of the aforementioned problems, can it still be insisted upon that democracy is the best alternative way of life or
form of government? These are, of course, rhetorical questions.
His faith in democracy is sustained, even while acknowledging the
difficulties involved in adopting it. What is the source or sources that maintain that faith is an interesting question to pursue. But, whatever the answer may be, part of it would be the
certitude that no better alternative have yet been found. Thus,
he continues to seek find instrumentalities of "democratizing"
individuals in society.

Among others, Dewey has always endorsed education not only

as a means of humanizing men but also as a way of "democratizing" them. He believes that "everything which is distinctively human is learned, not native, even though it could not be learned without native structures which mark man off from other animals."[22] The need for education can hardly be questioned. That it has a social function is similarly incontrovertible. It can be and is employed in directing and controlling societal activities. Yet, it can also be used to achieve non-democratic goals. Communist countries have successfully done so. The opinion that communism runs against the grain of natural human inclinations and that it will eventually fail has to be rethought, given the endurance and expansion of the communist ideology in the world.

Conversely, it is difficult to maintain that there is a native tendency toward the democratic life. Dewey himself would not press the idea too hard, considering that he rejects the very notion of fixed and original impulses. History and current experience show that people at various times and places learn to cherish whatever forms their environment take provided these do not antagonize basic biological and spiritual demands.

As his own writings reveal, Dewey is so passionately dedicated to democracy to the point of presenting it as the only reasonable alternative, if not the only justifiable choice. Visibly, his position is in consonance with his naturalism. But, as an experimental view, it fails to take into consideration the fact that men have been bred to accept various forms of social arrangements without rebellion and, sometimes, even with gratitude because their desires and ideals in life are, if not directly granted, made accessible. Needless to say, the societies in which these arrangements could be found are not necessarily primitive ones. Highly advanced cultures of past and present age in both East and West had existed and continue to exist without demanding the beneficence of democracy, at least not the kind of democracy Dewey sponsors.

For Dewey, however, the good life remains to be in waiting, in a world he calls the Great Community. But what is the real prospect of this vision? He himself provides no guarantee. He has moments of self-assurance as when he declares that the materials for its coming at at hand:

> We have the physical tools of communication as never before, The thoughts and aspirations congruous with them are not communicated, and hence are not common. Without such communication the public will remain shadowy and formless, seeking spasmodically for itself, but seizing and holding its shadow rather than its substance. Till the Great Society is converted into a Great Community, the Public will remain in eclipse. Communication can alone create a great community. Our Babel is not one of tongues but of the signs and symbols without which shared experience is impossible.[23]

More ardently, he exclaims:

> When the machine age has thus perfected its machi-
> nery it will be a means of life and not its des-
> potic master. Democracy will come on its own, for
> democracy is a name for a life of full and en-
> riching communion. It had its seer in Walt Whitman.
> It will have its consummation when free social
> inquiry is indissolubly wedded to the art of full
> and moving communication.[24]

But, he also has moments of misgiving:

> The will be no attempt to state how the required
> conditions might come into existence, nor to pro-
> phesy that they will occur. The object of the
> analysis will be to show that unless ascertained
> specifications are realized, the community cannot
> be organized as democratically effective public.
> It is not claimed that the conditions which will
> be noted will suffice, but only that at least they
> are indispensable.[25]

And, at some point, as if possessed by a gush of pessimism, he
declares that, perhaps, there will never be a Great Community!

His fear is that great modern societies of machines and
mechanically related men are incapable of recovering those 'lost
individuals.' This may have been the reason that compelled him,
at one critical point, to propose a return to the vitality and
depth of close and direct intercourse.[26] The conditions of association, he says, will have their final actuality in face-to-face
relationships by way of direct give and take. The reason is clear,
"...intelligence is dormant and its communications are broken,
inarticulate and faint until it possesses the local community
as its medium."[27]

A likely interpretation of this text is to consider the call
to return to local community as an invitation to establish a de-
centralized form of federated system of communities similar to
the Jeffersonian wards. This may very well be Dewey's intent,
since he does not regard modernization as inherently incompatible
with the moral values and social relationships of earlier generations. But, even understood in this manner, there is still left
the problem of tying togethether the various communities within
the federation. That this must be accomplished is obvious enough.
For, otherwise, each would fall way from the rest. How this tying
up can be achieved is an issue with no immediate solution. Dewey
himself offers none.

It is rather ironic that all the discourses on progress and

growth have to be silenced by a quiet plea to return to the simple and stable life of past and archaic associations. And what
remains of the ·hope for a Great Community? It now only appears
even less than a promise of the future. But, for Dewey, in more
hopeful times, it continues to be an ideal, one which moves his
world of process, as the Prime Mover(s) moved Aristotle's universe of substances not by efficiency but by attraction. Fit-
tingly, it stands as the culmination of his personal aspiration
for mankind. Unwittingly or not, he is projecting the object of
his natural piety which all along has been implicit in his works.

Dewey gives no warning that he is making a deliberate effort
to formulate a foundation to, or a full-pledged philosophy of religion. But positive indications are present that he is doing so.
It cannot be the case that he is introducing a distinctly or qua-
litatively higher form of experience (of the kind found in theis-
tic religions). In a philosophy that rejects transcendental or
surpernatural realm from the outset, no speculation of the kind
can be expected. Likewise, in a theory of experience that permits
no discontinuity, there no room for a separate seat of intellectual authority. Natural piety or religious attitude is a form of
natural experience in the same manner that an aesthetic one is.
Very likely, its distinctiveness lies in its intensity.

Descriptively, Dewey points to this experience as a sense
of harmony with and joyful wonderment at the mystery of the universe. It involves a basic change in one's relation to his entire
world, for it brings out a sense of wholeness and outward thrust.
In effect, it is a unification of the self with the totality of
conections he is engaged in. Faith has a meaning in this context.
It signifies "the unification of the self through allegiance to
inclusive ideal ends, which imagination presents us and to which
the human will responds as worthy of controlling our desires and
choices."[28] The ideals mentioned are chosen by men because of
their worthiness in guiding life. They are not real, but they
motivate and propel action.

The active relation between the ideal and the actual can be
interpreted as Dewey's meaning for the term 'god.' He speaks of
it as the unity of all ideal ends that stand related to all men
in spirit. Easily can this idea of 'god' be identified with the
concept of the Great Community! This is, by no means, a forced
reading. His entire philosophy requires it for completion. Also,
this is not an unfamiliar move in philosophy. Immanuel Kant has
already introduced it in the form of a regulative ideal. Thus,
in parallelism, just as much as God stands in Kantian theodicy
as that regulative ideal of practical reason, so also the Great
Community poses as the regulative ideal of all human experience
and action in Dewey's natural piety. Such a piety is fully expressed in communal living.

Knowing that one lives as part of a chain that extends to
the past and conects with nature, the thing to prize come about
by the grace of the doings and sufferings of the human community
in which he is a link. Therefore,

Ours is the responsibility of conserving, transmitting, rectifying, and expanding the heritage
of values we have received that those who come
after us may receive it more solid and secure,
more widely accessible and more generously shared
than we have received it. Here lies all the elements for a religious faith that shall not be confined to sect, class, or race. Such a faith has
always been implicitly the common faith of mankind. It remains to make it explicit and militant.[29]

Here, the cycle of Dewey's philosophical exploration reaches
closure. It starts in the datum of natural harmony man experiences with his environment - a condition that proves to be too vulnerable and precarious to be a situation of comfort. It ends in
the sense of wholeness with the world - a possibility that still
remains elusive and contingent. The reason is, (he tells us) it
rests in the hope for a common faith, but one, (he does not tell
us) that will never be, because it lacks the principle of unity
which only a real transcendent God can provide. There were attempts to bypass such a 'cul-de-sac,' suggesting that Dewey's
notion of community is open to transcendental reality. This is
a reasonable, if not altogether a promising counsel. For, this
could very well "provide a starting point for anyone who would
wish to extend further his insights."[30] Admittedly, an extension
(of some sort) to his 'biological pragmatism' or 'social instrumentalism' (whatever may be a more fitting name for his philosophical system) is called for, if merely to continue the "conversation" Dewey started and Rorty wishes to continue. Unfortunately,
Dewey himself did not express his preference. Quite likely, however, he would not find the idea of 'transcendence' compatible
with his impregnably closed naturalism.

###

EPILOGUE

John Dewey's thought has been presented in this essay as a systematic philosophy. The texts themselves and the reconstructive works of many of his notable commentators validate this interpretation. This is not, of course, saying that the set of arguments which led to the conclusion arrived at here are irrefutable. This is as subject to evaluation as any other readings; it can be accepted or rejected.   If accepted, the task of reading his works would now become less tedious, especially for the novice. If rejected, the burden of presenting a counterproof would then belong to the opposition. And if, in the final analysis, the weight of evidences does incline in that direction, then, so be it. Let this honest attempt be counted as a good effort in promoting Deweyan scholarship. Such an eventuality will not, however, be a happy occasion. For, if his works would have to be differently proposed (e. g., as random musings or unorganized comments or 'conversations),' the loss to the American intellectual heritage will be incalculable.

Among the few outstanding candidates, only Dewey, Peirce, and, James are eligible to truly represent what may be called "American Philosophy," as a distinctive school of thought in Western tradition, set apart from the British Empiricism, Linguistic Analysis, Existentialism, Phenomenology, Scholasticism, and the like. The title "School of Pragmatism" is also acceptable, provided the differences in their respective versions of it are adequately considered. The problem with the concept 'pragmatism' is not only, however, the variety of meanings it holds for each of its exponents. It has, likewise, been the object of abuse in the past by unsympathetic and superficial critics and teachers of philosophy who nonchalantly identify it with 'utilitarianism.' The fact is, Dewey is not a utilitarian in the sense that Jeremy Bentham is, just as he is not a pragmatist in the sense that William James is.

Yet, there are some common and identifiable threads linking Dewey to James and Dewey to Peirce. These, it may be suggested, justify presenting them as a 'school,' in the same manner that the others mentioned are. There is also something 'culturally' common among all three which cannot be found in others, even in thinkers of 'pragmatic' inclination. There are some things in all of them, though dominantly in Dewey, that are derived from, and are reflective of, the american intellectual and social landscapes - the environment and, oftentimes, the subject-matter of his commentaries, such as the conceptions of 'participatory democracy,' 'value as consequence,' 'experimental' and 'experiential,' the use of scientific paradigms (biologism and psychologism), the concern for knowledge, education, economics, and culture.

That there should be an identification and recognition of American philosophy is important (not to suggest that it be invented, but that it be discovered). It is important because North America (spefically the United States) is a social, political, economic and cultural phenomenon. How it became such, from an historical perspective, is an interesting object of study for americans and non-americans alike. How it emerged, grew, and was kept alive from its ideological beginning is an even more intriguing consideration. Understanding the ideas that gave birth to its laws and institutions and how these have guided the lives and relations of a diverse group of people is significant both in itself and for the lessons that can be drawn therefrom. And for this end, the primary sources cannot be any other than its founding fathers and its philosophers.

For the continuance (if not necessarily the growth) of philosophy, it is also important that American philosophy, once discovered, be promoted. The critical exchanges in either negative or positive directions among different schools of thought have kept philosophy alive through the centuries; these have also proved cathartic and salutary. In the same manner, serious consideration of the challenge Dewey puts on traditional philosophy will prove particularly rewarding, because his is, perhaps, one of the most confrontational. His polemics strike at the very roots of traditional philosophy, e. g., its assumption of a substance metaphysics, the logic of transecendentalism, the validity of dualism, etc.

But there is another harvest to be reaped in discovering American philosophy, one that is greater than the aim of sustaining philosophical discussion. Of all the philosophical systems in the West, the works of Dewey, James, and Whitehead (and, perhaps, Bergson) come closest to providing a language that could bridge the communication gap separating Western from Eastern thought. Western mainstream (mainly Hellenic and Anglo-European) philosophy has traditionally maintained a substantialist metaphysics in which 'things' rather than 'events' inhabit reality. The so-called 'process philosophers' (in which the above mentioned names are the most prominent), in adopting 'events' rather than 'things' as their ontological unit, approximate the philosophical setting of Eastern writers, thereby making conversation between the two traditions possible.

The return of an investment in comparative study of the Eastern and Western sources is equally handsome. Such a study will prove profitable not only in gaining exposure to unfamiliar categories and modes of thought and language but also in discovering conceptual and linguistic affinities through which previously locally conceived but elusive notions may become comprehensible. For example, a revisit of Dewey's **Experience and Nature** after exposure to Confucius' **Analects** may ease the discomfort of relating to Dewey's effort of reconciling contrasting (sometimes opposing) terms such as, 'organism' and 'environment,' 'individual' and 'social,' 'public' and 'private,' 'freedom' and 'authority,' etc.

This outcome may be expected because of a number of important paralellisms in the two thinkers. Both Dewey and Confucius support an immanental cosmos, i. e., one which precludes any transcendent reality (cause, principle or being) - an organic

system within which the principles of order and value are themselves dependent on the contexts to which they apply. Both explain occurences not as the scene of fixed causes and necessary
effects but of events and relations in specific contexts, where
acts are as much consequences as they are agents. Both depict
disjunctions not in terms of dualistic opposition but of pola-
rity, expressing both significant and symmetrical relations.
Both live in a world where evey element is symbiotically related,
i. e., relative to and correlative with everything and every
other. Both sees the cosmos as a self-creating community.

The achievement of philosophical communication between East
and West will, indubitably, be one of the most celebrated events
in the history of human culture.

###

NOTES

Chapter I

1. "Unity of Science as a Social Problem," **International Ency-clopedia of Unified Science**, vol. 1 (Chicago: Univeristy of Chicago Press, 1939), p. 32.

2. John Dewey, **Experience and Nature** (New York: Dover Publications, Inc., 1958), p. 413.

3. Ibid.

4. Arthur E. Murphy, "Dewey's Epistemology and Metaphysics," in **The Philosophy of John Dewey**, ed. P. A. Schilpp (New York: Tudor Publishing Co., 1951), p. 217.

5. John E. Smith, "John Dewey: Philosopher of Experience," in **John Dewey and the Experimental Spirit in Philosophy**, ed. Charles W. Hendel (New York: The Liberal Arts Press, 1959), p. 108.

6. John Dewey, **The Influence of Darwin on Philosophy** (New York: Peter Smith, 1951), p. 1.

7. Smith, "John Dewey: Philosopher of Experience," p. 97.

8. John Dewey, "The Subject Matter of Metaphysical Inquiry," in **On Experience, Nature, and Freedom**, ed. Richard J. Bernstein (New York: The Bobbs-Merrill Co., Inc., 1960), p. 220.

9. Ibid., p. 221.

10. Ernest Nagel, **Logic Without Metaphysics** (Glencoe, Ill.:   Free Press, 1956), p. 6.

11. Sidney Hook, **The Metaphysics of Pragmatism** (Chicago, London: The Open Court Company, 1927), p. 106.

12. Cf. ibid., p. 107, for a useful illustration of this point.

13. Ibid., p. 108.

14. Ibid., pp. 108-109.

15. See ibid., p. 111 where Hook explains the importance of 'interest.' For one thing, he says: "In opposition to both of the conflicting views, interest is given its place as the differentiating mark of a specific organization so that the problem of bias and selection can no longer be dismissed as a piece of psychological impertinence." Its role in Dewey scheme of thought will be shown in Chapter IV.

16. See Lewis E. Hahn's footnote no. 69, in "Dewey's Philosophy

178

and Philosophic Method," in Guide to the Works of John Dewey, ed. Jo Ann Boydston (Carbondale and Edwardsville: Southern Illinois University, 1970), p. 40 for various studies made on Dewey's categories.

17. Ibid., p. 43.

18. The term 'deduction' is used here according to Hook's first suggested meaning. Cf. The Metaphysics of Pragmatism, p. 118.

19. John Dewey, Philosophy and Civilization (New York: Minton, Balch and Co., 1931), pp. 77-78.

20. Dewey, Experience and Nature, p. 159.

21. John Dewey, Logic: The Theory of Inquiry (New York: Henry Holt and Co., 1938), p. 388.

22. Dewey, "The Subject Matter of Metaphysical Inquiry," p. 221.

23. Ibid.

24. "The Development of American Pragmatism" in Studies in the Histories of Ideas by the Department of Philosophy of Columbia University, vol. II (New York: Columbia University Press, 1925), Supplement, p. 366.

25. John Dewey, Characters and Events, Essays in Social and Political Philosophy, ed. J. Ratner (London: George Allen and Unwin, Ltd., 1929), vol. II, p. 463.

26. John Dewey, The Quest for Certainty, A Study of the Relation of Knowledge and Action (New York: G. P. Putnam's Sons, Capricorn Books, 1960), p. 37.

27. John Dewey, Experience and Education (New York: Colier Books, 1963), p. 42.

28. Dewey, The Quest for Certainty, p. 224.

29. Dewey, Experience and Education, p. 27.

30. Dewey, Experience and Nature, p. 111. Note the striking similarity with Whitehead's notion of 'objective immortality'; Cf. Process and Reality, An Essay in Cosmology (New York: The Free Press, 1969), p. viii.

31. Hahn, "Dewey's Philosophy and Philosophic Method," p. 44.

32. Dewey, On Experience, Nature, and Freedom, p. 244.

33. Dewey, Essays in Experimental Logic (New York: Dover Publications, 1916), p. 87.

34. John Dewey, Human Nature and Conduct, An Introduction to

179

Social Psychology (New York: The Modern Library, 1930), p. 186. See also, Dewey, Philosophy and Civilization, p. 82.

35. Dewey, Philosophy and Civilization, p. 81, where these continuities are enumerated. Here, the category of continuity is explicitly described as hypothesis. A hypothesis is then defined as that which cannot be denied without a contradiction.

36. Dewey, "The Subject Matter of Metaphysical Inquiry," p. 227.

37. Dewey, Experience and Nature, pp. 253-254.

38. Hendrik Hart, Communal Certainty and Authoritative Truth (Amsterdam: Swet and Zeitlinger, 1966), p. 16.

39. John Dewey and Arthur F. Bentley, A Philosophical Correspondence, 1932-1951, ed. J. Ratner and J. Altman (New Brunswick: Rutgers University Press, 1964), p. 595.

40. John Dewey, Philosophy of Education (Problems of Men) (New Jersey: Littlefield, Adams and Co., 1958), p. 309.

41. John Dewey, "Evolution and Ethics," Monist VIII (April 1898): 329.

42. John Dewey, Freedom and Culture (New York: Capricorn Books, 1963), p. 21.

43. John Dewey, Democracy and Education, An Introduction to the Philosophy of Education (New York: The Free Press, 1966), p. 2.

44. Dewey, Experience and Nature, p. 245.

45. Albert William Levi, Philosophy and the Modern World (Bloomington: Indiana University Press, 1959), p. 503.

46. Dewey and Bentley, A Philosophical Correspondence, pp. 56, 201, 385, 489, 495, 545. See Bernstein's interpretation in On Experience, Nature, and Freedom, p. xxiv.

47. Dewey, Philosophy and Civilization, p. 77.

48. A phrase borrowed from Whitehead; it is the exact counterpart of Dewey's own "fallacy of selective emphasis." Cf. Dewey, Experience and Nature, p. 27.

49. John Dewey, Intelligence in the Modern World: John Dewey's Philosophy, ed. J. Ratner (New York: The Modern Library, 1939), p. 177.

50. The important social consequences of these two views of action is shown by Bernstein in John Dewey (New York: Washington Square Press, Inc., 1967), pp. 81-82.

51. Dewey, Philosophy and Civilization, p. 221.

52. Dewey, Experience and Nature, p. 259.

53. Dewey, Intelligence in the Modern World, p. 150.

54. Sterling P. Lamprecht, The Metaphysics of Naturalism (New York: Appleton-Century-Crofts, 1967), p. 12.

55. Dewey, "The Subject Matter of Metaphysical Inquiry," p. xlv.

56. Dewey, Philosophy and Civilization, p. 79.

57. John Dewey, "Context and Thought," in On Experience, Nature, and Freedom, ed. Richard J. Bernstein (New York: The Bobbs-Merrill Co., Inc., 1960), p. 101.

58. John Dewey, "Philosophies of Freedom," in On Experience, Nature, and Freedom, ed. Richard J. Bernstein (New York: Bobbs-Merrill Co., Inc., 1960), p. 265.

59. Dewey, Experience and Nature, p. 252.

60. Keith Campbell, Body and Mind (New York: Doubleday and Co., Anchor Books, 1970), p. 2.

61. Dewey, Philosophy and Civilization, pp. 301-302. See also, Dewey, Experience and Nature, p. 251.

62. Campbell, Body and Mind, p. 1.

63. Dewey, Experience and Nature, p. 252.

64. Ibid.

65. See below for the role of art in eradicating this artificial separation of classes.

66. See Sidney Hook, John Dewey, An Intellectual Portrait (New York: The John Day Co. 1939), p. 110 who brought up the same linguistic problem that Dewey complains about.

67. Dewey, Philosophy and Civilization, p. 302.

68. Ibid. This point is developed at length in Experience and Nature, p. 261.

69. These primary qualities are similar to John Locke's tertiary qualities.

70. Dewey, Experience and Nature, p. 9.

71. Ibid., pp. 10-11; 262-263.

72. Dewey, Intelligence in the Modern World, p. 826.

73. Dewey, **Experience and Nature**, p. 277.

74. Ibid., p. 273.

75. Dewey, **Philosophy and Civilization**, p. 78.

76. Ibid., p. 85.

77. Dewey, **Experience and Nature**, p. 253.

78. Ibid., p. 266.

79. Dewey, **Philosophy and Civilization**, p. 310.

80. Ibid., p. 311.

81. Dewey, **Experience and Nature**, p. 253.

82. Ibid., p. 254.

83. Ibid., p. 255.

84. Ibid., p. 258-259.

85. Ibid., pp. 259-260.

###

NOTES

Chapter II

1. Dewey, Experience and Nature, pp. 204-205.

2. Ibid., p. 169.

3. Ibid., p. 290.

4. In Dewey, Intelligence and the Modern World, p. 809.

5. Dewey, Experience and Nature, p. 276.

6. Paul D. Wienpahl, "Dewey's Theory of Language and Meaning," in John Dewey: Philosopher of Science and Freedom, ed. Sidney Hook (New York: The Dial Press, 1950), p. 278.

7. Levi, Philosophy and the Modern World, p. 302.

8. Dewey, Intellligence in the Modern World, p. 810.

9. Dewey, Experience and Nature, 170.

10. Ibid.

11. Levi, Philosophy and the Modern World, p. 301.

12. Saturday Review, 18 April 1967, p. 36.

13. Dewey, Experience and Nature, p. 184.

14. Ibid., p. 171.

15. Ibid., p. 185 (underlining mine).

16. John Dewey, "Meaning and Existence," [a reply to Everett W. Hall, "Some Meanings of Meaning in Dewey's Experience and Nature,", Journal of Philosophy XXV (March 29, 1928): 169-181], Journal of Philosophy XXV (June 21, 1928): 347.

17. Ibid.

18. Ibid., p. 348.

19. Dewey, Experience and Nature, pp. 169-178.

20. Ibid., p. 280.

21. Ibid.

22. Ibid., pp. 178, 185.

23. Ibid., p. 205.

24. Ibid., 174.

25. See Charles Tesconi, Jr., "Dewey's Theory of Meaning," Educational Theory 19 (Spring 1969): 169.

26. Dewey, Experience and Nature, p. 190.

27. Emmanuel G. Mesthene, How Language Makes Us Know (The Hague: Martinus Nijhoff, 1964), p. 59.

28. Dewey, Logic: The Theory of Inquiry, p. 401.

29. Ibid., p. 104.

30. Ibid., p. 105.

31. Donald A. Piatt, "Dewey's Logical Theory," in The Philosophy of John Dewey, ed. Paul A. Schilpp (New York: Tudor Publishing Co., 1951), p. 122.

32. Dewey, Experience and Nature, p. 169.

33. Gerald Steibel, "The Belief in Communication," Antioch Review XV (September 1955): 290.

34. Dewey, Intelligence in the Modern World, p. 386.

35. Ibid., p. 808.

36. Piatt, "Dewey's Logical Theory," p. 122.

37. Dewey, Intelligence in the Modern World, pp. 388-389.

38. Ibid., p. 389.

39. Ibid. In Democracy and Education, p. 15, Dewey refers to language as the chief instrument in learning.

40. John L. Childs, "The Educational Philosophy of John Dewey," in The Philosophy of John Dewey, ed. Paul A. Schilpp (New York: Tudor Publishing Co., 1951), p. 437.

41. John Dewey, "Anti-Naturalism in Extremis," in Naturalism and the Human Spirit, ed. Y. H. Krikorian (New York: Columbia University Press, 1944), p. 3.

42. Dewey, Experience and Nature, p. 36.

43. Dewey, Freedom and Culture, p. 102.

44. Ibid., p. 345.

45. Bertrand Russell, "Dewey's New Logic," in The Philosophy of John Dewey, ed. Paul A. Schilpp (New York: Tudor Publishing Co., 1951), p. 144.

46. Lowell Nissen, John Dewey's Theory of Inquiry and Truth (The

Hague, Paris: Mouton and Co., 1966), p. 90.

47. Russell, "Dewey's New Logic," p. 145. Nissen suggests it to be a geometrical asymptote. Cf. ibid., p. 93.

48. Dewey, Logic, p. 345.

49. John Dewey, "On Experience, Knowledge and Value," in The Philosophy of John Dewey, ed. Paul A. Schilpp (New York: Tudor Publishing Co., 1951), p. 573.

50. Ibid., p. 571.

51. Felix Kaufmann, " John Dewey's Theory of Inquiry," in John Dewey: Philosopher of Science and Freedom, ed. Sidney Hook (New York: The Dial Press, 1950), p. 229.

52. Dewey, "On Experience, Knowledge and Value," p. 573.

53. Dewey, Logic: The Theory of Inquiry, p. 532.

54. Ibid.

55. Ibid., pp. 118-119.

56. Russell, "Dewey's New Logic," p. 148.

57. Dewey, "On Experience, Knowledge and Value," p. 572.

58. Ibid., p. 591.

59. John Dewey, "The Problem of Truth," (I. "Why is Truth a Problem?"), Old Penn, Weekly Review of the University of Pennsylvania IX (February 11, 1911): 523.

60. John Dewey, Reconstruction in Philosophy (Boston: The Beacon Press, 1957), p. 205.

61. Dewey, Democracy and Education, p. 186.

62. Dewey, "The Problem of Truth," p. 524.

63. Richard Bernstein, "Knowledge, Value, and Freedom," in John Dewey and the Experimental Spirit in Philosophy, ed. Charles W. Hendel (New York: The Liberal Arts Press, 1959), p. 68.

64. Charles S. Peirce, Values in a Universe of Chance: Selected Writing of Charles S. Peirce (Garden City, New York: Doubleday and Company, Inc., 1958), p. 69.

65. Levi, Philosophy and the Modern World, p. 311.

66. Ibid., p. 313.

67. John Dewey, "The Objects of Valuation," Journal of Philosophy

186

XV (May 9, 1918): 257.

68. Levi, Philosophy and the Modern World, p. 308.

69. John Dewey, "The Logic of Judgments of Practice," in Essays in Experimental Logic (Chicago: University of Chicago Press, 1916), p. 368.

70. Bernstein, "Knowledge, Value and Freedom," p. 75.

71. John Dewey, "Theory of Valuation," International Encyclopedia of Unified Science, vol. II, No. 4 (Chicago: The University of Chicago Press, 1962), pp. 58-59.

72. Ibid. p. 60.

73. Levi, Philosophy and the Modern World, p. 308.

74. Vincent C. Punzo, Reflective Naturalism (New York: The Macmillan Co., 1971), p. 175.

75. Bernstein, "Knowledge, Value, and Freedom," p. 78.

76. Dewey, Experience and Nature, p. xv.

77. Irwin Edman, "Dewey and Art," John Dewey: Philosopher of Science and Freedom, ed. Sidney Hook (New York: The Dial Press, 1950), p. 48.

78. See, for instance, Chapter IX of Experience and Nature where Dewey shows the merging of philosophy and art.

79. John Dewey, Arts as Experience (New York: Minton, Balch and Co., 1934), p. 40.

80. Dewey, Experience and Nature, pp. 373-374.

81. Ibid.

82. Dewey, Art as Experience, p. 279.

83. Ibid., pp. 279-280.

84. Ibid., p. 281.

85. Ibid.

86. J. C. Friedrich Schiller, On the Aesthetic Education of Man, in a Series of Letters, trans. and ed. E. M. Wilkinson and L. A. Willougby (Oxford: Clarendon Press, 1967), Sixth Letter, p. 35.

87. Dewey, Experience and Nature, p. 367.

88. Ibid., p. 358.

---

89. Ibid.

90. Dewey, Art as Experience, p. 5.

91. Horace M. Kallen, Art and Freedom, vol. II (New York: Duell, Sloan and Pearce, 1942), p. 910.

92. Dewey, Experience and Nature, pp. 365, 381-382.

93. Ibid., p. xv.

94. Kallen, Art and Freedom, pp. 914-915.

95. Cited in Kallen, Art and Freedom, p. 915.

96. Dewey, Art as Experience, p. 292.

97. Terence W. Stace, The Philosophy of Hegel, A Systematic Exposition (New York: Dover Publications, 1955), pp. 448-449.

98. Dewey, Experience and Nature, p. 379.

99. Ibid., p. 378.

100. Dewey, Art as Experience, p. 289.

101. Edman, "Dewey and Art," p. 53.

102. Kallen, Art and Freedom, p. 914.

103. Henry William Beechley, The Literary Works of Sir Joshua Reynolds, II (London: Henry G. Bohn, 1852), pp. 257, 300.

104. Dewey, Art as Experience, p. 326.

105. Edman, "Dewey and Art," p. 65.

106. Kallen, Art and Freedom, p. 915.

107. Ibid., p. 916.

###

Chapter III

1. Horace M. Kallen, "Individuality, Individualism, and John Dewey," Antioch Review XIX (1959): 299.

2. George Santayana, "Dewey's Naturalistic Metaphysics," The Philosophy of John Dewey, ed. P. A. Schilpp (New York: Tudor Publishing Co., 1951), p. 247.

3. Dewey, Experience and Nature, p. 291.

4. Ibid.

5. Dewey, Democracy and Education, p. 17.

6. Levi, Philosophy and the Modern World, p. 303.

7. John Dewey, Reconstruction in Philosophy (Boston: Beacon Press, 1967), p. 194.

8. The term "social-individuals" is not in Dewey's lexicon. But the present writer believes it best expresses Dewey's thought on the issue of transactional individuality and human freedom.

9. John Dewey, "Philosophies of Freedom," in Freedom in the Modern World, ed. Horace M. Kallen (New York: Coward- McCann, 1928.

10. Dewey, "Context and Thought," p. 91.

11. Dewey, "Philosophies of Freedom," in On Experience, Nature and Freedom, p. 265. In Experience and Nature, he describes the situation more elaborately: "Personal individuality has its bases and conditions in simpler events. Plants and non-human animals act as if they were concerned that their activity, their characteristic receptivity and response, should maintain itself. Even atoms and molecules show a selective bias in their indifferences, affinities, and repulsions when exposed to other events. With respect to some things they are hungry to the point of greediness; in the presence of others they are sluggish and cold." P. 208.

12. Dewey, Experience and Nature, p. 208.

13. Ibid., p. 256.

14. Ibid., p. 257.

15. Ibid., p. 258.

16. Dewey, "Context and Thought," p. 101.

190

17. Ibid. p. 299.

18. Ibid. p. 239.

19. John Dewey, Individualism Old and New (New York: Minton, Balch and Co., 1930), p. 168.

20. Dewey, Freedom and Culture, p. 33.

21. John Dewey, "The Crisis in Human History," Commentary I (March 1946): 2.

22. For Dewey, the realistic socio-political questions are a) how individuals come to be connected in just the ways which give human communities traits so different from any other inferior assemblies, say of trees, of electrons, and the like; b) how to adjust groups and individuals to one another. These are precisely the issues that he takes up in both his social and psychological works as will be shown in the following chapters.

23. Dewey, Public and Its Problems, p. 188.

24. Dewey, Experience and Nature, p. 242.

25. Dewey, Democracy and Education, p. 53.

26. Dewey, Human Nature and Conduct, p. 137.

27. Dewey, Experience and Nature, pp. 242-243.

28. Dewey, Democracy and Education, p. 52.

29. Dewey, Intelligence in the Modern World, p. 824.

30. John Dewey, Creative Intelligence: Essays in the Pragmatic Attitude (New York: Henry Holt and Co., 1917), p. 59.

31. Dewey, Experience and Nature, p. 172.

32. Ibid., p. 244.

33. John Dewey, A Common Faith (New Haven: Yale University Press, 1934), p. 19. This point will again be taken up in the last chapter in connection with the conception of the "Great Community".

34. Dewey, Individualism Old and New, p. 65.

35. See page 268.

36. Dewey, Human Nature and Conduct, p. 10.

37. Ibid., p. 15; also pp. 70-71.

38. Ibid., p. 41.

39. Ibid., p. 30.

40. Ibid.

41. John Dewey and James H. Tufts, **Ethics** (New York: Holt, Rinehart and Winston, 1961), p. 378.

42. Ibid., p. 66.

43. Ibid., p. 21.

44. Ibid., p. 87.

45. Ibid., p. 128.

46. Dewey, **Problems of Men**, p. 82. See also p. 72. A similar idea is endorsed in **Democracy and Education**. The purpose of teaching science is precisely to liberate minds and open new avenues: "the function which science has to perform in the curriculum is that which it has performed for the race: emancipation from local and temporary incidents of experience, and the opening of intellectual vistas obscured by the accidents of personal habit and predilection," (pp. 269-270).

47. Ibid., p. 113.

48. Dewey, **Public and Its Problems**, p. 10.

49. Ibid., p. 132.

50. See Dewey, **Democracy and Education**, p. 13.

51. Dewey, **Democracy and Education**, p. 13.

52. Ibid., p. 14.

53. Ibid., p. 16. In **Philosophy and Civilization**, pp. 175-176, Dewey shows that mind is at least an organ of service for the control of environment in relation to the ends of the life process. The formation of desires and habits are controlled by the role an individual plays in society, i. e., by his occupation. For occupations determine the chief modes of satisfaction, the standards of success and failure. "So fundamental and pervasive is the group of occupational activities that it affords the scheme or pattern of the structural organization of mental traits."

54. Dewey, **Democracy and Education**, p. 17.

55. Ibid., p. 47.

56. Ibid.

192

57. Ibid. p. 12.

58. Dewey, Public and Its Problems, p. 195.

59. Ibid.

60. Ibid., p. 197.

61. Ibid., p. 200.

62. Ibid.

63. Ibid., p. 199.

64. Dewey, Democracy and Education, p. 89.

65. Ibid., p. 94.

66. Dewey, Public and Its Problems, p. 201.

67. Dewey, Democracy and Education, p. 418.

68. Ibid., p. 115.

69. Ibid., p. 11.

70. Ibid., p. 357.

71. Ibid., p. 34.

72. Ibid., p. 11.

73. Ibid., p. 226.

74. Ibid., p. 241.

75. John Dewey, Problems of Men (New York: Philosophical Library, 1946), pp. 48 and 56.

76. Ibid., p. 40

77. John Dewey, Education in the Social Order (New York, Chicago: League for Industrial Democracy, 1934), p. 3.

78. Dewey, Problems of Men, p. 56.

79. Ibid., p,. 55.

80. Dewey, Democracy and Education, p. 86.

81. Dewey, Intelligence in the Modern World, p. 381.

82. John Dewey, "Freedom of Will," in A Cyclopedia of Education, II, ed. Paul Monroe (New York: Macmillan Co., 1911), p. 706.

83. Dewey, Problems of Men, p. 113.

84. Dewey, Philosophy and Civilization, p. 151. In Human Nature and Conduct, p. 25, he mentions the connection between will and habit. He appears to be identifying them. "All habits are demands for certain kind of activity; and they constitute the self. In any intelligible sense of the term will, they are will. They form our effective desires and they furnish us with our working capacities. They rule our thoughts, determining which shall appear and be strong and which shall pass from light into obscurity." Later, he observes that direct effort of will is useless if objective conditions are not changed to form habits. This ambiguous statement seems to separate the two.

85. Dewey, Human Nature and Conduct, p. 307.

86. Ibid., pp. 305-306.

87. Dewey, On Experience, Nature and Freedom, p. 264.

88. Ibid., p. 263.

89. Dewey, Intelligence in the Modern World, p. 410.

90. Dewey, On Experience, Nature and Freedom, p. 282. Note that Dewey is using the term "individuality" in a different sense in this passage. It is identified with the naturally given preference or bias which is different from individuality as a human achievement.

91. Dewey, Public and Its Problems. p. 186.

92. John Dewey, Freedom and Culture (New York: G. P. Putnam's Sons, 1939), p. 6. In Liberalism and Social Action, p. 34, John Dewey expressed his belief that if the early liberals interpreted liberty as something subject to historical relativity, then they would have known that "as economic relations became dominantly controlling forces in setting the pattern of human relations, the necessity of liberty for individuals which they proclaimed will require social control of economic forces in the interest of the great mass of individuals."

93. Dewey, "Philosophies of Freedom," pp. 269-270. In Liberalism and Social Action, Dewey has similar statements to make. See pp. 31 and 41.

94. Dewey, Problems of Men, p. 114.

95. Dewey, "Philosophies of Freedom," p. 271.

96. Ibid., p. 274.

97. Ibid., p. 273.

194

98. Ibid.

99. Dewey, Problems of Men, p. 113.

100. S. I. Benn and R. S. Peters, The Principles of Political Thought (New York: The Free Press, 1968), p. 250.

101. Dewey, Problems of Men, p. 113.

102. F. A. Hayek, The Constitution of Liberty (Chicago: The University of Chicago Press, 1960), p. 13.

103. Ibid., p. 17.

104. Dewey, Democracy and Education, p. 357.

105. Dewey, Human Nature and Conduct, p. 311.

106. Dewey, "Philosophies of Freedom," p. 276.

107. Dewey, Experience and Education, p. 70.

108. Dewey, Human Nature and Conduct, p. 255.

109. Dewey, "Philosophies of Freedom," p. 276.

110. Ibid., pp. 276-277.

111. Dewey, Human Nature and Conduct, pp. 310-311.

112. Ibid., p. 309.

113. Dewey, On Experience, Nature and Freedom, pp. 279-280.

###

NOTES

Chapter IV

1. Dewey, Freedom and Culture, p. 6.

2. Ibid., p. 9.

3. Ibid., p. 23.

4. Ibid., p. 59.

5. Dewey, Intelligence in the Modern World, p. 349.

6. Dewey, Freedom and Culture, p. 60.

7. Ibid., p. 9.

8. Dewey, Intelligence in the Modern World, p. 411.

9. Dewey, Liberalism and Social Action, p. 89.

10. Dewey, Intelligence in the Modern World, p. 411.

11. Dewey, Liberalism and Social Action, p. 89.

12. Dewey, Freedom and Culture, p. 73.

13. Ibid., p. 57.

14. Antony Jay, Corporation Man (New York: Random House, 1971.)

15. Dewey, Individualism Old and New, p. 65.

16. Dewey, Public and Its Problems, p. 127.

17. G. W. Allport, "Dewey's Individual and Social Psychology," in The Philosophy of John Dewey, ed. P. A. Schilpp (New York: Tudor Publishing Co., 1951), p. 287.

18. Dewey, Individualism Old and New, p. 82.

19. Ibid., p. 52.

20. Dewey, Philosophy of John Dewey, p. 428.

21. Dewey, Public and Its Problems, p. 125.

22. Ibid., p. 216.

23. Levi, Philosophy and the Modern World, p. 326.

24. Dewey, Liberalism and Social Action, p. 326.

25. Dewey, Philosophy of John Dewey, p. 428.

26. Dewey, Public and Its Problems, pp. 215-216.

27. Dewey, Intelligence in the Modern World, p. 422.

28. Morton G. White and Lucia White, The Intellectual Versus the City (Cambridge, Mass.: Harvard University Press and the MIT Press, 1962), p. 167.

29. Dewey, Experience and Nature, p. 151. See also, Dewey, Art as Experience, p. 342.

30. Dewey, Public and Its Problems, p. 82.

31. Dewey, Intelligence in the Modern World, p. 400.

32. Dewey, Human Nature and Conduct, p. 307.

33. Ibid.

34. Dewey, Public and Its Problems, p. 39.

35. Ibid., p. 83.

36. Ibid.

37. Ibid., p. 85.

38. M. Berger, T. Abel, and C. Page, Freedom and Control in Modern Society (Toronto, New York, London: D. Van Nostrand Co., Inc., 1954), p. 73.

39. Dewey, Public and Its Problems, p. 15.

40. Ibid., p. 33.

41. Ibid., p. 28.

42. Benn and Peters, The Principles of Political Thought, p. 260.

43. Dewey, Problems of Men, p. 113. ('Bold') emphasis mine. The message does not equate the public realm with asociations. But it implies the impossibility of singular things or groups acting singularly, i. e., without being modified by or modifying others, even indirectly.

44. Dewey and Tufts, Ethics, p. 237.

45. Ibid., p. 173.

46. Dewey, Public and Its Problems, p. 64.

47. Ibid.

48. Ibid., pp. 64-65.

49. See Dewey, Intelligence in the Modern World, p. 378.

50. Charles Reich, The Greening of America (New York: Random House, 1970), p. 91. It may be noted that Reich gives no precise distinction between private and public realms. It is however, the interpretation of the present writer his (Reich's) thougths on the matter roughly parallel Dewey's view. At any rate, the question at this point is not how precise the distinction is made but whether or not the distinction should be upheld.

51. Ibid., pp. 94-95.

52. Dewey, Public and its Problems, p. 61.

53. Ibid., p. 118.

54. Benn and Peters, The Principles of Political Thought, p. 150.

55. Dewey, Public and Its Problems, p. 74.

56. Benn and Peters, The Principles of Political Thought, p. 271.

57. Dewey, Intelligence in the Modern World, p. 402. In Public and Its Problems, he has an identical statement: "The man who wears the show knows bets that it pinches and where it pinches, even if the expert shoemaker is the best judge of how the trouble is to be remedied," p. 207.

58. John Dewey, Reconstruction in Philosophy (Boston: The Beacon Press, 1957), p. 205.

59. Dewey, Intelligence in the Modern World, p. 384.

60. Ibid., p. 383. Obviously, the idea is favorable to the activity of funding scientific researches.

61. Dewey, Human Nature and Conduct, pp. 308-309.

62. A. H. Somjee, for one, reads the disappearance of the state in Dewey's political theory. It is, he claims, no longer the center of activity in Dewey's society. The center becomes the many associations (social, cultural, economic, educational, scientific, and family). Similarly, he sees in this condition the reduction of of the moral reference of the state to an indirect one. The Political Theory of John Dewey (New York: Teachers College Press, Columbia University, 1958), p. 97. See next section for an additional discussion of this issue.

63. Dewey, Intelligence in the Modern World, p. 383.

64. Ibid., p. 385.

198

65. See page 203.

66. See Robert Paul Wolff, In Defense of Anarchism and On Violence (New York: Harper and Row, Publishers, Harper Torchbooks, 1970). N. B.: The discussion here is not intended to be a point by point assessment of Wolff's thesis. The gist of his argument, which follows the traditional conception of freedom, is cited to compare it with Dewey's fresh approach. What will appear is a contrast - one that shows Dewey's advantage by not retaining the old framework adopted by Wolff.

67. Dewey, Democracy and Education, pp. 95 and 140; Dewey, Intelligence in the Modern World, pp. 343, 360, 362; Dewey, Problems of Men, p. 58.

68. Dewey, Intelligence in the Modern World, p. 379.

69. Dewey, Reconstruction in Philosophy, p. 186.

70. Dewey and Tufts, Ethics, p. 237.

71. Ibid., p. 249.

72. Ibid.

73. Dewey, Intelligence in the Modern World, p. 401.

74. Dewey and Tufts, Ethics, p. 249.

75. Dewey, Public and Its Problems, p. 82.

76. Dewey and Tufts, Ethics, p. 237.

77. Ibid., p. 125.

78. Dewey, "Philosophies of Freedom," pp. 283, 287.

79. Dewey, Intelligence in the Modern World, p. 489.

80. Dewey, "Philosophies of Freedom," p. 274.

81. Ibid.

82. Ibid., p. 285.

83. See Dewey, Intelligence in the Modern World, p. 416 for more discussion of this subject. In Human Nature and Conduct, pp. 305-306, he expresses the view that this effort should focus on industrial development: "Since industry covers the most pervasive relations of man with his environment, freedom is unreal which does not have as its basis an economic command of the environment.

84. John Dewey and Arthur Bentley, Characters and Events, Popular

Essays in Social and Political Philosophy, ed. Joseph Ratner (New York: Henry Holt and Co., 1929), vol. II, p. 789.

85. Dewey, Problems of Men, pp. 94, 96. This type of conflict, says Dewey, can be identified with the struggle between old and new forms and modes of association.

86. Dewey, Intelligence in the Modern World, pp. 435, 441.

87. Dewey and Bentley, Characters and Events, p. 787.

88. Ibid., p. 789.

89. Ibid., p. 784.

90. Ibid., p. 785.

91. Dewey, Liberalism and Social Action, p. 87.

92. John Dewey, "The Future of Liberalism or The Democratic Way of Change," in What is Democracy? Its Conflicts, Ends and Means (Oklahoma: Cooperative Books, 1939), p. 10.

93. Ramsey Clark, Crime in America, (New York: Simon and Schuster, 1970), p. 272.

94. Dewey, Intelligence in the Modern World, p. 448.

95. Ibid. p. 402.

96. Ibid., p. 414.

97. John Dewey, "The Underlying Philosophy of Education," in Educational Frontier, ed. W. H. Kilpatrick (New York: Century Co., 1933), p. 318.

98. Dewey, Problems of Men, p. 109.

99. Dewey, Intelligence in the Modern World, p. 358.

100. Dewey, Experience and Education, p. 52.

101. Dewey, Public and Its Problems, p. 148.

102. Levi, Philosophy and the Modern World, p. 326.

103. Wayne A. R. Leys, "Dewey's Social, Political and Legal Philosophy," Guide to the Works of John Dewey, ed. Jo Ann Boydston (Carbondale and Edwardsville, Ill.: Southern Illinois University Press, 1970), p. 236.

104. Dewey, Philosophy and Civilization, p. 328. See also Reconstruction in Philosophy, p. 201, where Dewey traces the establishement and supremacy of the state over other forms of association, indicating that its structure is determined by

200

historical conditions.

105. George R. Geiger, "Dewey's Social and Political Philosophy," in The Philosophy of John Dewey, ed. Paul A. Schilpp (New York: Tudor Publishing Co., 1951), p. 352.

106. See Dewey's "The Underlying Philosophy of Education," p. 317.

107. R. J. Bernstein, Interpreting Dewey on the subject accepts the subject wholeheartedly. See Bernstein, John Dewey, (New York: Washington Square Press, Inc., 1967), p. 135.

108. Dewey, Freedom and Culture, p. 102.

109. Marc Belth, The Concept of Democracy in Dewey's Theory of Education (Ann Arbor, Mich.: University Microfilms, No. 16, 271, 1956), p. 276.

110. Dewey, Philosophy and the Modern World, p. 326.

111. Dewey, Public and Its Problems, p. 211.

112. Dewey, Democracy and Education, p. 101. Whether or not the new forms of association, like the United Nations, and communications, like satellite relays, actually lend support to Dewey's expectations is hard to say. They may have helped national and international relations to some degree, but they certainly were not able to eradicate deeply seated differences and conflicts that stand on the way of a great community.

113. Dewey, Public and Its Problems, p. 213.

114. Ibid.

115. Dewey, Democracy and Education, p. 101.

116. Ibid., p. 151.

117. Dewey, Individualism Old and New, p. 95.

118. Ibid., p. 34.

119. Dewey, Public and Its Problems, p. 154.

120. Dewey, Philosophy and the Modern World, p. 323.

121. Ibid.

122. Dewey, Public and Its Problems, p. 218.

123. Dewey, Liberalism and Social Action, p. 55.

124. Walter Feinberg, "The Conflict between Intelligence and

Community in Dewey's Educational Philosophy," in Educational Theory, 19 (Summer 1969): 236-248, where the author raises specifically the point under consideration here.

125. Dewey, Public and Its Problems, p. 154.

126. Dewey and Tufts, Ethics, p. 383.

127. For further discussion of democracy and communal education, see Belth, The Concept of Democracy in Dewey's Theory of Education.

###

NOTES

Chapter V

1. Dewey, "The Problem of Truth," p. 523. Elsewhere, he has a more emphatic statement: "Indeed, capacity to endure publicity and communication is a test by which it is decided whether a pretended good is genuine or spurious." Dewey, Reconstruction in Philosophy, p. 205.

2. Dewey, Human Nature and Conduct, p. 210.

3. Ibid. pp. 216-217.

4. Dewey et al., The Meaning of Marx, ed. S. Hook (New York: Farrar and Rinehart, Inc., 1934), p. 56.

5. Hendrik Hart, Communal Certainty and Authoritative Truth (Amsterdam: Set and Zeitlinger, 1966), p. 140.

6. Peter T. Manicas, The Death of the State (New York: Capricorn Books, G. P. Putnam's Sons, 1974), p. 246.

7. Dewey, Art as Experience, p. 326.

8. Bronislaw Malinowski, Freedom and Civilization (London: George Allen & Unwin, Ltd., 1947), p. 31.

9. Sigmund Freud, Civilization and Its Discontents. Translated by James Strachey. (New York: W. W. Norton & Co., Inc. 1961). Cited in Robert E. Dewey & James A. Gould, Freedom: Its History, Nature, and Varieties (New York: Macmillan Co., Inc., 1970), p. 293.

10. Kallen, "Individuality, Individualism, and John Dewey," p. 299.

11. Santayana, "Dewey's Naturalistic Metaphysics," p. 247.

12. Robert C. Pollock, "Process and Experience," in John Dewey: His Thoughts and Influence, ed. John Blewett, S. J. (New York: Fordham University Press, 1960), p. 182.

13. Levi, Philosophy in the Modern World, p. 305.

14. Paraphrasing the basic assumption of Sullivan's interpersonal theory of psychiatry, George R. Geiger, John Dewey in Perspective, (New York: Oxford University Press, 1958), p. 157.

15. John Dewey, John Dewey at Ninety, ed. Harry W. Laidler, addresses and greetings on the occasion of Dr. Dewey's 90th birthday dinner, October 20, 1946, at the Hotel Commodore (New York: League for Industrial Democracy, 1949), p. 19.

16. Belth, The Concept of Democracy in Dewey's Theory of Educa-

tion, p. 266.

17. Hook, ed., **John Dewey: Philosopher of Science and Freedom,**
    pp. 343-344. Peter T. Manicas offers some concrete proposals
    for the actual organization of a democratic community. These
    are consistent with Dewey's general ideas, p. 249.

18. Dewey, **Public and Its Problems,** p. 147. See also **Individua-**
    lism Old and New, p. 99.

19. Dewey, **Reconstruction in Philosophy,** p. 202.

20. Ibid., p. 206.

21. John Dewey, "The Protagonist of Democracy," in Journal of
    Philosophy XVIII (June 9, 1921): 316.

22. Dewey, **Public and Its Problems,** p. 154.

23. Ibid.

24. Ibid., p. 184.

25. Ibid., p. 157.

26. Ibid, pp. 213 and 218.

27. Ibid., p. 219.

28. John Dewey, **A Common Faith** (New Haven: Yale University
    Press, 1934), p. 33.

29. Ibid., p. 87.

30. Robert J. Roth, S. J., **John Dewey and Self-Realization**
    (Englewood Cliffs, N. J.: Prentice-Hall, Inc., 1962),
    p. 143.

###

BIBILIOGRAPHY

Primary Sources

Books

Dewey, John. Art as Experience. New York: Capricorn Books, G. P. Putnam's Sons, 1958.

Characters and Evens, Popular Essays in Social and Political Philosophy. 2 vols. Edited by Joseph Ratner. New York: Henry Holt and Co., 1929.

A Common Faith. New Haven: Yale University Press; London: Oxford University Press, 1934.

Creative Intelligence: Essays in the Pragmatic Attitude. New York: Henry Holt and Co., 1917.

Democracy and Education, An Introduction to the Philosophy of Education. Edited by Paul Monroe. New York: The Macmillan Co., 1916.

Education in the Social Order. New York, Chicago: League for Industrial Democracy, 1934.

Education Today. Edited by Joseph Ratner. London: George Allen and Unwin, Ltd., 1941.

Essays in Experimental Logic. New York: Dover Publications, 1916.

Experience and Education. New York: The Macmillan Co., 1952.

Experience and Nature. New York: Dover Publications, inc., 1958.

Freedom and Culture. New York: Capricorn Books, 1963.

German Philosophy and Politics. New York: Henry Holt and Co., 1915.

How We Think, A restatement of the Relation of Reflective Thinking to the Educative Process. Boston: D. C. Heath and Co., 1933.

Human Nature and Conduct, An Introduction to Social Psychology. New York: The Modern Library, 1930.

Individualism Old and New. New York: Minton,

Balch and Co., 1930.

The Influence of Darwin on Philosophy. New York: Peter Smith, 1951.

Intelligence in the Modern World: John Dewey's Philosophy. Edited by Joseph Ratner. New York: The Modern Library, 1939.

Liberalism and Social Action. New York: Capricorn Books, 1963.

Logic: The Theory of Inquiry. New York: Henry Holt and Co., 1938.

My Pedagogic Creed. Washington, D. C.: The Progressive Education Association, 1929.

On Experience, Nature, and Freedom: Representative Selections. Edited by Richard J. Bernstein. New York: Liberal Arts Press, 1960.

Philosophy and Civilization. New York: Capricorn Books, 1963.

Philosophy, Psychology and Social Practice. Edited by Joseph Ratner. New York: G. P. Putnam's Sons, 1963.

Problems of Men. New York: Philosophical Library, 1946.

The Public and Its Problems. Denver: Alan Swallow, 1957.

The Quest for Certainty, A Study of the Relation of Knowledge and Action. New York: Capricorn Books, G. P. Putnam's Sons, 1960.

Reconstruction in Philosophy. Boston: Beacon Press, 1967.

Theory of Valuation. Chicago: The University of Chicago Press, 1939.

What is Democracy? Its Conflicts, Ends and Means. Oklahona: Cooperative Books, 1939.

Dewey, John, and Bentley, Arthur F. A Philosophical Correspondence, 1932-1951. Edited by Sidney Ratner and Jules Altman. New Brunswick: Rutgers University Press, 1964.

Dewey, John, and Dewey, Evelyn. Schools of Tomorrow. New York: E. P. Dutton and Co., Inc., 1962.

Dewey, John, and Russell, Bertran; Cohen, Morris; Hook, Sidney; and Eddy, Sherwood. The Meaning of Marx, A Symposium. Edited by Sidney Hook. New York: Farrar and Rinehart, Inc., 1934.

Dewey, John, and Tufts, James H. Ethics. New York: Holt, Rinehart and Winston, 1961.

Articles

Dewey, John. "The Crisis in Human History." Commentary I (March 1946): 1-9.

"Experience and Existence: A Comment." Philosophy and Phenomenological Research IX (June 1949): 709-713.

"Experience, Knowledge and Value: A Rejoinder." In The Philosophy of John Dewey, pp. 517-608. Edited by Paul A. Schilpp. New York: Tudor Publishing Co., 1951.

"Greetings to the Urbana Conference." Essays for John Dewey's Ninetieth Birthday. Edited by Kenneth Deane Benne and William Oliver Stanley. Urbana, Illinois, 1950, pp. 3-4.

"Inquiry and Indeterminateness of Situations." Journal of Philosophy XXXIX (May 21, 1942): 290-296.

"Intelligence and Power." New Republic LXXVIII (April 25, 1934): 306-307.

"Meaning and Existence." Journal of Philosophy XXV (June 21, 1928): 345-353.

"The Objectivism-Subjectivism of Modern Philosophy." Journal of Philosophy XXXVIII (September 25, 1941): 533-542.

"The Problems of Truth." I. "Why is Truth a Problem?" Old Penn, Weekly Review of the University of Pennsylvania IX (February 11, 1911): 522-528; II. "Truth and Consequences." Old Penn (February 18, 1911): 556-563; III. "Objective Truths." Old Penn (March 4, 1911): 620-625.

"The Objects of Valuation." Journal of Philosophy XV (May 9, 1918): 253-260.

"Propositions, Warranted Assertibility, and Truth." Journal of Philosophy XXXVIII (March 27, 1941): 169-186.

Secondary Sources

Bernstein, Richard J. John Dewey. New York: Washington Square
        Press, Inc., 1967.

Blewett, John, S. J., ed. John Dewey: This Thought and Influence.
        New YorK: Fordham University Press, 1960.

Boydston, Jo Ann, ed. Guide to the Works of John Dewey. Carbon-
        dale and Edwardsville, Ill.: Southern Illinois Univer-
        sity Press, 1970.

Geiger, George R. John Dewey in Perspective. New York: Oxford
        University Press, 1958.

Hart, Hendrik. Communal Certainty and Authoritative Truth. Ams-
        terdam: Swet and Zeitlinger, 1966.

Hayek, F. A. The Constitution of Liberty. Chicago: The Univer-
        sity of Chicago Press, 1960.

Hendel, Charles W., ed. John Dewey and the Experimental Spirit
        in Philosophy. New York: The Liberal Arts Press,
        1959.

Hook, Sidney, ed. John Dewey, Philospher of Science and Freedom,
        A Symposium. New York: The Dial Press, 1950.

Hook, Sidney. The Metaphysics of Pragmatism. Chicago, London:
        The Open Court Publishing Co., 1927.

Kallen, Horace M. Art and Freedom. 2 vols. New York: Duell,
        Sloane and Pearce, 1942.

Kilpatrick, W. H., ed. Educational Frontier. New York: Century
        Co., 1933.

Krikorian, Y. H., ed. Naturalism and the Human Spirit. New
        York: Columbia University Press, 1944.

Lamprecht, Sterling P. The Metaphysics of Naturalism, New York:
        Appleton-Century-Crofts, 1967.

Lapley, Ray. Value, A Cooperative Inquiry. New York: Columbia
        University Press, 1949.

Levi, Albert W. Philosophy and the Modern World. Bloomington,
        Indiana University Press, 1959.

Levitt, Morton. Freud and Dewey on the Nature of Man. New York:
        Philosophical Library, 1960.

Manicas, Peter T. The Death of the State. New York: Capricorn
        Books, G. P. Putnam's Sons, 1974.

Martland, Thomas R., Jr. The Metaphysics of William James and
John Dewey, Process and Structure in Philosophy and
Religion. New York: Philosophical Library, 1963.

Mead, George H. Mind, Self and Society. A Posthumous work
edited by Charles W. Morris. Chicago: Chicago University Press, 1934.

Mesthene, Emmanuel G. How Language Makes Us Know, Some Views
About the Nature of Intelligibility. The Hague:
Martinus Nijhoff, 1964.

Nathanson, Jerome. John Dewey, The Reconstruction of the Democratic Life. New York: Charles Scribner's Sons, 1951.

Nisbet, Robert A. The Quest for Community. New York: Oxford
University Press, 1970.

Nissen, Lowell. John Dewey's Theory of Inquiry and Truth. The
Hague: Martinus Nijhoff, 1966.

Punzo, Vincent C. Reflective Naturalism. New York: The Macmillan Co., 1971.

Roth, Robert J., S. J. John Dewey and Self Realization. Engle-
wood Cliffs, N. J.: Prentice-Hall, Inc., 1962.

Schilpp, Paul Arthur, ed. The Philosophy of John Dewey. New York:
Tudor Publishing Co., 1951.

Somjee, Abdulkarim H. The Political Theory of John Dewey. New
York: Teachers College Press, Columbia University,
1968.

Thayer, H. S. The Logic of Pragmatism, An Examination of John
Dewey's Logic. New York: The Humanities Press, 1952.

Thomas, Milton Halsey. John Dewey: A Centennial Bibliography.
Chicago: The University of Chicago Press, 1962.

White, Morton G. The Origin of Dewey's Instrumentalism. New
York: Columbia University Press, 1943.

Articles

Dykhuizen, George. "John Dewey's Liberalism." Educational
Theory XII (January 1962): 45-52.

Eames, Elizabeth R., and Eames, Morris S. "The Leading Principles of Pragmatic Naturalism." Personalist XLIII
(1962): 322-327.

Eames, Morris S. "Liberalism and the Problem of Alienation."

Religious Humanism 4 (Spring 1970): 56-60.

Feinberg, Walter. "The Conflict between Intelligence and Community in Dewey's Educational Philosophy." **Educational
Theory** 19 (Summer 1969): 236-248.

Fen, S-N. "Social Relations as the Content of Intellectual
Learning, Dewey's Point of View." **Social Studies** LV
(April 1964): 138-143.

Haworth, L. "Dewey's Philosophy of Corporation." **Ethics**, January
1962, pp. 120-131.

Kallen, Horace M. "Individuality, Individualism and John Dewey."
Antioch Review XIX (1959): 299-316.

Mayeroff, Milton. "Some Developments in Dewey's Concept of the
Unification of the Self." **Personalist** XLV (1964):
13-26.

Schultz, Frederick M. "Community as a Pedagogical Enterprise and
the Functions of Schooling within it in the Philosophy
of John Dewey." **Educational Theory** 21 (Summer 1971):
321-337.

Sheldon, W. H. "The Protagonist of Democracy." **Journal of Philosophy** XVIII (June 9, 1921): 309-320.

Steibel, Gerald Lee. "The Belief in Communication." **Antioch
Review** XV (September 1955): 286-299.

Tesconi, Charles, Jr. "Dewey's Theory of Meaning." **Educational
Theory** 19 (Spring 1969): 166-174.

White Morton G., and White, Lucia. "The Plea for Community:
Robert Park and John Dewey." In **The Intellectual
Versus the City**, pp. 155-178. Cambridge, Mass.:
Harvard University Press and the MIT Press, 1962.

Unpublished Works

Avalos, Beatrice. **The Problem of Man and Community in Contemporary Thought**. Thesis, St. Louis University, 1961.

Belth, Marc. **The Concept of Democracy in Dewey's Theory of Education**. Ann Arbor, Mich.: University Microfilms
Publication No. 16, 271, 1956.

###

###

Firth, Brian William

THE CONSTITUTION OF CONSENSUS
Democracy as an Ethical Imperative

American University Studies: Series 10, Political Science. Vol. 8
ISBN 0-8204-0412-8   hardback US $ 29.90/sFr. 44.80

Recommended prices - alterations reserved

Ratification of the Constitution annihilated one Congress and created another. It also established that the States had a right to exist, and a right to abolish the Congress, the President, the Supreme Court. Nevertheless, for almost two centuries «conservatives» (first Federalists and then Republicans) have been telling us that the Congress is equal to the State legislatures, the U.S. courts to those of the States.

And indeed they must be believed, if it is true that the U.S. judges have the authority of the judges or commissioners of the court of the Continental Congress, viz. to decide by majority. If Congress can act without the judges being agreed, then it can act without the States being agreed.

There are, however, three grounds for rejecting this position. First, the historical record. Second, the evidence of the Constitution itself. Third, the fact that no (reasonable) man could hold the law to be so.

Contents: The judges of the U.S. are believed to have the authority of those of the Continental Congress and 26 of the States, to decide over a dissent: but this is a solecism – A synthesis of *government of law* for educated readers without specialized knowledge.

PETER LANG PUBLISHING, INC.
62 West 45th Street
USA – New York, NY 10036